THE IRONIC GERMAN

THE
IRONIC GERMAN

A STUDY OF

THOMAS MANN

by

ERICH HELLER

An Atlantic Monthly Press Book

Little, Brown and Company

BOSTON · TORONTO

FOR

FRANCIS BENNETT
PAUL AND HJOERDIS ROUBICZEK
GRAHAM STOREY

with my affectionate memories of those days at Cambridge
when the idea of this book was first conceived

Preface

THOMAS MANN, as he told us, sometimes felt that his *Joseph and his Brothers* ought perhaps to have been given a different name: *Jacob and his Sons*. I have similar qualms concerning the title of my book: for it is not only about Thomas Mann. His intellectual ancestry plays as big a part in it as does the patriarch in the story of his children; and as the story of Joseph, written by Thomas Mann, was bound to become also the portrait of a whole epoch, so this book about Thomas Mann could not help seeing his work in the context of the age of which he was certainly one of the most representative writers. For this reason I should like to think that my study, being not only about Thomas Mann, is yet not less but, on the contrary, *more* about him. It would be gratifying if at the end the reader were as sure as I am myself that none of my apparent digressions ever loses contact with Thomas Mann's mind and achievement—as little as the tales of Jacob are without bearing upon Joseph's destiny.

My thanks for permission to use previously published material are due to *The Times Literary Supplement*, *The Listener*, and Messrs. J. M. Dent & Sons, Ltd. I am grateful to Martin Secker & Warburg Ltd. in London and to Alfred A. Knopf, Inc. in New York for permission to quote from the English translations of Thomas Mann's works. In many instances I have taken the liberty of modifying the translations, either to indulge my own preferences, or, more frequently, for the sake of a particular emphasis suggested by my interpretation.

Even if I cannot individually acknowledge all the help I have received in writing this book from friends, colleagues, and pupils, I sincerely hope they will know how grateful I am to them. I must, however, mention Professor Hermann J. Weigand, of Yale University. His scholarly enthusiasm for my subject,

7

and his kindness in keeping me in touch with his own work, have been a constant encouragement to me.

Any acknowledgment of what I owe to my friend and colleague Dr. Anthony Thorlby is bound to be inadequate. He has given me a most generous measure of his time, learning, and inspiration. If ever there was a 'creative critic', it was he with regard to this book. He has a large share in whatever may be its virtues, and none in its shortcomings. I should also like to thank Mr. Roger Senhouse and Mr. R. J. Taylor for much valuable help; and if this book still shows any linguistic flaws after the assistance, most gratefully acknowledged, which I received from Miss Eithne Wilkins at the proof-reading stage, this is due entirely to my perseverance in making mistakes.

On its way to the printers my manuscript, legible only by virtue of her sympathetic intuition, has passed through the hands and typewriter of Miss M. F. McKnight. I am much indebted to her for her friendship, care, and patience.

The awkward problem of footnotes and references I have tried to solve by separating the former (marked by asterisks) from the latter (marked by numbers). The references are relegated to the Appendix, where they may, to some extent, fulfill the function of an Index of names and titles; but they contain *no comments, and no information apart from the sources of quotations.* The numbers in the text, therefore, should not impede the progress of the incurious reader.

E. H.

Contents

I

Introduction: A Tribute *

1

IT was some time in the late 'twenties that I first came across
Thomas Mann. I grew up then in a Europe which, only
just recovering from a great war, was making ready for a new
catastrophe. *Tonio Kröger* (1903) was the story I read, and I
was instantly captivated. There was a quality in the writing
which I should describe with the word 'interest' if it had not
lost its meaning in an age that tends to find most interesting
what matters least. Yet the original meaning of the word is
'it matters'. *Tonio Kröger* spoke to me, and not only to me, with
the urgency of *tua res agitur*, and was not less compelling for
not urging anything in tone or gesture. Nor was the immediate
appeal due to the flattery to which young readers are so easily
susceptible when they find their private worries and idiosyncracies sanctioned by the publicity of literature. For this *'tua
res'* was truly a *'res'*, a thing, an intimation of destiny. It
mattered.

But what matters? Tonio Kröger's was the familiar voice to
which one had come to respond without effort or embarrassment;

* Some of this was written on the occasions of Thomas Mann's eightieth
birthday on 6 June 1955 and his death on 12 August 1955. I have not
changed it. It is, therefore, in a more direct and personal manner, what
the whole book is meant to be implicitly : tribute to the work of a writer,
and testimony to a literary fascination which, with the passage of time,
has grown stronger both in affection and critique; and what would be
the worth of critique if it were not sustained by one kind of affection or
another, an affection striving to justify itself before reason and be vindicated by the findings of critical justice?

11

the educated voice which had learned so well to ask 'what matters?' with every overtone of scepticism, distrust, and finely controlled diffidence; it was one's own inner voice which early in life had whispered irreverent protests against the speech-day platitudes of the classics master, and later in life would speak in hushed asides, anxious not to be drowned by the hollow echo from inside the larger words. His was the language which felt its way in cautious articulation through the maze of broken pieces left behind by the explosion of the grand vocabulary. Wary, disillusioned, ironical, skirting in a movement of sad elegance the capital letters of the high virtues which had taken on the look of capital lies, *Tonio Kröger* yet spoke of great and everlasting things. For it is the story of a young man who, in his time and place, asks the question which matters most, the old, simple and hard question of how to attain the good life. And as it is in his time and place that he is asking the question, he is forced also to ask: is the good life at all attainable?

Today the student of German literature is likely to grow a little restive when asked to contemplate once more the celebrated Tonio Kröger problem of 'the artist with a guilty conscience', the scruples of the bourgeois writer. The horns of the old dilemma—Art and Life—have perhaps become rather blunt with so much critical attention, and artist and society may be entitled to a little rest from the persistent dialectical bother. But it will always be timely to talk, if talk one must, about that which lies behind the immediate personal occasion of Tonio Kröger's uneasiness. For his is only one particular case of the uneasiness which, in one form or another, stirs and drives most of the heroes of Thomas Mann's stories and novels over the thousands of pages of their eloquent destinies. The surprising momentum of Tonio Kröger's apparently slight tale is due to the fact that it contains elements of great specific gravity. For it is only one step of the spirit from Tonio Kröger's Hanseatic home-town to the far-away lands of Thomas Mann's *Joseph and his Brothers* (1933–43), from the young bourgeois writer's troubled mind to the souls of the Hebrew

patriarchs setting out on their pilgrimage in search of an
answer to the question,

> Why ordainedst thou unrest to my son Gilgamesh,
> Gavest him a heart that knoweth not repose?—

cursed and blessed as they are—so we read in the prelude to
the tetralogy—with 'the inability to rest, the compulsion to
ask, listen and seek, to wrestle for God, to quest in labour,
full of bitterness and doubt, for the true and the just, the
whence and the whither, our real nature and calling, and the
will of the Highest'.[1]

If 'interest' means 'it matters', it also has the ring of 'being
in between'. 'In between'—it is the dwelling-place of Thomas
Mann's chief characters, the residence too of anxiety and disquiet, of irony and humour, of tragedy and comedy; that is to
say, the accustomed place of man. Tonio Kröger stands in
melancholy bewilderment between his tradition and his emancipated consciousness, between a world without knowledge and
a knowledge without world. Life, he calls it, and art, and might
call it innocence and guilt. For clearly, it is a ripple from the
first fatal plunge. Adam has eaten of the tree of knowledge,
and life has been a problem ever since. The good life? The
union of the good, the true, the beautiful? But to know the
truth is perhaps to know the worst, and beauty may have been
before the serpent had its say.

Knowledge as the enemy of life, as the tempter to death, as
the ally of disease—this is an ever-recurring theme in Thomas
Mann's works, and certainly the central inspiration of his
beginning; and because the seriousness of this preoccupation
is reflected in everything he has ever written, even his early
stories stand out from the modishly morbid and comfortably
pessimistic literary environment in which they first appeared.
His first novel, *Buddenbrooks* (1901), is the story of the fall of a
family. It is, at the same time, his first allegory of the Fall of
Man. The Buddenbrooks are doomed because they have come
to know. And it is no whim of literary ornamentation that
invokes the memory of Hamlet in *Tonio Kröger*. 'There is

something I call being sick of knowledge . . .,' says Tonio, 'when it is enough for a man to see through a thing in order to be sick to death of it—the case of Hamlet. . . . He knew what it meant to be called to knowledge without being born to it. To see things clearly, even if through tears, to recognize, notice, observe, even at the very moment when hands are clinging and lips meeting, and the eye is blinded with feeling— it is infamous, indecent, outrageous. . . .'[2]

It is at times of great change that the tragedy of knowledge is re-enacted with new vigour. Both the histories of Doctor Faustus, who goes to Hell because he wants to know, and of Hamlet, who lives in Hell because he knows, were the inventions of an age when yet another little paradise was abandoned and new kingdoms of the world were conquered. Both mark the end of a tradition and the tragic consciousness of a new departure. For to live within a tradition means to enjoy once again, if only in some small measure, the privileges of innocence. Tradition is the wise agreement not to ask certain questions, to narrow the domain of the questionable, and grant the mind a firm foundation of answers which can be taken for granted. Thomas Buddenbrook is Thomas Mann's merchant-Hamlet. In his mind the robustly unquestioning tradition of bourgeois living dissolves into a host of questions and doubts, paralysing his will, turning his actions awry, and making him into an actor who performs his burgher life as a kind of moral pretence—as though the real thing were something else, a thought, a play, an uncertain intimation of the spirit. And with his son Hanno the play is the thing, and music becomes the only reality: music, and death, the great romantic liberators of the soul, the powers that move in with noble excess where the balance between question and answer is upset—the balance called tradition.

When the individual soul loses the measure of certainty and the prospect of continuity vouchsafed by tradition, time and death take on another and more troublesome aspect. Emancipation from the common lot is bought at the price of a heightened awareness of transience. In a world of radically conscious individualities, time and death become more aggressive foes. Consciousness, time, and death—these are the themes ⚹ of Thomas Mann's second novel, *The Magic Mountain* (1924). Once more it is a story of initiation and expulsion, of lost innocence and the pains of selfhood. Hans Castorp, an engineer from Hamburg, an 'unremarkable' young man, unquestioning and undoubting, enters an Alpine sanatorium for tubercular diseases, begins to doubt and question, and becomes 'remarkable'.

At the touch of Thomas Mann's artistry the scene, gradually and almost imperceptibly, is made transparent. The strictly realistic exploration reaches the frontiers of the myth, and, remaining realistic, pushes through. Hans Castorp has fallen among the sick. The sanatorium is Europe. It is also the world. Man is the patient. A progressive radical and a reactionary Jesuit talk and talk, quarrelling for the soul of Hans, a soul that is already at the mercy of a Russian woman. The discord of the talkative angels merely enhances the attraction of the temptress. The thermometers rise, showing the fever of knowledge. Hans Castorp knows. The world is now his world, and time is his time. When his soul is in motion, time expands; when his soul is drowsy, time speeds on in an empty race. Three weeks of awakening are longer than seven years of rumination. In Hamburg Hans Castorp was within life; here, on the mountain, he faces it. Down in the plain his responsibilities were within the world. Up here he is responsible for the world. Day after day he sits on a grassy slope and 'governs'. For he knows, and knowledge is power; yet, ironically, it is also loneliness, feebleness, and sickness to death. *The Magic Mountain* is the summing-up of the mind of modern Europe. None of its intellectual inclinations, moods, and fashions is missing, but all are transcended in a myth of profound irony. I have heard critics say that it is too talkative a book and, like other books by Thomas Mann, too ostentatiously knowledgeable for a work of the imagination. This criticism misses the very point of the work. For it is knowledge that ⟩ is the subject-matter of the novel, and the mind that comes to know is its protagonist.

It was almost predictable that Thomas Mann would write a
Doctor Faustus (1947). There was Goethe's example, there was
Germany in the grip of evil; but *Doctor Faustus*, above all,
provided the classic mould of the tragedy of knowing, the
modern version of the Fall. All the earlier works of Thomas
Mann are, implicitly, a critique of that liberally enlightened
optimism which believes in knowledge as the purest source
of moral and spiritual improvement; and this could not be
otherwise in the case of a mind so deeply imbued with the
knowledge of the tragic aspect of knowing. This critique was
even made explicit at the time of the First World War. The
book which Thomas Mann wrote then, product of a crisis so disturbing that he was unable to continue his work as a novelist,
was *Meditations of a Non-Political Man* (1918). Today it
reads like a log-book which, while the writing is unsettled by
the shock of an unexpected collision, yet records an important
stage in the voyage of exploration. It is a defence of romanticism against the enlightenment, of music against the pale
sobriety of rationalist articulation, and of pessimistic irony
against the rhetorical blatancy of moralistic politics. Yet even
while the book was being written, history played a disastrous
trick on the romantic philosophy: it smuggled it into the hands
of mindless thugs who, in its degraded name, began to prepare
their unspeakably corrupting conquest of Germany and the
world; and Thomas Mann met the challenge.

In *The Magic Mountain* the critique of liberalism is freely
confronted with the critique of that critique, and an opening
is sought for the transcending of the dialectical deadlock. In
Doctor Faustus, however, it finds its tragic consummation.
Both its heroes, the German composer Adrian Leverkühn and his
country, are the victims of a war waged within souls untouched
and untouchable by the blessing of Joseph. For Joseph, the
Joseph of Genesis, and hero of Thomas Mann's longest and
greatest book, becomes the symbol of peace beyond the agonies
of the destructive feud. He too knows, but what he knows is
not the worst. He too has left his home, but without losing
the sustenance of its soil. Like Hanno Buddenbrook and Tonio

Kröger, Joseph is set apart. Yet with him it spells no doom. It means the vocation to mediate. Just because he is such an accomplished dreamer himself, he is also the best interpreter of dreams. A hermetic messenger without dark alchemy, a prophet 'without foaming at the mouth', he stands before Pharaoh and says: 'For the mould and model of ancient custom comes to us from the depths which lie beneath; it is that which binds us. But that which grants us selfhood comes from God and is of the spirit; it is free. And it is the secret of civilized life that the ancient mould and model, within which we are bound and rooted, shall be filled with the divine freedom of selfhood, and there is no true civility without the one or the other.'[3]

Yet closest to Thomas Mann's heart is the chapter which, I feel, is also closest to the heart of the matter we have been discussing: the chapter called 'Of Love which denies the Blessing'. Its hero is Jacob, not Joseph; Jacob who has travelled to Egypt to see his long-lost son again. Holding him in his arms, he confides that the blessing will not go to him. For Joseph's story is only the guarantee of a promise, an anticipation on earth of the fulfilment that cannot be brought about by mortals and last. The father's blessing will go to Judah, the son with the anxious soul, who is destined to continue the pilgrimage of the race through regions poorer in wealth and spirit than the land of Egypt at that blessed moment of her history.

There is suffering still to come; but let there be also laughter. Enter the clown, as Verdi's *Falstaff* enters through the gate of mature wisdom. With *Felix Krull* (1954) the world received from Thomas Mann the gift which German literature has almost proverbially withheld from it: the great comic novel. Felix Krull is Joseph's distant cousin: Hermes, the rogue, the thief, the darling vagabond, stealing Apollo's cows but also playing upon the lyre. It is as a lift-boy that he mediates between below and above, and as an illicit lover that he reads dreams and makes them come true; and if he rises in the world, it is as a false count. Indeed, he is no promise of salvation, but holds

B

up its comic mask to a world which is so uncertain of truth that it cannot but be deceived.

2

It is a commonplace of literary judgment that modern German literature is, on its highest elevations, too problematical and speculative, and, on its more easily accessible levels, too provincially mediocre ever to gain as secure a place in the world of letters as that indisputably held by English, French, and Russian writers. There is, it is true, the monumental reputation of Goethe; but his work is more a landmark of the educated European mind than a familiar part of its equipment, more a weighty document of humanity than frequently chosen reading matter. There is Hölderlin, hardly translatable, whose name is evoked, and often in vain, as marking the root of modern poetic rootlessness and the grand mystical home of the homelessness of the spirit. There is, of course, Rilke, Orpheus of the voiceless inner life and lyrical redeemer of the waste land of reality. And there is, finally, Kafka, worshipper in the god-deserted church of Europe, narrator of a common agony and surveyor of the land without hope. Monumental classicism, spiritual uprootedness, lyrical mysticism and the superb prose-exploration of a pathological predicament—this, it seems, is all that the literary world, within its present scope of interest and general information, is prepared to acknowledge as the German contribution. It can hardly be regarded as the acknowledgement of a sound body of national literature.

Yet such a national literature, beset by all manner of problems and unsteadied by a stormy and altogether anomalous historical situation, does exist, and if, after all, something of its spirit has reached the contemporary world outside Germany, this is due to the work of Thomas Mann. He is, as novelist and teller of stories in the grand manner, the late heir of the central tradition of modern German literature. It may seem arbitrary to look upon the nineteenth-century German novel and *Novelle* as 'central', and to say that, if there is a centre

at all, it is to be found in the *Bildungsroman*, the narrative
unfolding of the formation of character, in such works as
Goethe's *Wilhelm Meister*, Gottfried Keller's *Der grüne
Heinrich* and, with a difference, Stifter's *Der Nachsommer*, or
in those shorter works, enacted in what we have come to call a
'realistic setting' and dominated by atmosphere, social conflict,
abrupt adventures of soul and mind, or dramatic moral decisions, works associated with the names of Jean Paul, C. F.
Meyer, Jeremias Gotthelf, Wilhelm Raabe, and Fontane.   This
arbitrary choice, however, can be excused on the grounds of
the blatant absence of any central and common dedication in
the more spectacular employments of German literary genius
by poets and writers such as Novalis, Kleist, E. T. A. Hoffmann,
or Büchner.   If, in addition, we agree that the period in question was the age of the bourgeois, then we may be doubly
justified in regarding as central the literature of the *Bürger*—
the German word for bourgeois, which is yet so different in its
connotations from the more political and sociological meaning
of the French term.

Thomas Mann was born in 1875 at Lübeck.   In this old and
secluded town of the Hanseatic League the traditional forms and
attitudes of bourgeois existence survived with a higher degree
of self-assurance and conservatism than in many of the German
or European metropolitan centres.   Moreover, Thomas Mann's
family belonged to the merchant-patrician aristocracy of that
city of medieval Gothic, commercial urbanity, sea-bound trade,
Baltic equanimity, inbred snobbery, and provincial crankiness.
The decay of this burgher community and his own estrangement from it (ascribed partly to what he inherited from a
southern-exotic mother) was Thomas Mann's first inspiration.
Lübeck was for him what Dublin was for James Joyce.   Yet
while Joyce soon acknowledged, through his very passion for
literary experimentation, the end of a certain tradition, Thomas
Mann remained even artistically a burgher.   He too experimented, but his experiment was to present, within the *traditional*
forms of novel and *Novelle*, the dissolution of all established
patterns of living.   Where other writers pursued newly discovered

complications of life with equally complicated mechanisms of style and form, especially constructed for the purpose, Thomas Mann simply knotted more tightly the old net of the story-teller. Compared, say, to Proust or James Joyce, his presentation of highly problematical matters hardly raises any literary problems.

This is in itself a highly ironical situation, and it is indeed irony that pervades the whole work of Thomas Mann. When in 1901 the very long novel *Buddenbrooks* appeared, its author was twenty-six. It was a time when a young writer was expected to join the *avant-garde*. Revolutionary literary manifestos poured forth from the pages of the fashionable journals; everywhere new gestures of style and expression were rehearsed, campaigns were arranged for ultimate conquests of mind, soul, and 'reality', agonies and triumphs were celebrated with cosmic, if somewhat breathless, trumpets. In the midst of this naturalist, symbolist, and expressionist turmoil there appeared a novel that showed the unmistakable imprint of a master in the peaceful art of literary manufacture from a period before the machines of the industrial revolution in literature had come into their own. Nobody would have guessed that it was written by a young man. Its epic detachment, steady tone of irony, unmilitant conciliatory psychology—*tout comprendre*, while the rebellious mood of the day was *ne rien pardonner*—and, above all, the fact that its writer had the time and patience to produce a piece of exquisitely elaborate craftsmanship, seemed to point to a vigorous survival from a past epoch. Yet after an initial resistance of the reading public the book was read, read indeed to the point of becoming a persistent best-seller. No other book on this level of artistic refinement took with such spectacular success the very hurdle which was its theme: the barrier between sensibility and vitality, between Art and its potential public, Life. There is, in this epoch, no comparable case of uncommon literary genius endearing itself so massively to the common reader. The only other example of a profitable peace between the highbrow periphery and the centre of popularity, Hofmannsthal's *Rosenkavalier*, was achieved in a highly self-conscious effort and certainly not without music assisting in the enterprise. (And what music! The most bewitching invention of that virtuoso dispenser of robustness and decadence.)

It was Hofmannsthal who once defined most succinctly the disquieting quality of the literary situation against which the singularly 'quiet' achievement of Thomas Mann should be contemplated. Hofmannsthal's essay 'A Letter'[4] is a personal confession in the guise of an imaginary letter written by the young Lord Chandos, a fictitious Elizabethan nobleman and poet, to Francis Bacon. At the same time, it is more than a self-revelation of Hofmannsthal's; it reflects a deep disturbance of the age itself, at least in so far as it is represented by its literature. This is how Hofmannsthal describes the disturbance. The traditional order of things fall apart, and their meanings lie buried under the fragments. Elements, once bound together to make a world, now present themselves to the poet in monstrous separateness. To speak of them coherently at all would be to speak untruthfully. The commonplace phrases of the daily round of observations seem all of a sudden insoluble riddles. 'The sheriff is a wicked man; the vicar is a good fellow; our neighbour must be pitied, his sons are wastrels; the baker is to be envied, his daughters are virtuous'—all this strikes Hofmannsthal's Lord Chandos now as utterly unconvincing, completely lacking in the quality of truth. 'My mind', he writes, 'compelled me to view all things with uncanny closeness; and just as I once saw a piece of skin from my little finger under a magnifying lens, and it looked like a landscape with mighty furrows and caves, so it was now with people and what they said and did. I failed to see it with the simplifying eye of habit and custom. Everything fell to pieces, the pieces to pieces again, and nothing could be comprehended any more with the help of customary notions. Single words, torn apart, floated around me; they coalesced into eyes which stared at me, and made me stare back. Then again they became a vortex which . . . dragged me into bleak emptiness.' In sentences such as these Lord Chandos apologizes to Francis Bacon for the silence into which he has lapsed, a silence which seems to be the betrayal of the early promise he had given of great poetic gifts.

This 'Letter' is Hofmannsthal's version of a crisis experienced by many a serious writer of the period, and therefore it would be easy to enlarge upon it with numerous quotations from Proust, Valéry, and James Joyce, from Rilke and Musil, and all would sound like mere variations on Hofmannsthal's theme, or indeed as much like repetitions of it as does, for instance, this passage from Kafka: 'And I had hoped to learn from you what it actually is that is happening to things which whirl all around me like a snowfall, while in front of other people even a little brandy glass seems to be planted upon the table as firmly as a monument.' [5]

The singular achievement of Thomas Mann becomes clear if we compare his work with that of the descendants of Lord Chandos who, despite all the hardships of the mind described by Hofmannsthal, have come into a large literary fortune: Proust, Joyce, Rilke, Musil, or Kafka. What matters here is not literary merit or distinction, but the fact that it would be difficult indeed to find a place for Thomas Mann in an order of literature determined by their works. For they were engaged, to different degrees and with different outcomes, in the task of forging a new and complex manner of literary coherence from the very impossibility—as Hofmannsthal put it—of thinking and speaking coherently any more. Time will show whether they have discovered vast expanses of virgin soil for the human mind to cultivate after the exhaustion of its accustomed domiciles, or whether they have designed and built inspired monuments at a dead end. There were times when Thomas Mann himself feared that, compared with theirs, his works might give the impression of 'stale traditionalism'.[6] Indeed, they might—were it not for his irony, which is not merely an attitude of mind conveyed through ironical diction, but decisively modifies the traditional form itself. This is true even of his earliest and seemingly most conventional novel, *Buddenbrooks*. When an *avant-garde* woman artist from

Munich had finished reading the book, she said to Thomas Mann: 'I was not bored by your novel, and with every page I read I was astonished that I was not bored.' [7]

She was both not bored and astonished at not being bored because *Buddenbrooks* already foreshadowed the daring literary device of Thomas Mann's later works: the calculated and artistically mastered incongruity between the meaning of the story told and the manner of telling it. From *Death in Venice* (1911) to *Doctor Faustus* and *Felix Krull* Thomas Mann experimented ever more audaciously with this ironical juxtaposition of manner and substance, and fruitfully scandalized the mind by simulating, with the sustained conventional form, the security of a tradition, while the very things thus recorded gave the lie to the pretence. The method is perhaps most successful in *Death in Venice*, where a composition of classical order and serenity is used to tell a most unclassical tale of disorder and decomposition, and where the writer, with the irony of a moralist, conjures up, by means even of occasional Greek hexameters and German lyricisms, the very religious centres of the worship of beauty: classical antiquity and the Venice of romanticism, of Platen, of Richard Wagner, in order to set against such memories the story of an artist who falls a victim to the fatal ambiguity of the Beautiful, dying a *Liebestod* before the backcloth of a sea as blue as the Archipelago, but in the vicinity of a plague-ridden city. Again—and this time on an incomparably larger scale—we see the method at work in *Doctor Faustus*, where Serenus Zeitblom, one of the last humanists in Hitler's war-torn Germany, is the bewildered, helplessly uncomprehending and yet strangely competent recorder of the most un-humanistic occurrences on an extreme frontier of the mind, an uncanny meeting-place of Art, Politics, and Hell. The same technique is employed in *The Holy Sinner* (1951), the short-story epilogue, in a humorous key, to *Doctor Faustus*, in which an Irish monk, apparently naïve and un-initiated, is the narrator of a story of sensual outrage, inscrutable doom, and complicated blessing.

This method, of course, results in parody; yet it is parody

of rare distinction and significance.   It is at once creation and critique, high entertainment and intellectual exploration— something like an attempt to realize the German romantic expectation of *Universalpoesie*; and it is the protest of the burgher-moralist, declared through the preserved form itself, against those forces which threaten with extinction the accustomed ways of living and literary pleasure: the moral protest of Tonio Kröger against the artist's new freedom sadly won from a society in which he lives as an exile, a freedom that so easily deteriorates into *libertinage*, cynicism, and irresponsible playfulness, or—as was to be revealed later by the Adrian Leverkühn of *Doctor Faustus*—to an alliance with the very powers of evil.

Thomas Mann was as 'contemporary'—if I may use this queer term of praise with which some critics appear to have replaced the older virtue of timelessness—as any of the major writers of the age, and knew and felt as much as they did the impasse of which Hofmannsthal's Lord Chandos speaks.   He could not have written the tragedy of Doctor Faustus had he himself been a mere Serenus Zeitblom, humanistic country-cousin to the metropolitan desperadoes of art.   There is, in *Doctor Faustus*, Wendell Kretzschmar, Leverkühn's stuttering music teacher, sitting at the piano in front of his little audience desirous of musical education, and playing and explaining to them Beethoven's Sonata Opus 111; and into its sublime noise he shouts and stutters his comments: 'Here . . . the appearance of art is thrown off—in the end art always throws off the appearance of art.'   And why, his listeners would ask, was there no third movement?   Well, simply because the sonata happens to come to an end in the second movement, to an end without return.   'And', we read, 'when Wendell Kretzschmar said "the sonata", he meant not only this one in C minor, but the sonata in general, as a species, as a traditional art-form; it itself was here at an end, brought to its end, it had fulfilled its destiny, reached its goal . . . it was the end of the sonata form.' [8]

Thus Wendell Kretzschmar.   But when Thomas Mann made

him say 'the sonata', he meant not only this particular form of
musical composition, he meant any form of art and any form
of literature. 'In the end art always throws off the appearance
of art'—and may be forced to abdicate altogether when life
itself assumes so fantastic a shape that the imagination can
no longer compete, stuttering its farewell without return and
petering out into silence. Thomas Mann more than once ap-
proached the Lord Chandos point of paralysis. What saved
him was the particular character of his moral intelligence; for
with him moral intelligence was the very fibre of the aesthetic
sensibility—a morality spontaneously resolved to preserve the
continuity of form as the symbol and promise of something
absolute and indestructible. In this he differed, for instance,
from Hofmannsthal, who had to support his literary stam-
ina with an extraneous moral resolution. With Thomas
Mann the moral nature was, right from the beginning, an
organic element within the creative process of making literature.

Thomas Mann once said that among all the reviews of
Buddenbrooks there was one which, at the time, he found the
most gratifying, not because it praised the novel but because
it contrasted his own 'pessimistic moralism' with the 'luxurious
aestheticism' of another new book, a novel by d'Annunzio.
'It was *this* newspaper cutting which I carried about with me
and was fond of showing. For that was it. This was myself
and this was how I wished to be seen by others; and this wish
was full of opposition—opposition to a philosophy and
literary practice which I felt to be alien to me, hostile, irresponsible, . . . indeed, *infamous*.' [9]

It was in this spirit of opposition that Thomas Mann set out
to build a traditionally solid house on a metaphysically condemned site. Of course, there is profound irony in such an
enterprise, the irony of giving a traditional form to the very
experience of its disintegration, of clinging to a convention in
the clear knowledge of its incongruity, and of desperately
resisting despair. His reward was the humour of *Joseph*, the
laughter of *Felix Krull*. It was not easily earned. In a letter

he wrote one year before his death, he said he would like to have engraved on his tombstone Goethe's words:

So kamst du durch, so ging es allenfalls,
Machs einer nach und breche nicht den Hals

meaning that he only just succeeded in getting through life and art without breaking his neck. By the skin of his teeth, and with a literary intelligence as fine as the finest his age has known, he has, for a blessedly long moment of creation, snatched the image of man from Lord Chandos's distorting mirror. From complications of every conceivable and many an inconceivable kind, from innumerable phrases, endlessly prolonged, ironically twisted and elaborately guarded against the onrush of the bleak waters, we yet emerge with those brief sentences, which were the despair of Lord Chandos, still meaningfully intact or intact again, sentences such as 'The sheriff is a wicked man' or 'Our neighbour must be pitied'. At the beginning of his life as a writer Tonio Kröger said: 'As I write, the sea whispers to me and I close my eyes. I am looking into a world unborn and formless, a world that needs to be ordered and shaped; I see into a whirl of shadows and human figures. . . .' [10] At the end the human figure stands before us in greater clarity than anyone would have dared hope amidst the whirls and the shadows; it even speaks the old and still familiar language; it even smiles. Reason enough to be grateful.

II

Pessimism and Sensibility

1

THOMAS MANN'S first novel, *Buddenbrooks*, a work entirely in the manner of literary realism, is at the same time a philosophical novel in the sense that the imagination which has conceived it bears the imprint of Schopenhauer's thought. As Dante's *Divina Commedia* is the poetry of a universe which had received its theological interpretation by St. Thomas Aquinas, or as Lucretius's *De rerum natura* poetically speaks of the nature of things in accordance with the doctrine of Epicurus, so Thomas Mann tells a story about people who live in a world philosophically interpreted by Schopenhauer (and re-interpreted on the basis of identical metaphysical assumptions by Nietzsche—with considerable effect, as will be seen, upon Thomas Mann). Schopenhauer's philosophical system itself reads like an imaginative invention, profoundly felt and contemplated, persuasively told, and in its own way as ironical as the best stories written by Thomas Mann.

The plot of Schopenhauer's philosophy, like the plot of all good stories, turns upon a contrast and an opposition: the conflict between the world—a world the true nature of which is the *Will* to be what it is, a will willing *itself* without sense or reason—and the mind of man; for the mind of man, the result of a mysterious accident in an otherwise smoothly-running universe, is endowed with the gift of recognizing the Will for what it is; it is free to take offence at the Will's unreason and senselessness, and oppose all its works. It can will against the Will and, in an act of heroic self-realization, withdraw from the

27

'World-as-Will' in order to settle somewhere where there is no Will, and therefore no world, and therefore—nothing. It is at this point that Schopenhauer's philosophical system issues in paradox, with irony taking over from logical consistency. For this nothingness which is where the Will ends—and logic must indeed insist upon this nothing if the Will is to be truly the Alpha and Omega of everything which has any real existence—reveals itself as the fullness of the spirit; and Schopenhauer's prose, the prose of a great writer, rises to dithyrambic heights in praise of this 'nothing':

All that stretches before us then is nothingness. Yet our nature, which shrinks from being dissolved into this nothingness, is merely the will to live, that Will which is the essence of ourselves, and also of our world. The fact that we so strongly abhor this nothingness is but another way of realizing that it is life we so strongly will, indeed that we are nothing if not this very will to live, and know nothing but it. Yet if we avert our eyes from our own want and bondage, and turn to those who have risen above the world, and in whom the Will, having wholly recognized itself and found its own presence in everything else, achieves the freedom of self-negation, and who then only wait for the Will's last vestige, which still enlivens their bodies, to vanish with them, we shall behold—no, not the turmoil of strife and ambition, not the endless changes from desire to anxiety and from pleasure to misery, not the insatiable and undying expectation which makes up the dream of life dreamt by the will of man—but the peace which passes all understanding, the soul as calm as an untroubled sea, and that deep stillness, inviolable confidence and security, the mere reflection of which, on faces such as Raphael and Corregio have painted, is a complete and certain gospel: what is left is knowledge, what has gone is the Will. It is through the contemplation of such saintliness, which . . . is brought before our eyes by art and vouchsafed with the stamp of inner truth, that we must shake off the dark oppression of this nothingness . . .[1]

The sustained breath of such sentences, whose perfect rhythmic organization is hardly communicable in translation, brings down the whole metaphysical fabric: how can this blind Will be the true principle of the world if its negation leaves us not with 'nothing' but with the enjoyment of eternal bliss?

However, on the logical ruins of Schopenhauer's philosophy there was to go up many a structure of considerable aesthetic distinction, and all of them were to be marked, not necessarily to their artistic disadvantage, by the flaw in the original design. This is true, as we shall see, of Thomas Mann's dealings with art and artists from *Buddenbrooks* to *Doctor Faustus*. It would even be possible to show that the very point at which Schopenhauer's mind, leaving the dark oppression of the world, leaps into the 'void' of saintly contemplation, at the end of the nineteenth century became, and right into the twentieth remained, the focus of aesthetic attention and artistic practice.

The dramatic opposition within the world of the Buddenbrooks is identical with that of Schopenhauer's philosophy; and indeed it is this philosophy which, together with Nietzsche's thought and Wagner's music, has formed the contours of Thomas Mann's mind much more powerfully than any of the other influences pursued by the literary historian. To Goethe, for instance, he found his way rather late in life; once there, it is true, he never left his orbit, circling around him with intense curiosity, artistic wonder, and intrigued fascination. But this cannot be compared with that greedy enthusiasm of mind and imagination engendered by his first contacts with Schopenhauer, Nietzsche, and Wagner.

In Goethe he sought and found the vindication by genius of his own ironical state of mind, a mind which, as if by preordained attraction, had surrendered to the intellectually irreconcilable and equally irresistible claims of Schopenhauer and Nietzsche; and he turned to Goethe for ideas, kindred, profound, and yet not catastrophic, to hold against those by which he was held, and for support in his determination to reach a creative compromise. Fondly toying with a 'Goethean pattern' in his own life, he fancied the project of an *imitatio mystica*, enacting it from time to time with an earnest sense of comedy and with that cleverly engineered suspension of disbelief which has proved so infectious in the case of many a critic: *Tonio Kröger* might be his *Werther*, and never mind *Buddenbrooks* which, preceding *Tonio Kröger*, has no possible parallel among Goethe's productions; *Death in Venice* would then be to *Tonio Kröger* what *Torquato Tasso* is to *Werther*, a '*gesteigerter* Kröger' to a '*gesteigerter* Werther'. And are not Hans Castorp, hero of the great '*Bildungsroman*' *The Magic Mountain*, and Wilhelm Meister somehow related as companions in the school of life? Goethe, it is true, did not write four volumes of *Joseph and his Brothers*, but as a boy he once began to spin out the brief biblical account, and said in *Dichtung und Wahrheit*: 'How lovable this story is, and how natural! But it seems too short, and one feels called upon to develop it in detail' [2]—a remark rendered almost comic by the thoroughness with which Thomas Mann has remedied the ancient shortcoming. The *imitatio mystica* is, of course, at its height in *Lotte in Weimar*, a piece of daring empathy, a creative essay of the first order, in which literal quotation and literary invention of Goethe's thought and speech are worked into a blend of imaginative biography and fictitious autobiography, of 'fiction' and 'truth', '*Dichtung*' and '*Wahrheit*'. Yet nowhere is the peculiar character of this 'mystical imitation' as flagrantly revealed as in the work that more than any other provokes the comparison with Goethe—*Doctor Faustus*; for what this new Faustus, the composer Adrian Leverkühn, at the tragic climax of his life says of Beethoven's Ninth Symphony —'It must be unwritten, revoked. And I shall do it' [3]—also comprehends the relationship of Thomas Mann's novel to Goethe's dramatic poem. Despite the common model, *Doctor Faustus* is at the furthest possible remove from the world of Goethe. If, with its Nietzschean hero, it is the despairing return to Schopenhauer's pessimism and his demonic interpretation of music, it is yet a homecoming to a sphere from which in truth Thomas Mann had never quite escaped.

'An unforgettable initiation of the soul', 'a metaphysical intoxication'—this is how Thomas Mann described the effect upon him, at twenty, of Schopenhauer's philosophy.[4] Small wonder then that *Buddenbrooks*, his early masterpiece, derives its intellectual plot from Schopenhauer; and so completely had philosophy become assimilated into the *imaginative* order of the writer's mind that, despite this philosophical spell, he succeeded, almost for the only time in his long career, in writing a novel without once alarming the susceptibilities of those readers who want 'life' and not 'ideas'. On the plane of literary history, then, it is a consistently realist or, for what the term is worth, naturalist novel, unthinkable without the example of the great masters of the genre, but more directly inspired by minor Scandinavians and above all by *Renée Mauperin* of the Goncourts; and in so far as this 'naturalist novel'—'for Germany perhaps the first and only one', as its author once said [5]—is also a humorous novel, its literary manner owes something to Dickens and the Low German writer Fritz Reuter. In fact, the accumulated European experience in the art of composing a novel is brought to bear upon a domestic German story—a marriage between the cosmopolitan and the narrowly national which is announced on the first page in the first words of old Buddenbrook ('*Je den Düwel ook, c'est la question, ma très chère demoiselle*') raising at once, with this mixture of Low German and French, the problem of translation, a difficulty which was to increase with every successive work, made the rendering of Thomas Mann in another language an almost heroic literary venture, and its relative success a triumph of devoted labour as well as of sheer substance over the inevitable injuries done to its organic form.

A French critic, reviewing *Buddenbrooks* in the *Mercure de France* of 1908, was convinced that it was untranslatable, with the translator's work bedevilled not only by the use of dialect (particularly important in the juxtaposition of North German and South German mentalities) and other linguistic perplexities, but also by the very 'structure' of the book; and this structure is an organization of ideas which, giving the lie to a conventional prejudice, enhance, rather than reduce, the life of the story. These ideas, having been enveloped by the living organism of the work and rendered as invisible as the anatomical sketch behind the body on the painter's canvas, form the intellectual plot of the novel and, to a large extent, determine its status. It is this *intellectual* plot which makes the reader *feel* that, in following the lives of these Lübeck burghers in their provincial seclusion, he yet comes face to face with a comprehensive view of the world.

The intellectual consistency of its plot endows the story with a kind of relentless logic which is rare in modern literature. *Buddenbrooks* is an old-fashioned book in the sense that its characters are in the undisturbed possession of their fates. Their stories *belong* to them in a manner which Thomas Mann later emphasized in the foreword to *The Magic Mountain*, saying that the extraordinary story of the simple-minded hero, although told for its, not his, sake, is yet *his* story, 'and not every story happens to everybody'. This is only worth remarking because modern novels are full of dispossessed persons: characters deprived of 'fate', and either at the mercy of 'crass casualty', as Thomas Hardy called it, or, as with Proust, Joyce, or Kafka, in search of their 'lost time', their 'mythological pattern', their 'unattainable reality', or else, as with Gide and the existentialists, violently appropriating an unauthorized destiny through an *acte gratuit* or an existential choice.   In *Buddenbrooks* no time is lost, no reality is in suspense, and no act is gratuitous.   Indeed, the Buddenbrooks in their decline come to doubt all certainties, but their author envisages all their doubts against no uncertain background: a firm order of reality within which the human person occupies a definable place.   Hence the fate of the individual, what he does and what happens to him, is only the dramatic unfolding of what he is meant to be.   Fate and character, therefore, are indissolubly one.   Thus the novel, in all its unsparing pessimism and sceptical irony, conveys a sense of meaningful order existing not only in and through the aesthetic organization of the written work but in the world itself.   For, beginning with *Buddenbrooks*, Thomas Mann's artistic practice was a struggle against the temptation of that aesthetic purism which has determined the nature and shape of so much in literature and poetry ever since Flaubert sought relief from the strain of a senseless reality in the purity of prose, yearning to write a book that was uncontaminated by 'life', a 'book about nothing at all which, free of any external connection, would support itself entirely by the internal force of style'.[6]   What Thomas Mann, rather naïvely, was in the habit of calling his own '*Bürger-lichkeit*', his sense of having roots in a definite social order at odds with the free play of the imagination and the adventurous-ness of art, was only a way of voicing his moral protest against an aesthetic passion paradoxically inspired and sustained by the void of 'real' meaning.

Buddenbrooks is a story without surprises.   What is sur-prising is the subtle art with which the young writer manages the gradual illumination of inevitability through an organically continuous sequence of shocks of recognition.   Of course there are lapses, passages where the author is carried away by the persuasiveness of his plot, indulging in melodramatic allegor-izing.   Thomas, the third in the line of Buddenbrooks (and he is to be the last to honour their tradition of business and citizen-ship), has married Gerda.   It is an unconventional choice. Gerda, extravagantly refined, detached, musical, is bound to remain a stranger among the Buddenbrooks; and how im-probable it is that she will produce sons to fall in with the Buddenbrook ways!   Indeed, her child, young Hanno, is to suffer from nightmares, will be lonely among his school-fellows, show no interest whatever in the concerns of the firm, soon be enslaved by music, and die before his time.   Here we meet Gerda for the first time as Thomas's wife:

> The door opened, and there stood before them in the twilight, in a pleated piqué house-frock, white as snow, a slender figure. The heavy dark-red hair framed her white face, and blue shadows lay about her close-set brown eyes. It was Gerda, mother of future Buddenbrooks.[7]

Similarly, there is a scene which yields its meaning with a keenness as unrestrained as this allegory of nightfall and sweet-scented decay.   Hanno, the child who is so strikingly lacking in the virtues of a future burgher and businessman, finds himself one day alone in his father's study.   Thomas, his father and by now Senator of his city, has been occupying himself with the family papers, and the last page, showing the family tree,

c

lies on top of the pile. Hanno reads it and then, in dreamy half-consciousness, takes pen and ruler and draws a double line underneath and across the whole page. When Thomas discovers the misdeed:

> 'What does this mean? What is the matter with you? Answer me! Why do such a mischievous thing?' cried the Senator, and struck Hanno's cheek lightly with the rolled-up paper.
>
> And little Johann stammered, retreating, with his hand to his cheek, 'I thought—I thought—there wouldn't be any more.'[8]

But such lapses into the obvious are surprisingly rare, considering the youth of the author and the enthusiasm of logicality with which the plot of the novel must have filled him. On the whole he safely relies upon the inner logic of his characters for evolving their fates, and on the unity of fate and character for establishing the coherence of the world he has created; and so closely-knit is this coherence that, in retrospect, the suspense in which the reader is held appears almost like the mere appeal to solve a mathematical equation, with the unknown quantity withheld and yet intrinsically given. The casual affliction of a toothache: if its victim is Thomas Buddenbrook at a certain point in his life, it 'contains' his death. Once the perfect correspondence between the inner and the outer story of a character is established, the writer can afford to pass on to the reader a piece of information apparently detached from the narrative, inviting him, as it were, to put it in the place where it is needed for the completion of the picture. This is what Thomas Mann actually does in the case of Hanno Buddenbrook's death; and a comparison of the logic of death in *Buddenbrooks* with, for instance, E. M. Forster's calculated casualness in allowing his characters to die, would support what has been said about the solid order of Thomas Mann's world in contrast to the disordered universe of some of his contemporaries. When Hanno Buddenbrook's end comes, it is not only he who dies: the whole tradition of the Buddenbrooks has played itself out. His death is a logical necessity.

This point calls for critical caution. Tidy and representative deaths are, of course, not in themselves an artistic merit. On the contrary, such is the character of the age and the intellectual temper of its literature that any obvious 'scheme' is more likely to be the contrivance of a second-rate mind. Sophistication and refinement of sensibility, on the other hand, excel in the subtle aesthetic organization of chaos, and in salvaging the last semblance and memory of order through a hard-won victory of form over all but form-proof matter. And it is precisely this new kind of artistic excellence of which the young artist Hanno Buddenbrook is the embodied promise—a fact which proves the imaginative richness and intellectual authenticity of the idea of order underlying the composition of the novel. It is an idea of order which comprehends, as it were, the *creative* aspect of negation. For Hanno is not merely the last of the Buddenbrooks, but also the first precocious practitioner of an art which only after their death, and after the death of the artistic convention within which their story is told, can come into its own. It is an art which, conscious of originating in destruction, anxiously cherishes the hope of a new freedom, even if before long Thomas Mann himself was to write, in *Doctor Faustus*, the tragic story of how that hope was shattered and that freedom renounced. *Buddenbrooks*, however, does not simply tell of the end of a family, or mark the end of the literary tradition to which as a realist novel it strictly adheres. It also points, by virtue of the logic of its intellectual plot, to those creative forces which are released by the collapse of the old order. It is because of this that the logical tidiness of the novel is far from being antiquated. By gathering into its own conventional organization the very idea of an art which is bound to overthrow the convention, *Buddenbrooks* ironically refutes the charge of conventionality.

We have come to know Hanno, the sad, hypersensitive, excessively musical child and only heir to the house of Buddenbrook, have seen how he suffers at the hands of his teachers and schoolmates, and now watch him at home, playing the piano and losing himself in a musical fantasy of pain, yearning, and a relief so shattering that life itself seems to yield to its finality; and the next chapter opens with the sentence: 'Typhoid fever takes the following course',[9] and continues to describe the symptoms of the disease with the objectivity of a medical text-book. The reader, with a shock, obeys the implied order, putting the piece of detached information into the place where it is needed to bring a story to its logical conclusion. This transformation of matter into organic life depends for its success upon the unity of concrete story and intellectual plot, upon a logical order of ideas binding together both the fates and the characters of the figures in the novel. Thus the 'first and only naturalist novel' in German literature is also a philosophical novel. And as the philosophy derives from Schopenhauer, so the two cosmic antagonists in Schopenhauer's thought—the World-as-Will and the World as the human mind which, forming the true idea of this Will-World, comes to deny it—appear in the guise of life and spirit.* Yet the novel also exploits, on two decisive occasions and each time with splendid aesthetic ruthlessness, the logical break in the philosopher's system; and the tactics of these moves are suggested first by Nietzsche, and then by Wagner.

2

Buddenbrooks is the story of a Hanseatic burgher family, grain merchants who play an important part in the social life of their

---

* I shall use the word 'spirit', not 'mind', as a translation for the German 'Geist', that ubiquitous term which comes so readily to German tongues and pens, and often seems to signal the very absence of the thing it ought to mean, or at least the failure of the mind in forming a precise idea. Nevertheless, it is indispensable and meaningful, as is shown, for instance, by Rudolf Hildebrand's article on 'Geist', a truly useful piece of philology, in Grimm's *Deutsches Wörterbuch*. My reason for using 'spirit', not 'mind', in translating it, is that 'Geist', though being, on the whole, more mundane and secular than 'spirit', is yet a decidedly more spiritual concept than mind. For in common usage the word 'mind', just like 'reason' or 'intellect', appears to claim for the faculty it denotes merely the kind of superiority over the world of matter which enables it to recognize, understand, and control. 'Geist', on the other hand, suggests more than this. It suggests freedom and independence, and thus, being akin to 'genius' or 'creative imagination', man's share in a freely creative power.

city. It is a story of four generations: Johann Buddenbrook senior, Consul Johann Buddenbrook junior and his stepbrother Gotthold, the first black sheep of the clan, then the Consul's three children, Thomas, Christian, and Antonia, called Tony, and finally Thomas's only son Johann, called Hanno. The action is concentrated in forty years, from 1835 to 1875. It is a time of great political and social change in Europe. Within the lifetime of the Buddenbrooks fall the dramatic events of 1848, 1866, and 1871, with their repercussions making themselves felt even in the Baltic remoteness of Lübeck, the unnamed but obvious residence of the family.

'The Decline of a Family'—this is the subtitle of the novel, and clearly their decline represents the dissolution of a whole social order, of a European era politically and culturally dominated by the burgher, the pre-industrial bourgeois. There are interpreters of *Buddenbrooks* who call on Karl Marx rather than the family doctor to diagnose the true nature of Thomas Buddenbrook's toothache and Hanno's typhoid fever; and indeed, the novel itself suggests the fatal role which class-consciousness itself plays in the undoing of a doomed class. There might have been a few more healthy generations of Buddenbrooks if Thomas had married his first mistress, the girl from the flower-shop who later becomes Frau Iwersen, the strong mother of numerous children, and who, at the time of Thomas's death, is 'as usual, expecting'.[10] Instead, their parting comes as a matter of course, because, as Thomas says, 'one is carried along—you see. If I live, I shall take over the business, and make a good match.' [11] Or if his sister Tony had taken as husband Morten Schwarzkopf, the son of the Master-Pilot of Travemünde, student and social reformer, athletic, charming, sincere, and hopelessly beneath her station, instead of obeying, at once and without a struggle, her father's letter: 'My child, we are not born for our little personal happiness. We are not free, separate, independent individuals, but like links in a chain . . .' [12] Of course, she marries the man the family has chosen, the disastrous Bendix Grünlich, and a few of Morten Schwarzkopf's rebellious phrases about the aristocracy and the reactionary local newspaper, so disarmingly out of place in her mouth, are all that will remain of Tony Buddenbrook's first and only love.

It is easy, therefore, to regard *Buddenbrooks* as a sociological novel, although Thomas Mann himself would not have it so. He even claimed that he remained long unaware of one of the most important social facts of the age: the emergence of the capitalist bourgeois.   In discussing his 'old-fashioned' allegiance to the tradition of the burgher, he once wrote : 'True, I must have been almost asleep while the German burgher changed into the bourgeois.' [13]   Yet the Marxist critic Georg Lukacs is right when he objects that 'with this remark Thomas Mann under-rates his own production'.[14]   For the novel does show clearly enough how the most reckless type of bourgeois moves in where the burgher leaves off; it is the Hagenströms, unscrupulous parvenus of the new financial hierarchy, brigands of the stock exchange, who take over the house and firm of Buddenbrook, carried into their position on the current of 'historical neces-sity'.   Yet the determinism at work in the novel cannot be defined after the fashion of 'historical laws'; it is of a different order.   No *historical* necessity can be abstracted from the destinies of its characters lest violence be done to the nature of the work.   As Thomas Mann has created them, they partake, in pity, pathos, and humour, of the paradoxical distinction of man: to feel that he is the free agent of his fate even when his mind persuades him of its ineluctability.   'We are like links in a chain', writes Consul Buddenbrook to his daughter in order to remind her of her *moral* duty to part with Morten Schwarzkopf; and 'one is carried along', says Thomas Budden-brook to his mistress when he feels he has to make the *decision* to break with her.   Indeed, it is in Thomas Buddenbrook that this very paradox turns into tragedy: he is consumed by the conflict within himself between the sense of being 'carried along' to his doom and the sense of being free to avert it.

In Schopenhauer's cosmic drama the crisis of the Will occurs as soon as man emerges from unreflective Nature, bringing into the world the fatal gifts of reflection and introspection.

In *Buddenbrooks* this drama is, as it were, re-enacted, on the human level itself, through the gradual refinements of consciousness. Thomas is to the Buddenbrooks what, in Schopenhauer's philosophy, Man is to Nature. For through Man, as Schopenhauer puts it, 'the Will comes to know itself and, astonished at its own activities, begins to enquire into its own character'.[15] Its perplexity is the greater as now, for the first time consciously, it faces death and is overwhelmed by the thought of its finite existence, the vanity of all its labours, and the illusoriness of its freedom. In Thomas the will of the Buddenbrooks suffers a similar embarrassment. Yet Thomas, ever more convinced by his reflective consciousness that the sense of futility which has taken possession of him is but the voice of inescapable catastrophe, seeks to employ all his moral resources in support of the Will, the will to be a Buddenbrook. On one occasion he even tests his moral courage and tries to assert his freedom with all the perverse logic of doom by entering, for the good of the firm, into a dubious business contract from which his moral character shrinks. Of course, he is defeated.[16] For no wilful blindness can obscure a sight once seen by the reflective eye, and no manoeuvre of perversity heal the damaged integrity of the will. But before the spirit of reflection reaches such momentum in Thomas, it has first to rehearse its strength in his father, Consul Johann Buddenbrook.

The novel begins with little skirmishes between 'Will' and 'Idea' taking place in the drawing-room of the Buddenbrooks. Old Buddenbrook, the Consul's father, represents the Will in its perfect integrity. His mind is precisely what Schopenhauer says it is in its simple and harmonious adjustment to the needs of the Will, 'a lantern illuminating the way of the Will'; and very far from being the luminous power to which Schopenhauer likens the mind of genius: 'the sun revealing the world'.[17] On the contrary, no ray of light is to be wasted on regions better left in the dark lest the Will be deflected from its straight path. Not even in children will old Buddenbrook tolerate useless exercises of the imagination. His

grand-daughter, little Tony, has just discovered a new theory
about the respective activities of lightning and thunder: 'If the
lightning sets something on fire, then it's the lightning that
strikes.   If it doesn't, why, then it's the thunder.'   The family
circle is amused; not so the grandfather.   With Voltairean
rational jealousy he wishes to know who puts such nonsense
into the child's head.   His son defends the autonomous right
of a child's imagination, but he: *'Excusez, mon cher!   Mais
c'est une folie!*   I don't like children's minds getting muddled
like this.' [18]

With Johann Buddenbrook junior the 'lantern' begins to
be unsteady and light is allowed to fall on 'useless' parts of the
land.   His religion is pietistic, his sense of business not immune from morbid scruples, his politics idealistic, and his
relationship to nature romantically nostalgic.   All these inclinations of the son's are utterly alien to the father and ridiculed
by him as so much extravagance.   Later that evening, at the
dinner given to celebrate the completion of the magnificent
new family house, the *leit-motif* of decline and doom is sounded
for the first time.   The conversation turns on the bankruptcy
of the local firm Ratenkamp and Co.   Someone suggests that
it was all due to Ratenkamp's choice of an unreliable partner.
Johann junior is not content with so simple an interpretation.
With his face assuming a gloomy expression, he suggests that
Ratenkamp acted as if hypnotized by a sense of catastrophe.
So, someone asks, things would have turned out just the same
if there had been no new partner?   Perhaps not, the Consul
replies, but still, Ratenkamp chose the partner 'inevitably',
driven by something 'inexorable', and in order to 'fulfil his
destiny'.   Not surprisingly, the party is embarrassed by this
portentous note, and old Buddenbrook intervenes to change
the subject: *'Assez,* Jean, that's just one of your *idées.'* [19]
Idées are not to the old man's liking, nor is any other sort of
'nonsense' and sentimentality.   One of the guests mentions
the garden the Buddenbrooks own just outside the gates of the
town.   It's a mere nuisance, old Buddenbrook protests, deteriorated as it has into a wilderness, a jungle.   One should

tidy it up, cut the grass, trim the bushes, shape them into cones and cubes. His son protests. It would spoil everything if nature were to be deprived of all her freedom. 'What the deuce,' cries old Buddenbrook, 'if the "freedom of nature" belongs to me, haven't I the right to do with it what I please?' [20] For the Will dislikes all wills not its own.

His will is wonderfully intact, and unassailable by his son's romantic fancies; he is, in so far as this state of innocence is attainable at all within the human species, that 'perfect objectivation of the Will' and its 'perfect enjoyment of itself' which Schopenhauer discerns in Nature. But in Buddenbrook junior the Will, to adapt Schopenhauer's description of the human mind emerging from the mindless state of the world, acquires the power and compulsion to 'reflect upon itself. At this point, however, it is bound to be struck by the dubiousness of its own existence, and cannot escape the question of what is the origin and purpose of it all.' [21] And although the younger Buddenbrook's will is still far from losing itself in this perplexity, it is yet baffled already, on decisive occasions, by the demands of 'ideas' interfering with its business—the Buddenbrook business. Consul Buddenbrook's character is, in Thomas Mann's rendering, a superb study of the subtle hypocrisy contrived by the spirit in its self-righteous subservience to the Will.

Late at night, after the departure of the guests, the embarrassing affair of Gotthold is discussed between father and son. Gotthold, old Buddenbrook's son by his first wife, has fallen foul of the family: he married against his father's will, started business on his own, and disgraced the name of Buddenbrook by opening a shop. A quarrel ensues over his future inheritance. Johann junior is to be the sole heir of the new house. Gotthold demands a considerable compensation. His letters hint at 'certain influences' working against him. This is aimed at his stepbrother Johann, himself divided between his self-interest, his sound business sense, objecting to a substantial weakening of the firm's resources, and his Christian conscience. On the day of the dinner-party yet another letter from Gotthold has arrived.   Consul Buddenbrook has with-held it from his father until now.   At last the old man reads it and asks for his son's opinion: 'Father, surely you under-stand my dilemma.   For the sake of family harmony I ought to suggest—but . . .'   The conversation goes on for some time, with many a 'but' and 'however' from Johann junior, with many an angry resolution, on the part of his father, to refuse Gotthold's demands.   Then:

> 'Father,' said the Consul softly, 'this affair with Gotthold causes me much anxiety.'
> 'Nonsense, Jean!   Why anxiety?'
> 'It has been a very happy day for all of us.   We celebrated our new house.   We felt proud and glad at what we have accom-plished . . .   But this bitter feud with my brother, your eldest son—it's like a crack in the house we have built.   A family should be united, Father.   It must keep together.   "A house divided against itself will fall." '
> 'Fiddlesticks, Jean!   He is an insolent fellow, that's what he is.'
> There was a pause.   The last candle in the room burned lower and lower.
> 'What are you doing, Jean?   I can hardly see you.'
> And the Consul said drily: 'I'm calculating.'

And in the sobering light of commercial arithmetic—one of the most reliable weapons the Will can hope to find in the arsenal of the intellect—his sense of business recovers from the attacks of conscience:

> 'I must advise you not to give in.'
> 'Thank goodness!   *Fini.   N'en parlons plus!   En avant!*   Let's get to bed.' [22]

Johann Buddenbrook is the first Buddenbrook to suffer the pains of self-awareness, and the last whose will is still strong enough to force its way through the gathering crowd of ideas. It is a costly victory.   He spends what is all but the last re-sources of the will in a manœuvre to disentangle it from a delicate situation demanding a far subtler strategy than the case of Gotthold.   By dutiful persuasion he has caused his daughter Tony to marry the exquisitely repulsive rascal Bendix

Grünlich, who struck him as a man of good manners, sincere feelings, and commercial promise. But, of course, he is an impostor. After a few years, the inevitable occurs: a bankruptcy of disquieting dimensions. Johann Buddenbrook could still save him, as he had, unconsciously, saved him once before by giving him Tony, her dowry; and the credit invested in the name of Buddenbrook. To save him now would mean a very considerable drain on the firm's capital. His 'will' says no, but what about his conscience, his 'ideas'? He knows Tony did not love Grünlich when she married him. But meanwhile a child has been born; and may she not have come to love Grünlich in the years of their marriage? And the marriage itself? Johann Buddenbrook is a sincere Christian, believing in the sanctity of the institution. True, the law provides the possibility of divorce in such a case. But is he not himself responsible for this marriage, and is it not, therefore, his duty to make its continuance possible? He must see his daughter. She shall decide.

Thomas Mann has succeeded in involving, as it were, three *dramatis personae* in the scene between Johann Buddenbrook and his daughter: Tony, Johann Buddenbrook's true will, and Johann Buddenbrook's moral idea.

'Listen, my dear child,' said the Consul, stroking her hair. 'I want to ask you something very serious. Tell me: you love your husband with your whole heart, don't you?'

'Of course, Papa,' said Tony with a face of innocent hypocrisy —precisely the face of the child Tony when she was asked: 'You won't tease that old woman again?' The Consul was silent for a while. Then he asked again: 'You love him so much that you could not live without him, under any circumstances, even if by God's will his situation should change and he could no longer provide you with all these things?' And his hand described a quick movement over the furniture and portières, over the gilt clock on the étagère, and finally over her own frock.

'Certainly, Papa,' repeated Tony, in the soothing tone she nearly always used when any one spoke seriously to her.

And then he reveals to her Grünlich's circumstances. The

word 'bankruptcy' rings in her ears more fearful than death.
It means tumult, shame, misery, and despair.

> 'I am asking you,' he said gently, 'if you are ready to follow
> your husband into poverty?' He realized at once that he had
> instinctively used the hard word to frighten her, and added: 'Of
> course, he may recover.'
> 'Certainly, Papa,' she answered. But it did not prevent her
> from bursting into tears. . . .
> 'You mean it?' he asked . . .
> 'I must, mustn't I?' she sobbed. 'Don't I have to——?'
> 'Certainly not,' he said. But, from a sense of guilt, corrected
> himself:
> 'I should not necessarily force you, my dear Tony. Assuming,
> of course, that your feelings do not bind you indissolubly to your
> husband. . . .'

Tony wants to know whether Grünlich is to blame for his
misfortune. Very probably, he says, but again corrects himself: 'That is—no, I don't know, my child. I have not yet
discussed things with him or his banker.' And then he asks
again whether she loves her husband.

> 'Oh, what a question to ask, Papa! Of course, I have never
> loved him—he has always been repulsive to me. Surely you must
> have known that?'
> It would have been hard to say what Johann Buddenbrook's
> face expressed. His eyes looked shocked and sad, and yet he
> pressed his lips hard together so that great wrinkles appeared at
> the corners of his mouth and on his cheeks, as used to happen
> when he had brought a piece of business to a profitable conclusion.

Although it is not so very hard to say what Johann Buddenbrook's facial expression meant, this is yet admirably done:
his eyes reflecting the moral idea, and his mouth the deep
satisfaction of the will at having its way. For the day is all
but won. Before long Tony will be not only ready but
determined to leave Grünlich and return with her child to
the parental home. And what tactics on the part of Buddenbrook! The crucial question has been withheld until now
when the field is already cleared of serious opposition: can

Grünlich's downfall be avoided? Of course, Johann Buddenbrook could pay his debts:

> 'How much is it?' she asked.
> 'What does it matter, my child? A very large sum.' And
> Consul Buddenbrook nodded several times, as though the weight
> of the very thought of such a sum pushed his head up and down.
> 'Also, I should not conceal from you,' he went on, 'that the firm
> has suffered losses already, quite apart from this affair, and that
> the surrender of a sum like this would be a blow from which it
> would not easily, by no means easily, recover. However, I do
> not say that in order to——'
> He did not finish. Tony had leapt to her feet, had even taken
> a few steps backward, and with the wet handkerchief still in her
> hand, she cried: 'Enough! Never!' She looked almost heroic.[23]

At this moment she seems to be a reincarnation of her
grandfather's forceful will, repeating almost the very words
with which he once concluded a similar conversation: '*Fini.
N'en parlons plus! En avant!*' Among her generation of
Buddenbrooks she is alone in having preserved the naïveté of
the will. But in her the will is only saved from defeat because
the combat does not take place: spirit has withdrawn from
the fight. It is not that she has no ideas. On the contrary,
she has quite a number of them, but all mercifully miss their
Schopenhauerian target: the Will. They are almost exclusively
engaged in the activity which, according to Schopenhauer,
produces the comic: the registration of a phenomenon in an
incongruous category.[24] Had she no ideas at all about what
is happening to her and her family, she would be pathetic.
She is comic—and one of Thomas Mann's most successful
comic creations—because she has hopelessly incongruous
ideas. If the Great Flood were upon her, she would find
complete relief in being angry about the inadequacy of the
weather forecast. She enacts the 'tragedy of her marriage'
with immense gusto and a ceaseless flow of conversational
reflections on the meaning of matrimony and the dignity of
suffering—'dignity' is the idea by which she lives. Then she
marries again: Herr Permaneder from Munich, a hop merchant,

exceedingly Bavarian and 'very jolly'. But soon the Buddenbrooks in their northern abode receive a telegram from the
south: 'Don't be frightened. Am coming at once. All is over.
Your unhappy Antonia.' [25]

Her second marriage has come to an end in the manner of
a farce. Yet she puts the farcical phenomenon in the category
of the tragic. One night Permaneder is late in coming home
from an alcoholic party. In the hall he meets Babette, the
maid. Tony is roused from her sleep by the noise of flirtatious aggression, steps out of her bedroom—and sees. It
might be by Wilhelm Busch, but Tony reacts tragically.
'Carried away by a frenzy of desperation, she heaped upon his
head her disgust, her abhorrence, her profound contempt and
loathing for him and all his ways.' [26] And leaves him, never
to return, never—for he shouts a word at her, an unrepeatable
word, which 'shall never pass my lips'. It seems to be capable
of shattering the very idea of 'dignity' and blotting out the
light of her world. This magic curse is, as the reader is told
much later, a Bavarian commonplace of masculine annoyance:
'Geh zum Deifi, Saulud'r dreckats!'—as untranslatable as are
all the more urgent requests, conveyed in popular parlance,
that someone should go to Hell. It must indeed put an end
to the second marriage of Antonia Buddenbrook, who exists
by what is dignified alone, safely wedded to the tradition of
her family, and blissfully at rest in the embrace of a vigorous
illusion. In her the 'will' of the Buddenbrooks attains once
more to a firmly defined form—it is a comic one. Her father,
the Consul, would pore for hours on end over the family
records, filled as he is with vague misgivings of instability,
and in need of the comfort of history, some soothing token of
continuance. 'Compare yourself! Discover what you are!'
These words from Goethe's Torquato Tasso—the appeal to a
despairing man to recover his strength in the contemplation
of his eternal type—would not be lost on Johann Buddenbrook (and were, by the way, to serve as the motto of Thomas
Mann's Meditations of a Non-political Man). Yet Tony is all
present. She does not grow or change. True, after the first

divorce she takes to saying 'I am only an old, ugly woman', but in her mouth it sounds like the part a child has learned for a school play.   For she is the parody of a final principle superior to time or change, in fact, the comic incarnation of Schopenhauer's 'idea of the species' within which the individual partakes of a kind of 'immortality in time', and the power of which is such that 'at every moment we may be serenely sure that, despite time, death and putrefaction, we shall all be here, always'.[27]

Tony Buddenbrook is like a comic version of the 'unfathomable mystery', which Schopenhauer perceives in animals: 'Just look at the first you see.   Look at your dog: how unafraid it is, how calm!   Millions of dogs had to die ere it was its turn to live.   But the perdition of those millions has not affected the idea "dog", it has not been dimmed in the very least by all that dying.   This is why the dog stands before you in all its vivacity and vigour, as if this very day were its first, and none could be its last, and its eyes are alight with the radiance of an indestructible principle. . . .'[28]   Tony's indestructible principle is the idea of a species called Buddenbrooks, and not even the demonstrable end of this species can shake her certainty.   It is by virtue of this principle, so blissfully incommensurable with the actual state of affairs, that, in her touching silliness, she is immune from time and many a death.   Dignified amidst indignities, unharmed by bankruptcies, divorces, or even Bavarian insults, she outfools the tragedy, just as her brother Christian is the melancholy fool of the piece, the natural outcast of the species.

If Tony, then, is a parody of 'life', a 'willing' self operating in a void and unreachable by the questioning insinuations of the spirit, Christian, who owes his name most certainly to Nietzsche, is Thomas Mann's first essay in caricaturing the spirit which has broken away from the business of seriously living and willing.   Moreover, the memory of Christian was destined to become an essential element in Thomas Mann's vision of the artist, so much so that the true nature of the moral scruples with which Thomas Mann surrounds the artistic vocation can hardly be grasped without the help of Christian Buddenbrook. When the reader first meets him, a boy coming home from school on the evening of the dinner-party, accompanied by one of the guests, the town poet Jean Jacques Hoffstede, whom he had met in the street, he is introduced by Hoffstede as 'a devil of a fellow, a little *incroyable*, eh? I will not conceal my *engouement*. He must study, I think— he is witty and brilliant.' And he is all this, and something of an actor too, mimicking his teachers with a genuine gift of caricature. Old Buddenbrook is, of course, suspicious of his talents: '*n' Aap is hei!*', he says in Low German, and adds mockingly: 'Why not say at once that he should become a poet, Hoffstede?' [29] Indeed, what should he become? A merchant? An actor? A writer? Like all Buddenbrooks he tries to become a merchant, but fails miserably. Nor do his histrionic talents lead to anything, save the part of *raconteur* of the gentlemen's club, and connoisseur of actresses. With increasing age he surrenders more and more to neurotic introspection, describing his numerous ailments with such dramatic force that his listeners are hypnotized into almost suffering the same symptoms: the 'vague agony' down the left leg where 'all the nerves are too short', the sudden inability to swallow, the irresistible urge to jump out of the window.

All in all, he is the creature of the species Buddenbrook at the lowest point of its vitality, and becomes the victim of that 'hypochondria and spleen' which Schopenhauer describes as the invariable psychological result of the natural will sagging without the succour and sanction of moral resolution; and because Christian is such a victim, he is also the caricature of the *décadent* who in Nietzsche's diagnosis would ultimately usurp, enfeeble, and destroy the cultural tradition of Europe. Christian has the makings, if not the format and nervous energy, of Nietzsche's aesthetic nihilist who, having lost the taste of reality and the power of vital feeling, exhausts himself in the pursuit of sensations, self-destructive and recaptured only by means of ever stronger stimulation. [30] This type abounds when a tradition loses its vital coherence and its will

to survive. For eccentrics become the norm when the centre
no longer holds; and when the limits of a pattern are reached,
what else can there be but border-line cases? Where there is no
order, the extraordinary becomes trivial, uniqueness common,
the freak typical, the outsider the rule, and in the general
confusion any raucous sounds of anger may easily be mistaken
for a calling to higher things.

It is at such a time that the artistic impulse itself is laid
open to suspicion due to the inflationary abundance of cheap
talent—and nothing is more conducive to the rash breeding
of talent than the dissolution of solid substance. Who can
be quite sure then that the apparent artistic impulse is
really a creative urge so powerful that no less creative manner
of activity could satisfy it? That it is not merely a restless
groping for aesthetic satisfaction to compensate for the loss
of any meaningful social routine? Or, still worse, the aspiration of wounded pride, the desire of the unemployable to prove
his productive worth? Or are the motives inextricably mixed
and, alas, reflected in the fumbling uncertainty or coarse
triviality of the works then produced? Thomas Mann never
ceases to ask such questions. They issue from the questionable shape of Christian Buddenbrook, the *bourgeois déraciné*,
the man of the vague agony, deserter of life, and travesty of
the spirit.

In an argument with Thomas Buddenbrook, Christian tries
to explain his ways to his angry brother. Yes, he was wasting
his time on trifles, on the theatre, on flirting. But had Thomas,
before he was married and head of the firm, never indulged in
such pleasures? 'Yet this is the difference between us,' he
continues, 'you have always known how to combine it with the
serious business of living. But I don't know how to do it.
You see, I am quite exhausted and used up by the other things,
the trifles. There is nothing left over for the serious stuff. . . .'
And Thomas flies into a rage: 'For heaven's sake, have you
no pride? How can you go on living in a way which you don't
even dare defend? But that's just like you: all that matters
to you is to see a thing, understand it, describe it . . .' [31]

D

So much of the image of Christian entered later into Thomas Mann's interpretation of the artist that in his first portrayal of a writer, in *Tonio Kröger*, Tonio describes artists like himself in all but identical words: 'This is the *credo* of the artist: once a thing is made articulate, it is finished. If the whole world is expressed, it is finished, redeemed, done with.' And adds his moral protest: 'But I am not a nihilist.' [32]

3

'But I am not a nihilist'—it is the Nietzschean protest against Schopenhauer's philosophy of redemption, and, consistently enough, it is uttered by Tonio Kröger in opposition to a *credo* of art the first author of which was Schopenhauer. For art, according to Schopenhauer, is the product of that purely contemplative and selfless state in which the World-as-Will, that is, the world as we know it, is 'finished', 'redeemed' and 'done with'. This strikingly incongruous sequence of epithets is yet a perfect rendering of the metaphysical incongruity which is at the heart of Schopenhauer's thought, an incongruity which was to be exploited in every possible manner by artists and thinkers coming under the spell of Schopenhauer—for instance by Richard Wagner, Nietzsche, and Thomas Mann. And as, through Christian Buddenbrook, the name of Nietzsche intrudes into the discussion of a work of which it has been said that its intellectual plot derives from Schopenhauer, it is timely to enquire once more into the precise location of the imaginative intelligence behind the novel *Buddenbrooks*.

Schopenhauer's pessimism, as we have seen, appears to be absolute. For it interprets the whole world as the objective manifestation of a principle which, by its very nature, must be unyielding to the demands made by the reason and the moral faculty of man: the demands for sense and goodness. Yet, on the other hand, this apparently limitless metaphysical pessimism is strictly and self-defeatingly limited. It comes to an end—somewhere. True, Schopenhauer places this 'somewhere' at the frontiers of the world. Yet if this world were really the whole world, the human mind too would reach its extreme limit there. Instead of which, Schopenhauer's pessimistic mind not only passes those boundaries but also sheds its pessimism in the process, suddenly acquiring 'inviolable confidence', hope, and faith.

Faith in what? In 'nothing', says Schopenhauer—and indeed can, metaphysically and logically speaking, say nothing else. Yet this 'nothing', as we have seen, holds all the good things of the world, and saints and artists call it their home. Yes, artists too. For artists, if only in their moments of creation, share in the saintly condition of utter self-forgetfulness, liberation from the Will, and pure objective vision. But what, one asks, is there to see? The Platonic ideas, says Schopenhauer, which, as the eternal forms of all transient things, are the 'true object of art'.[33] And what are these eternal forms of all transient things? The primary and lasting models of the Will objectifying itself. And what is the Will? We know the gloomy answer. And yet the eternal forms of this disastrous Will, when devoutly contemplated, lead the saint towards the ecstatic adoration of their creator, and the artist towards their imitation in works of art, the supreme pleasure of the human mind.

It is sheer alchemy, and so superbly carried out by Schopenhauer that aesthetically the performance almost justifies the extraordinarily faulty metaphysics; and it is this alchemy which has bewitched the mind of many an artist of the nineteenth century. For it seems the magic consummation of the *Zeitgeist* itself, metaphysically vindicating its most persistent moods: the deep distrust of the worth and value of life, the brave desire to know and speak the abominable truth about it, and the enchantment with the imagination as a form of existence. To be undeceived into deception, disillusioned into illusion, to despise the will and yet be most energetic in creation, to have 'done with the world' and yet 'redeem' it, as Tonio Kröger says—it is such contradictory wishes that find their philosophical guardian in Schopenhauer. 'What is left is knowledge, what has gone is the Will', he says of the supreme condition of the human mind. But *is* it, even on his own terms, knowledge? By no means. For knowledge, knowledge of what really is, could only make a sorry tale. What Schopenhauer's saints and artists see and know and revere cannot possibly be the inmost truth of the world, which, in all consistency, could only be deplorable. But what does call forth their hosanna is the metamorphosis of reality miraculously worked by the creative imagination—in fact, the creative imagination itself. Here lie the roots of all later theories insisting upon a strict separation of the aesthetic act and judgment from the habits acquired by the mind in its dealings with the empirical world; and, of course, the roots too of Thomas Mann's preoccupation, from *Buddenbrooks* onwards, with the opposition between life and art. Yet the peculiar irony in which he envelops this problem arises from his sympathy not only with Schopenhauer but also with Nietzsche's way of following up and 're-valuing' the pessimistic philosophy.

The young Nietzsche's *The Birth of Tragedy* shows all the signs of his 'metaphysical intoxication' with Schopenhauer's philosophy of art (and it is to art that three-quarters of *The World as Will and Idea* are devoted). In language both rhapsodic and intellectually brilliant he applies the Schopenhauerian scheme to his own metaphysico-historical interpretation of the genesis of tragedy, letting it culminate in Richard Wagner's operas. Anticipating a very great deal of what others were to say later about the 'impersonal' nature of a work of art, he follows Schopenhauer in believing that the artist, as artist, is 'liberated from his individual will, having become, as it were, a pure medium', a medium of redemption: for it transforms reality into 'pure appearance', into that 'aesthetic phenomenon' of which Nietzsche says that it alone 'justifies for ever world and existence'.[34] The justification, however, was not to last. Before long, Schopenhauer's 'nothingness', the disconcertingly empty and negatively transcendent abode of goodness and beauty, was to be taken quite literally by Nietzsche; and, in consequence, he denounced Schopenhauer's system as a nihilistic scandal. If the 'aesthetic

phenomenon' emerged from 'nothing', then it bore no semblance to truth; it was a beautiful lie, made up to enable a
feeble race to endure reality: 'We have *Art* in order *not to
perish of Truth.*' [35] If the world is nothing but the objectifica-
tion of a senseless principle, well then, let us not play truant,
not shirk reality, in order to dream the nursery dream of
redeeming nothingness. And Nietzsche went even further
and asked: The world has no meaning? True! But what of
it? This can worry and intimidate only the wretched victims
of the conspiracy in which, over the centuries, Platonic metaphysics and Christianity have joined forces to defeat the good
and strong life through the insidious attack upon it by nay-
saying weaklings in search of a reason and spiritual pretext
to keep alive. Thus Schopenhauer's World-as-Will, *denied* in
the saintly contemplation of 'eternal forms', becomes Nietzsche's
World-as-the-Will-to-Power, *affirmed* in the superhuman acceptance of a reality in need of no moral justification and immeasurably superior to any demands for sense or meaning.
Yet Nietzsche, even while reversing its adjudication of values,
never completely abandons Schopenhauer's metaphysical scheme
of things. It is, therefore, not surprising that *Buddenbrooks*,
while preserving the Schopenhauerian plot, yet ironically
oscillates in its critique of life between Nietzsche's affirmation
of the Will and Schopenhauer's moral denial of it.

This ironical fluctuation determines not only the course of
the story, its pessimistic humour and mocking pathos, but also
—and increasingly so from one work to the next—Thomas
Mann's style, with its preference for hyphenated adjectives,
frequently linking the heroic with the pathetic, the affirma-
tive with the derisory, and the construction of his sentences
which are so reluctant to reach a definite terminus, and finally
drop their burden at a long-withheld full-stop with a resigned
sigh and smile at the weary nature of a syntax unable to carry
on for ever the contemplation of doubts surrounding every
assertion. As for *Buddenbrooks*, the tone of the writing would,
for instance, suggest that it is, of course, better to be old
Buddenbrook in the integrity of his will than the weakling

Christian with his superior power to 'see and express' things as an 'aesthetic phenomenon'. But then, compared with his other grandson Thomas, does old Buddenbrook not seem crude and almost brutal? Are Thomas's vulnerability, his openness to the insinuations of the spirit, and the manner of his struggle and defeat not all but heroic? Does the complexity of his character, so dangerous to the species Buddenbrooks, not also endow it with an unprecedented depth and richness? Is the end of a business firm, the novel seems to ask, a price too high to pay for the efflorescence of musical genius in Hanno? Does the energy set free by the decline of the Will simply hasten the destructive process and 'finish' life, or is it capable of enhancing its worth and 'redeeming' it? This is how *Buddenbrooks*, in the exercise of a poetic justice in which the moral and the aesthetic sense are blended in an intriguing and ironical manner, now gives, and now withdraws, its assent to Schopenhauer's condemnation of the Will, now welcomes, and now refutes, Nietzsche's advocacy of Life.

On one occasion, immediately upon the death of their mother, Thomas and Christian quarrel more bitterly than ever before. Christian announces his intention to marry his mistress and adopt her children. Meeting with angry opposition from his brother, he bursts into an impassioned tirade against Thomas's forced sense of propriety, his 'tact' and 'dignity', his lack of compassion and love. And Thomas, more overwhelmed than angry, replies: 'I have become what I am because I did not want to become like you. If, inwardly, I have kept away from you, this has been in self-defence. I have had to be on my guard. Your nature and character are a danger to me— that is the truth.' [36] And it is the truth. For Thomas's will, the will to be a Buddenbrook, precariously manœuvres on the verge of exhaustion, only just warding off the danger of collapse, or of petering out in the feeble anarchy of '*idées*', Christian's meagre legacy from his father, the Consul. Yet on another occasion, it is precisely '*idées*', and of a sort that would no doubt have struck old Buddenbrook as extravagant nonsense, which Thomas calls to the help, so badly needed, of his belief in 'being a Buddenbrook'. It is at the deathbed of his uncle Gotthold, the first sinner against the tradition, that he muses upon the 'sense of poetry' necessary to sustain the loyalty to the firm with which Gotthold broke: 'Did you not know that one can be a great man even in a little place, a Caesar in a modest trading town on the Baltic?' And he even invokes an echo from Goethe's *Faust*, reflecting that '*alles ist nur ein Gleichnis auf Erden*' [37]—that everything transient is but a symbol. But all this is merely in the nature of variations in a minor key on the theme of life and spirit, Will and Idea. The theme itself reaches its full force in Thomas Buddenbrook's nocturnal vision of life, death, and immortality. It is then that the opposing voices of Schopenhauer and Nietzsche are most strangely and skilfully interwoven in an ironical celebration of life *and* death, of denial *and* affirmation.

4

At this point, it may be helpful to ask whether a literary discussion is justified in relying, to some extent, upon a philosophical argument. The justification is simple: there is no universally valid way of saying what the relationship is between 'philosophy' and 'literature'. But there may be, perhaps, a particular way of showing that in a particular case it is legitimate, or even unavoidable, to speak of a philosophy in speaking of a literary work.

To say that philosophy and literature have, or ought to have, nothing to do with each other suggests, firstly, that we know precisely what, in every single instance, they both are, and, secondly, that we have a clear notion of what is implied by 'having nothing to do with each other'. To put it positively: there are beyond any doubt some works of literature that have a great deal to do with some philosophies. We need only remind ourselves of Lucretius and Epicurus, Dante and St. Thomas Aquinas. But, of course, 'a great deal' need not be what our *literary* understanding of such a work gains by an understanding of its *philosophical* connections. Again, it would be easier to arrive at a decision about this, if we were, in fact, surer of the precise difference, in every respect, between literary and philosophical comprehension. It is very likely that there is such a difference, but whatever it is, I have no doubt that it is more relevant to the comprehension of poetry than to the appreciation of a work in prose. Yet in neither case can the difference be satisfactorily defined in the abstract. It can only be adumbrated in relation to definite works. For even an apparently 'general' literary theory fares best when dealing with the type of work by which it was inspired. It is not too difficult, for instance, to make some sense of the dramatic theories of Aristotle in the light of Greek tragedy, and it would be easier still if we knew all the dramas with which Aristotle was most familiar; but to 'justify' Shakespeare by Aristotelean principles is as laborious and tedious an exercise of the intelligence as it would be—and indeed was—one of downright idiocy to condemn him on their strength. In the same way, a great many recent dogmas of literary criticism, particularly those bent upon establishing the jealous category of the 'purely aesthetic' as opposed to 'thought' or 'moral intention', or the criterion of the 'ambiguous', have simply served to rehabilitate certain neglected poets of the past, or accommodate certain new departures. The universal application of such standards is bound to make a mockery of literary taste, and of the body of literature a figure of earnest fun.*

Like most excursions, this too was strictly unnecessary. It would have sufficed to say that the peculiar understanding of life which is embodied in a work of literature—and it is this *understanding* which determines also the *formal* aspects of the

---

* In a recent essay, T. S. Eliot confirms this from his own experience as poet and critic: 'The best of my *literary* criticism . . . consists of essays on poets and poetic dramatists who had influenced me. It is a by-product of my private poetry-workshop; or a prolongation of the thinking that went into the formation of my own verse . . . My criticism has this in common with that of Ezra Pound, that its merits and its limitations can only be fully appreciated when it is considered in relation to the poetry I have written myself' (*The Sewanee Review*, Autumn 1956, pp. 529–30, and *On Poetry and Poets*, London, 1957, p. 106).

work: its organization and its style—may have crystallized in the contact between the writer and a philosopher, between an imagination and a thought. In such a case the philosophy will be as relevant to the nature and quality of the writing as is its vocabulary, rhythm, or syntax. Indeed, every major literary work has a *syntax of ideas* upon which it may ultimately depend for its rank and status. If, moreover, the philosophy in question is not so much a systematic essay in the solution of problems as, like Schopenhauer's, an attempt to gain absolution from them, an act of liberation from the stresses and distresses of the mind; if, in fact, it is 'no philosophy at all', as many of our contemporary philosophers would misguidedly be ready to protest, then its assimilation in a piece of literature may proceed as naturally and spontaneously as that of a scene of nature in a romantic poem. The quality of a writer's feeling for ideas will then decide the quality of his writing as much as, in another case, a writer's feeling for the sea or a landscape. However, it may be objected that 'nature' differs from 'ideas' in that she possesses an attribute which we also expect from imaginative literature: concreteness. It is a fallacious expectation: the kind of concreteness we expect is not that of nature; what strikes us, metaphorically speaking, as 'concrete' is the artist's idea of nature. Besides, is love—to choose another example from the common subject-matters of literature—concrete? Only in so far as it moves human beings to act out their destinies. And it is possible for an idea to move a man passionately, and possible for a man to fall in love with an idea. This is precisely what, in *Buddenbrooks*, one day happens to Thomas. There is hardly another way of describing his state of mind when, having chanced upon the book, he reads the chapter 'On Death' from the second volume of Schopenhauer's *The World as Will and Idea*; and it is by no means, as we have seen, an arbitrary literary contrivance that the scene which marks the climax in the story of Thomas Buddenbrook, and may be regarded as the climax of the novel, is linked to this philosopher (who, incidentally, remains unnamed). It is an inevitable consummation, demanded by the syntax of ideas inherent in this most 'concrete' narrative.

Senator Thomas Buddenbrook, forty-eight and maintaining, with ever-increasing effort, the appearance of success in the face of the undeniable decline of his business and his vitality; incongruously opposing the sense of decay with the meticulous elegance of his attire and an addiction to *eau-de-Cologne*; anxiously watching his only child Hanno, who is so ill-equipped by nature for the future task of conducting the increasingly difficult affairs of the firm; and filled with a vague but intense fear, which he wishes he could call jealousy, of 'the mysterious little scandal above his head', over his office, where, in the drawing-room, his wife Gerda, looking astonishingly young and as if preserved by her own coolness, is joined ever more frequently in duets by a young lieutenant with a passion for music—Thomas Buddenbrook, then, is possessed by a restlessness which often drives him from his desk into the garden, where he aimlessly wanders about, or sits lethargically in the pavilion. It is here that he casually opens the second volume of a 'metaphysical system', and, although unskilled in this kind of reading, is immediately engrossed in it. Thomas Mann describes the effect upon Thomas Buddenbrook in a manner reminiscent of the words he used, in the autobiographical sketch already quoted, of his own initiation into Schopenhauer's philosophy. Thomas Buddenbrook's mind and soul, oppressed as they were by the premonition of death, now feel 'immeasurably expanded' and as if 'intoxicated with the alluring promise of an unheard-of enchantment'. And during the night that follows he suddenly wakes, gazing out of his darkness into an 'unfathomably deep prospect of light', and hears his own voice saying: 'I shall live!' 'End and dissolution? Pitiable words, and thrice pitiable he whom they fill with terror! What would end and dissolve? Why, this my body and individuality, this clumsy, obstinate, hateful incumbrance, *preventing me from being something other and better*.' The italics are of the interior monologue itself, which is Schopenhauerian word for word; or almost word for word—for

Schopenhauer knows no 'other and better' unless it be the condition of saintliness. But for the time being Schopenhauer dominates the nocturnal vision until this point is reached: 'Do I hope to live on in my son? In a creature yet weaker and more timid and insecure than myself? Blind and childish folly! What is a son to me? I need no son! Where shall I be when I am dead? Wherever there will be an "I"! Ah, it is so radiantly clear, so overwhelmingly simple: I shall be in all those who for ever and ever will say "I".'

This again is Schopenhauer, almost verbatim, and comes from the very chapter which Thomas Buddenbrook read that afternoon. But although those are the words of Schopenhauer, the jubilant emphasis belongs entirely to Thomas Buddenbrook or Thomas Mann. Schopenhauer, it is true, does in that chapter deal with death and immortality, but an immortality without grace or comfort: an immortality which rests in the assured survival of the species. For the species, Schopenhauer believes, is the only level of life at which a measure of individuation is safeguarded by the arrangements of the cosmic Will. The individual itself is produced, and killed again, in careless profusion, as wasteful as the exquisite craftsmanship spent on countless shells that litter the beaches of the sea. It is the species that alone matters to the Will, the species and its procreation, excessively guaranteed by a superfluity of sex-craving entities. Therefore, it is in sex that Schopenhauer, anticipating Freud, discovers 'the focus of the Will' and thus the source of the individual's greatest raptures and distresses. For sex is the point at which the individual is exposed, in powerful immediacy, to a force vastly transcending himself: the will of the species, the promise of life everlasting. But what an eternity is this? An eternity stretching, according to Schopenhauer, into the dismal immensity of time without hope of salvation, an eternity into which the individual has to be tricked by the delirium of sex, 'a fever, longing still/For that which longer nurseth the disease'. By virtue of Schopenhauer's passionately lucid prose, mockery turns to sublimity in sentence after sentence devoted to the grand fool and slave of the

Will: man in love, deceived by the mirage of self-fulfilment into subservience to a master so cruelly indifferent to the individual's selfhood.

Yet it is in this vision of a bleak Schopenhauerian eternity, strung together on the endless thread of generations, that Thomas Buddenbrook conquers the fear of death: 'I shall be in all those who for ever and ever will say "I".' What can such survival mean to him? Has he himself found happiness in saying 'I'? Is it not exactly here whence issues Schopenhauer's plea to renounce for good all 'I-saying' and seek that state of purest contemplation where the willing self is at last abandoned in saintly 'nothingness'? Clearly, Thomas Buddenbrook has—and how significantly!—misunderstood *The World as Will and Idea*, and may indeed have read yet other books, although we are not told.

For his soliloquy continues thus: '. . . but above all in those who say it in the full vigour of joy. Somewhere in the world a child is growing up, endowed with great gifts, free to use them, well-built and untroubled, innocent, ruthless, and serene, one of those whose sight makes joy more joyous and despair more desperate. This is my son! *This is myself*, soon, soon, as soon as death frees me from the wretched delusion that I am not he as much as I am myself. . . .' This, of course, is no longer Schopenhauer. It is a romantic distillation from Nietzsche, the blondest version of the Superman. And the following words, still under the spell of Nietzsche, also anticipate Tonio Kröger: 'Have I ever hated life, life in its innocence, cruelty, and strength? What foolish confusion! Myself I have hated because I could not bear it! But I love you. . . !'[38]

It is Thomas Mann's Tonio Kröger, the writer, who, as a youth, begins where Thomas Buddenbrook, the merchant, ends: in love with life in the shape of a boy, 'well-built and untroubled, innocent, ruthless, and serene'; and Tonio Kröger who, as a man, concludes his self-confession by once again speaking of that love, 'hidden away in his inmost being', for 'the blond and blue-eyed who are happy in their untroubled lives, lovable and ordinary'—a love of which he says that it

alone is capable of turning 'a *littérateur* into a poet'.[39] But
of Tonio Kröger more will be said later.

Thomas Buddenbrook's vision and monologue is perhaps
the only passage in the book that gives the attentive reader a
clue to the author's age, which, for the rest, is so extraordinarily,
indeed uniquely, concealed behind such epic composure and
ironical detachment as is usually held to be the literary temper
of maturity.   At this point, however, youthful emotion is in
control of scene and style.   Moreover, it is one of only two
scenes in the novel which are dominated by the vocabulary
of the passion of love; and as happens to be the case in the
other scene too, its passion is also the rapture of death.   And
for the writer of *Buddenbrooks*, the spiritual status of love
and death, these twin enchantments of the romantic imagination, is—and largely remains throughout his later works—
determined by his experience of Schopenhauer, Nietzsche, and,
as we shall see, Richard Wagner.   Although Thomas Mann
himself once said that only Schopenhauer and Wagner influenced *Buddenbrooks*, while Nietzsche had to wait until
Tonio Kröger,[40] it is yet true that the peculiar irony of his
first novel is the attitude of a mind hovering in creative indecision between the extremes of Schopenhauer and Nietzsche.
If there could be any doubt about this, it would be dispelled
by Thomas Buddenbrook's vision.

The impetuosity and spontaneity with which Thomas Buddenbrook passes the dramatic crossing of the Schopenhauerian
and Nietzschean ways without, as it were, noticing the sign-
posts, is as impressive as it is revealing.   What it reveals is
an inclination of the modern mind shared not only by the
national heirs of the two philosophies.   It is clear that Thomas
Buddenbrook, if he followed Schopenhauer, should resolutely
turn from that never-ending vista of life, that desolate continuity of the Will, which he glimpses in the eyes of all those
who 'for ever and ever will say "I" ', and seek the dominion
of 'nothingness' where all 'I-saying' ends in the absolute negation of our Will-ruled existence.   But in no time whatever,
and before the sentence is finished, he is in a place where it is

no longer the World-as-Will which gives offence, but we ourselves in our imperfection, with our wills enfeebled by sensibility and doubt; in a place where, with Nietzschean psychological daring, he sees through the Schopenhauerian denial of Will and self, recognizing its dubious motives, such as weakness, fear, maladjustment, impotence, and the wounded love of life proclaiming in self-defence the superiority of the spirit. At one moment Schopenhauer is accepted: the world is Will, and the spirit is its enemy. At the next moment Schopenhauer is ousted by Nietzsche: the Will is good, and the enmity to it is wicked. However, Thomas Buddenbrook does not put the alternatives quite so radically; indeed, he feverishly runs them into one. And what is it that has enchanted the bleak world of Schopenhauer and, at the same time, breathed the warmth of romance into Zarathustra's glacial landscape? Has God returned to the creation, or else some other meaning, majestic and unanswerable? A god, perhaps, but his name is Eros. And Eros does not ask if life is worth living. He bestows that worth through the irrefutability of desire. Is life, then, desirable? Eros does not care: the desire of love is worth living. It is by this dubious route that Thomas Buddenbrook reaches the point at which the dejected spirit turns for consolation to the life-force and to beauty, pessimism to vitalism and aestheticism—and he passes this turning-point so smoothly because he has moved with the logic of a European movement.

It is indeed amazing how far and fast Thomas Buddenbrook out-dreams the book that causes him to dream. Yet it is the book that is as much to blame as the dreamer. For Schopenhauer's *World as Will and Idea*, being the most inspired statement of European pessimism, advances, with all its fineness of thought and beauty of reasoning, a simple belief: what is real, is worthless; what is valuable, lacks reality. And where reality and value are thus seen and felt to be mutually exclusive, there *all* values, indeed truth itself, must in the end lose any *real* significance. Then the transition is speedy, and so smooth it is hardly perceptible, from one metaphysical illusion to another: from redemption through the denial of the Will to redemption through the Will's increase, from art as salvation to art as damnation (and Thomas Mann's damned composer Faustus-Leverkühn descends in a straight line from the Buddenbrooks) or from Eros as a saviour to Eros as a curse (and with the saving grace of Thomas Buddenbrook's new love for life we draw close to that death which lurks for Gustav Aschenbach in Venice).

'I love you!' exclaims Thomas Buddenbrook, with Nietzsche now prompting a text which was begun by Schopenhauer. Love—whom? His neighbour? It depends; if he is young, well-built, strong, and handsome. Clearly, it is Eros who speaks, a divinity common enough, and calling, it would seem, for no strenuous exercise of philosophical reason. Nevertheless, the situation is questionable in the extreme. For here the erotic delight is uttered with the accents of a quasi-religious expectation. Also, it is conceived in no friendly spirit. Its ecstasy is not the love of life enhanced by passion. On the contrary, it rises from the depths of despair, intoxicating with 'the alluring promise of an unheard-of enchantment' a mind lost in the dejected contemplation of a world which, right to its core, seems the denial of all love. Thus it is a profoundly impossible love, a love in a world without love.

Perhaps there are, after all, only two themes which are new in modern literature, distinguishing the nineteenth and twentieth centuries from any previous literary epochs: this kind of love and the tedium of the frustrated spirit. They are all but identical themes and Thomas Mann is master of both. In *The Magic Mountain* he gives a whole chapter to the 'great god Ennui', playfully apologizing for the unusual attribution of a demonic quality to the state of boredom (not knowing, perhaps, that ennui had already been 'demonized' by Baudelaire) and allowing this demon to rule the scene after the withdrawal of the infirm Venus, Clavdia Chauchat. But as early as *Buddenbrooks* the boring god descends from his leaden skies, joining the autumnal Kurgarten gathering of Lübeck gentlemen, with Thomas and Christian Buddenbrook among them, who have outstayed the season in the seaside resort of Travemünde. The rain filling the silence of the deserted place with its 'ceaseless, forlorn and desolate murmur', and the belated guests wearily, pointlessly and lasciviously conversing,[41] are the homely image of that very life which waits for the transfiguring illumination through pessimistic metaphysics or the Dionysian pathology. The common denominator of those two themes, the demonic doldrums and the sickly Eros, is the metaphysical devaluation of the world. Schopenhauer has given it its systematic philosophy, which differs from the ancient Manichaean pessimism in that it has no room for the *reality* of transcendence, and Nietzsche 'transvalued' it in the fundamentally desperate and therefore hysterical cult of the ecstatic life-force. These, then, are the two near-identical themes which have made their common entry into modern literature: tedium, and the pessimistic ecstasy of love which is no love but an erotic entanglement impatient of resolution, a passion hopeless not because its object is unyielding, but simply because there is no hope. Disillusionment is of its essence because what it seeks is an illusion. It is the love of the destitute spirit, the *Minnesang* of unredeemable separateness, Rilke's 'Ah, they only obscure with each other their individual fates!' Whether it is, with Proust, Marcel's terrible bedridden craving for Albertine, or, with Thomas Mann, Gustav Aschenbach's *Liebestod* in plague-infested Venice; whether, in *The Magic Mountain*, Hans Castorp's yearning for Clavdia Chauchat, sustained by the horizontal manner of tubercular existence, or, in *Doctor Faustus*, Adrian Leverkühn's sickness-seeking embrace of the prostitute (or, at its worst, in *The Black Swan*, the cancer-begotten infatuation of an elderly woman for a young man), in every case it is the invalid love rising from the invalidity of life—not unlike the music of young Hanno with which, at the end of the novel, Thomas Mann celebrates the death and transfiguration of the Buddenbrooks.

This is how Thomas Mann describes Hanno's improvisations at the piano on the last evening before his fatal illness.

(The description, alas, all but defeats translation, but is in its original more than a promise of Thomas Mann's extraordinary power, at its height in *Doctor Faustus*, to render in words a certain kind of music.)

> . . . The cadence, resolution, fulfilment, perfect serenity came, and with rapturous exultation everything unfurled into a harmony, which in an ineluctably sad ritardando melted into another. It was the motif, the first motif, he was playing. And what now began was a feast, a triumph, a boundless orgy of this single phrase which glittered in all its colours, plunged through all the octaves, wept, quivered in a tremolando, sang, rejoiced, sobbed— to emerge victorious, arrayed with all the rushing, foaming, sparkling splendour of the orchestra. There was something brutal and stupid, and at the same time religious and ascetic, something like utter devotion and self-sacrifice in the fanatical worship of this trifle, this scrap of melody, this brief, childish, harmonic invention of one-and-a-half bars; something impious about the excessiveness and insatiability with which he relished and exploited it; something cynically desperate, like the will to perish in an ecstasy, about the avidity with which he drew from it all the sweetness it would yield. . . .[42]

It is the kind of music of which Hanno's schoolboy friend, the young Count Mölln, once said, 'I know what it means'— and blushed;[43] it is an adolescent version of Richard Wagner's music to which the child Hanno had been introduced by his mother, much to the alarm of her friend, the old church organist of the town, who thinks it an 'infamous' sort of art: 'Look how the child sits there listening! Are you determined to poison his mind?'[44] In Hanno's swan-song to the Will, conceived in the same key as his father's vision and endowed with the same enthusiastic vocabulary which, on these two occasions alone, breaks the ironical restraint of the book with a note of lyrical abandon, the Schopenhauerian plot, already deflected in the direction of Nietzsche, receives its dramatic Wagnerian twist. Of course, this strange and highly significant derailment of Schopenhauer's train of thought was anticipated by Wagner himself when he wrote his *Tristan*-music to a text inspired by the philosopher's metaphysical pessimism. The

E

letter he wrote on the subject (1 December 1858) is one of the most revealing jokes in the history of ideas. For in it he reports that, after reading once more 'friend Schopenhauer's *magnum opus*' he felt moved 'to extend and, in some details, even to correct it'. And the extension and correction consist in nothing less than the discovery that there exists 'a way of salvation leading to the perfect appeasement of the Will', a way which is much simpler and more direct than Schopenhauer's ascetic and strenuous road of renunciation. This salvation lies in love, not, however, an 'abstract love' but a love which 'has its roots in sex'. Like young Count Mölln, one knows what he means. The letter is written in Venice, where he composes Isolde's *Liebestod*, and is addressed to Mathilde Wesendonck. Nevertheless, the naïveté with which he calls 'a correction of some details' what is in fact the complete reversal of Schopenhauer's thought is disarming indeed. And yet his *Tristan* superbly succeeds in artistically realizing this intellectual sleight of hand, and does so as naturally as Thomas Mann, on a much smaller scale, succeeds in blending, at the very climax of his novel, absolute philosophical incompatibilities.

What is involved here is more than a meeting of opposites; the extraordinary fusion is sanctioned by the inner, the supra-intellectual, logic of Schopenhauer's pessimism: the logic of the Will *aesthetically* affirmed even in its *philosophical* denial, the logic of that Schopenhauerian transcendental realm, called 'nothingness', which, after it is emptied of any religious reality, almost asks to be invaded by human desire or the aesthetic faculty of man. To minds inescapably cast in the mould of the Christian tradition there seem to be, after the end of the belief in a life higher than life, above all three possibilities: pessimism, vitalism, or aestheticism. Their common fountain-head is Schopenhauer's philosophy. In pessimism, life loses all the value it once possessed as the school and training-ground for absolute existence; in vitalism, its worth is infinitely inflated into an autonomous Absolute through philosophical acts of violence by far in excess of the resources of ecstasy the human soul can muster from day to day; in aestheticism it is recommended for magical transfiguration through the aesthetic vision. How profoundly related these three possibilities are, can be seen in the manner in which *Buddenbrooks*, from its pessimistic ground, rises first to Thomas's Nietzschean dream of life everlasting, and then to Hanno's Wagnerian delirium in which a weakened will, far from denying itself in obedience to Schopenhauer, gathers and spends all its remaining strength in a musical consummation of the desire for the significant life—the voluptuous embrace of death.* Did Thomas Mann know what he did, or was it a fruitful accident of the imagination, when, in recording the sad lot of the diabetic James Möllendorpf, he produced the perfect caricature of this voluptuous suicide of the Will? For 'in this diabetic old man the instinct of self-preservation had become so weak that, in the last years of his life, he succumbed more and more to a passion for cakes and pastries. . . . He rented a room in a district of the town quite out of keeping with his social position, a little hole of a room, whither he would secretly betake himself to consume sweets. And there they found the dear departed, his mouth still full of cake. . . .'[45] A *Liebestod* on the level of diabetes and confectionery.

In his middle years Thomas Mann once likened *Buddenbrooks* to a musical instrument he had constructed 'in the vigour of youth' freely to play on it in his later life.[46] When he said this, he could hardly have known how true it was to become. We have lingered so long over *Buddenbrooks* because it contains almost all the elements of vision and thought of which the later works are made. If his playing becomes ever more assured, if the pieces are ever more complex and ambitious, the performance is yet rendered on the strings strung across the body of his first novel.

* In the autobiographical sketch previously quoted, Thomas Mann, in speaking of the 'metaphysical intoxication' induced in him by Schopenhauer, also mentions that his own 'belated and powerful sexual awakening had much to do with it' (*Die Neue Rundschau*, 1930, p. 743). This may serve as a confirmation of what I have said about Schopenhauer's philosophy 'naturally' inviting the kind of misinterpretations, 'extensions,' and 'corrections' it has received.

III

The Embarrassed Muse

1

EVEN before *Buddenbrooks* was accepted for publication Thomas Mann began *Tonio Kröger*. As early as 29 December 1900, in a letter to his brother Heinrich, he mentions his plan for the 'elegiac *Novelle*' which six weeks later (13 February 1901) is tentatively given the title 'Literature'; and he adds in brackets: '*Illae lacrimae!*' In the same letter he says: 'When spring comes, I shall have survived a winter full of inward excitement. This very unliterary and unsophisticated experience has proved one thing to me: there is still something left in me which is not mere irony, something which is straightforward, warm, and good. No, not everything in me has been distorted, corroded, laid waste by cursed literature. Literature is death, and I shall never understand how one can be enslaved by it without hating it bitterly.' The experience to which he refers is 'not a love affair, at least not in the ordinary sense, but a friendship which is—incredible though it seems to me— understood, reciprocated, rewarded, and yet assumes at times, particularly in hours of depression and solitude, too painful a character. . . .' [1] (There is little doubt that this friendship is the same that is mentioned in the autobiographical sketch of 1930: '. . . a kind of resurrection of my feelings for that fair-haired schoolmate'—the Hans Hansen of *Tonio Kröger*—'but much happier, thanks to far greater intellectual closeness.' [2] Some forty years later, in *Doctor Faustus*, the memory of this early Munich experience obviously helped to form the relationship between Adrian Leverkühn and Rudi Schwerdtfeger.)

The main theme of *Tonio Kröger* was unmistakably engendered by the mood of that letter; for the rest, the *Novelle* is as close to *Buddenbrooks* as a fresh shoot to the original plant. Once more we are with a Hanno Buddenbrook who, having survived his music and typhoid fever, struggles with the 'curse' of literature, that ghost from the Flaubertian estate, which has haunted many an artistic dedication and turned writing into the enemy of the '*cœur simple*', the heart alive with innocent love and unchilled by irony. *Tonio Kröger* is the lyrically delicate vessel of a heavy freight and yet carries its burden with the accomplished sense of balance which is the gift of aesthetic mastery. Again, the plot is a plot of ideas, and the story itself is so slight it is hardly worth recounting. Tonio (for his mother comes from somewhere 'deep down on the map') Kröger (for his father is Consul Kröger, grain merchant in an old German city on the Baltic—Lübeck again) is a boy chosen, against his will, by the spirit of art. He is bad at his lessons, but good at reading, dreaming, and writing verse. The fountain and the old walnut tree in the garden, the yellow dunes and green waves of the Baltic Sea—these are the things he loves. But he also loves his schoolmate Hans Hansen, fair, blue-eyed, well-built, and 'ruthless', the very boy, it seems, in whom Thomas Buddenbrook yearned to live on after death. Will Tonio ever succeed in winning him over and make him feel, for instance, what he himself feels when reading Schiller's *Don Carlos*, the scene above all where the courtiers are speechless at the news that in his cabinet the King, the great, hard, and powerful King of Spain, weeps because the man he loved and trusted has deceived him? Or does Tonio even wish to succeed? Is it not just because Schiller and weeping kings mean nothing to Hans Hansen that he loves him so dearly? Just as a little later he loves fair, healthy, and stupid Ingeborg Holm, destined to remain unimpressed by his being a poet—and loves her not least because she will for ever laugh at his clumsiness, and would laugh even 'if he had produced all by himself the nine symphonies, *The World as Will and Idea*, and the Last Judgment'.[3]

Tonio Kröger grows up to be a successful writer. Having

learned early in life, as early as his love for Hans Hansen, that 'he who loves most is the most easily defeated and must suffer',[4] and knowing also that warmth of feeling is not the temperature in which the written word prospers, he sets out to kill his heart in adventures of the flesh and excesses of intellectual detachment.   And he works—'not like a man who works that he may live; but as one who is bent on living only in his work' because 'one must die to life in order to be entirely a creator'.[5]   Yet his conscience keeps protesting, for he is not, as we have heard already, 'a nihilist'.   In Munich, where he now lives, his painter friend Lisaveta, at the end of a long conversation which holds the central place in the story, diagnoses his complaint in words which have become an examination platitude of modern German literature: 'You are a burgher who has lost his way.'[6]   Whereupon the burgher decides to have a holiday with the burghers: he goes to a place by the Baltic Sea, stopping on the way in his native town which he has not seen for thirteen years, and where his family mansion now houses a public library.   He is in danger of being arrested in Lübeck: the police look for an imposter presumed to be *en route* for Denmark; and Tonio Kröger is strangely reluctant to clear up the misunderstanding: 'After all, were they not almost right, these guardians of civic order? In a sense he quite agreed with them',[7] just as once upon a time he used inwardly to agree with his father's scolding him for his bad performances at school.

In Denmark, after some early autumn days spent on the beach and bemused by solitude, he finds Hans Hansen and Ingeborg Holm again, or rather their images re-embodied in two young members of a party which has come to his hotel for a night of dancing.   Watching them at the dance—through a glass door, as befits this writer's vision of 'life'—Tonio Kröger is in a trance of memories and 'his heart is alive once more'.   'But what is it that lies between that past and this present, and has made him what he now is?   A waste land, coldness, desolation; and ah, sensibility! And Art!'[8]   Next day Tonio writes, as he has promised, to Lisaveta: '. . . a burgher who has strayed into art, a bohemian homesick for the tidy house of his childhood, an

artist with a guilty conscience. . . . I stand between two worlds.
I am at home in neither. . . . You artists call me a burgher, and
the burghers try to arrest me. . . . For surely it is my burgher
conscience which forces me to see in art . . . something profoundly ambiguous, suspect and dubious, and makes me fall in
love . . . with the blond and blue-eyed . . . and commonplace. . . .
If anything can turn a *littérateur* into a poet, then it is this
burgher love of mine. . . .'[9]

This is all there is of a story in *Tonio Kröger*, a work which
could hardly be called a *Novelle* if one insisted upon Goethe's
definition of the genre as the narration of a spectacular event.*
It gently defies all rules worked out for this class of literature,
very much in the manner of Chekhov's eluding the orthodox
laws of drama. There is no 'event', and what occurs could not
be less spectacular. Amazing is merely the literary charm which
resolves in lyrical simplicity an exceedingly problematical state
of mind, the lucid presentation through incident and reflection of
a poetic mood intricately composed of thought and emotion.
Tonio Kröger is more in the nature of an extended poem in
prose; in a sense, it is even rhymed, with the repetition of certain
motifs assuming the unifying function of rhyme.

The *leit-motif*—Thomas Mann's acknowledged debt to
Richard Wagner—already played its part in the composition of
Buddenbrooks, either in the form of the Homeric *epitheton
ornans*, an unchanging attribute of a person's appearance,
character, or manner of speech, or of identical words to describe
significantly similar situations. In *Tonio Kröger* the same
technique is used with even subtler effect. There is not only
the rhythmical recurrence of images, sounds, configurations:
the wild flower in Consul Kröger's button-hole, the peculiarly
inclined attitude of Tonio's head and his habit of softly whistling
when he is in a sad or pensive mood, the gypsies in their green
wagon opposing with vagrant rootlessness the burgher's respectable domesticity—there is, in fact, all the *Buddenbrooks*-
proven strategy of the story-teller to make his medium Time

---

* '. . . eine ereignete unerhörte Begebenheit' (conversation with Ecker-
mann, 29 January 1827).

yield a little to his vain desire to establish the whole story, like a picture or a sculpture, at every moment of its duration. But there are also innovations. For instance: at the beginning of the story the author describes the feelings which Hans Hansen's one gesture of affection inspires in the boy Tonio; and at the end the writer Tonio Kröger uses the very same words, as it were in his own right, to speak of that love of life which may still save his problematical literary existence.[10] By so taking the words out of his author's mouth, Tonio seems to say: 'It is truly *my* story that has been told', just as the author, on his part, demonstrates in this manner that it is recognizably *his* world in which the story takes place. Such reassurance is badly needed where the loss of real existence—'dying to life'—is felt to be the condition of artistic creativeness. Thus the *leit-motif*, tidy symbol of a significantly ordered life, becomes for Thomas Mann the seal of possession secure beyond loss, as well as proof, valid beyond doubt and deprivation, of having mastered reality through knowing the secret of its organization. To make sure that the world makes sense despite all insinuations to the contrary, indeed to make it yield sense if it is unwilling to do so on its own, wholly to possess it on the strength of the created order of the work of art, and yet always to doubt the efficacy of this act of appropriation—it is this kind of creativeness, both possessive and melancholy, which Thomas Mann's style suggests. This style, passionate and pedantic, seeking real certainty through imaginative conquests and ironically bringing their value into question again, has its happiest moments when language, in its unavoidably onesided outspokenness, yet approaches the state of music and carries the echo of those complex harmonies in which the soul, possessed and possessing, is momentarily at rest. Essentially musical, the *leit-motif* is but the crystallization of an all-pervasive element in Thomas Mann's literary mind. In *Tonio Kröger* it conveys, more effectively than any explicit utterance, the foremost problem of the hero: how to defend his work, and indeed himself, against the encroachment of non-entity. And entity consists in meaningful organization, visibly vindicated by the *leit-motif*.

Does Tonio Kröger truly 'love life', the 'ordinary' and 'commonplace', and does he love it with a love which merits the name by which he calls it: *Bürgerliebe*, burgher love? He is, to judge by his story, manifestly deluded. As is proper for a tale the theme of which is a man's separation from ordinary human existence, no other being, apart from himself, comes to life in it. Hans Hansen is a mere creature of Tonio's youthful Eros, a blond and blue-eyed apparition invoked by an erotic craving the burghers would be anxious to disown. The same is true, within safer conventions, of Ingeborg Holm. Lisaveta, in her turn, is hardly more than his sister-confessor. And the rest of the story's population is made up of amusing caricatures of bourgeois society: Herr Knaak, the ludicrous dancing teacher and master of bourgeois ceremonies, or Herr Seehaase, the embarrassed hotel proprietor in Lübeck, or the Hamburg business man on the boat whose oceanic observations on the starry universe are sadly interrupted by the oceanic effects of a surfeit of lobster. Certainly, more lovable than these, in the story's own emotional climate, are the fountain and the walnut tree, undemanding instigators of lyrical feeling, and then again the sea, element of infinite fluidity—symbol, for Thomas Mann, of life blissfully halted at the stage of boundless potentiality and not yet subject to the rigorous restriction of finite forms, intimation of the inarticulate, immeasurable, infinite, and closest approximation within the material world to the eternal void and nothingness.

Is such the love of a burgher, or the love for the burgher's world? Clearly, what Thomas Mann calls 'burgher' is simply a name, suggested to him by his social origins, for a certain ethical attitude. It takes the form of a moral protest against all those practitioners of art who, at the beginning of this century, artistically and intellectually throve on the disintegration of their social *milieu*, mistaking libertinism for liberty, licentiousness for poetic licence, a disorderly soul for the mark of genius, and untrammelled self-expression for the prerequisite of artistic accomplishment. And it is his moral indictment of the artist's 'dwelling in possibility', as Emily Dickinson put it, an expression of the moral discomfort suffered in the inability or unwillingness to commit himself to a definite form of existence which, with the seriousness of an irrevocable choice, would cut off the free play of the imagination, and reduce to a sadly lingering sense of loss the inexhaustible offerings of the 'fluid element'. Yet the refusal to make the confining choice, to forgo the continuous exploration of 'possibility', involves, so it seems to the moral consciousness of Tonio Kröger and his author, a far greater loss: the loss of 'real life', or, as Kierkegaard put it, the loss of 'existence'. Tonio Kröger is deeply suspicious of the moral status of the mere aesthetic recorder; it is this suspicion which produces what Thomas Mann later called his 'amorous affirmation' of 'the unproblematical and innocent form of existence', of 'everything which is not spirit and art'. And in the *Novelle*, according to *Meditations of a Non-Political Man*, 'the name of life . . . was given, sentimentally enough, to the world of the burgher'.[11] Had Thomas Mann known Kierkegaard at the time he would have discovered that Tonio Kröger lived not so much in a half-way house between burgher and artist as in that border-region between the aesthetic and the ethical state in which Kierkegaard saw the proper home of irony.

The sentimental vagueness of the concept 'burgher' in Thomas Mann's earlier writings is indeed most conspicuous. It seems an elusive but powerful organism capable of absorbing into its indefinitely expansive system a vast variety of incommensurable things: a measure of Christian piety and a measure of Will to Power, Goethe's doctrine of resignation and Nietzsche's dithyrambic excesses, Stifter's untempestuous ideal and Wagner's musical demon, Schopenhauer's will to saintliness and Bismarck's *Realpolitik;* it seems, in fact, an inexhaustibly magnetic 'And', an 'And in itself', and thus perhaps truly deserving of the name of 'life'. But having eaten the fruits from a whole orchard of trees of knowledge, it certainly no longer has the blue eyes of innocence. 'A burgher gone astray'—if to be a burgher is to walk in such a maze, what else can one do but lose one's way? And Tonio Kröger may be right in reflecting that 'if he went wrong it was because for some people there is no such thing as a right way'.[12]   Yet as the right way is nevertheless in some obscurely commanding sense the way of the burgher, the way of the burgher can only mean that 'actuality of commitment' which is immune from the lures of the 'realm of possibility', and acknowledges the moral superiority of life actually lived over all forms of aesthetic reflection.

Tonio Kröger's burgher love, the artistic affection for everything that is not art, is a sentiment akin to that which leads to the *'trahison des clercs'*, and Thomas Mann is right in saying that in his *Novelle* Nietzsche's philosophy of Life gains the upper hand over Schopenhauer's denial of it, tilting the scales of Will and Spirit, which stood ironically balanced in *Buddenbrooks*, in favour of Life.   Yet in spite of this, Spirit does not entirely lose in status what Life seems to gain; on the contrary, Tonio Kröger submits to the 'curse' of literature as one accepting a mission.   Going to Denmark, he too will 'stand on the platform of Elsinore where the spirit appeared to Hamlet, bringing misery and death to that poor and noble youth'.[13]   The spirit which had insidiously crept into the life of the Buddenbrooks, unsteadying, bewildering, corroding it, now seems to issue a clear if tragic commandment: die to 'life' for the sake of 'art'!

Blurred as the image of the burgher remains in *Tonio Kröger*, the sense of loss and sacrifice in the artist becomes poignantly clear.   To Lisaveta it seems that Tonio is devoutly dedicated to his vocation.   'Don't talk about vocation,' he replies, 'literature is not a calling, it is a curse.'[14]   And this curse lies in the necessity to be almost 'something extra-human, inhuman, to cultivate a strange aloofness, indeed indifference towards human existence in order to be able, or even tempted, to play with it aesthetically, portray it in good taste and to good effect. The very gift of style, form and expression, is nothing but this cool and fastidious attitude towards human life; its very condition is impoverishment, a desperate lack of spontaneity. . . . The artist is finished as soon as he becomes a man and begins to feel. . . .   I tell you I am often sick to death of having to represent what is human without myself having a share in it.'[15]

And Tonio goes still further in his denunciation of the artist's 'inhumanity': 'To see things clearly, if even through tears, to recognise, notice, observe, even at the very moment when hands are clinging and lips meeting, and the eye is blinded with feeling— it is infamous, indecent, outrageous. . . .' [16] And 'He is mistaken who believes he may pluck a single leaf from the laurel tree of art without paying for it with his life.' [17]

2

Is Tonio Kröger's vision of life, art, and artists true? The very question is likely to stir up a nest of hornets buzzing with literary criticism. For is it at all a permissible question? Were it not, to speak with Horatio (and Tonio who quotes him), to consider too curiously, to consider so? The organization of the story, the subtle intertwining of motifs, the appropriateness of the idiom, the subjective coherence and plausibility of the hero's mind, be he right or mistaken—these are valid criteria of literary worth. True. Yet after all is said and done, there lingers curiosity concerning the nature of that which is organized, the sense in the intertwining, and what exactly it is to which the idiom is appropriate. In the case of *Tonio Kröger* these are, as it were, doubly literary considerations. For, firstly, its hero is a questioning mind, and the quality of his questions must determine not only the manner of their literary presentation but also the status of the literary work; and, secondly, the problem he raises is literature itself. And the sense of truth with which, and the level of truth on which, a writer creatively perceives this problem is a measure of his genius. Moreover, our understanding of *Tonio Kröger*, and of the position this obviously only semi-imaginary young writer holds in the real history of literature, may gain considerably if we realize that our reluctance to ask the question of truth would be due to our belief in the essential correctness of Tonio's diagnosis of literature and life. It is a diagnosis shared, consciously or not, by many a literary critic. For only if 'life' and 'letters' are pre-ordained strangers, only then are questions arising from the business of 'living' out of place if applied to 'writing'. And certainly, if life has to 'die' so that 'literature' can live, then the critic paying attention to anything that is not 'strictly literary' merely busies himself with attending funerals.

There can be little doubt that *Tonio Kröger* expresses a subjective truth about the relationship of art and life, a truth so intensely felt that the prolonged argument in the middle of the *Novelle* is not only smoothly absorbed into the lyrical substance of the work, but is also reflected in its atmosphere and embodied in its incident. This would in itself suffice to carry conviction even if we did not know that the Tonio-experience was so compelling that it claimed a large share in almost all the future productions of Thomas Mann. 'A man of character has his typical experience which will recur again and again',[18] said Nietzsche: and the typical experience of Thomas Mann is that which is the sole subject-matter of *Tonio Kröger*. It is an experience so strong that Mann's last great works, *Doctor Faustus* and *Felix Krull*, are in the nature of an apotheosis, the one tragic, the other comic, of the Kröger-theme; and so typical that it insisted, in *Lotte in Weimar*, upon bending the incommensurable nature of Goethe's genius into some gestures of conformity with the Lübeck archetype. The immense literary fruitfulness of this subjective truth is, however, due to its coinciding with a vast and weighty historical truth, a coincidence which gives to Thomas Mann's achievement, however it will fare with the incalculable judges of eternal value, its singular historical importance. To see Thomas Mann's work in its historical perspective means to see not only more than it, but also more of it.

We have heard Tonio Kröger curse as 'infamous' and 'outrageous' his fate of having to cultivate a 'strange aloofness' from human existence, of having to see, observe, and represent life without vitally sharing in it. It is a fate which Schopenhauer blessed. The genius of art, he said, consists in the faculty of 'pure contemplation', in the power of the mind to conquer the Will and lose itself entirely in the vision of the object to be represented: 'Genius is perfect objectivity.' It is a person's ability 'to become immersed in seeing and observing, to recall the mind from that service for which it was originally meant: the service to the Will, that is, to lose sight of his own interest and volition, of all his own aims and purposes, and hence to disown for some time his whole personality and survive alone as a pure subject of knowledge, as a medium of lucid vision. . . .' [19] It would be interesting and profitable to analyse this grand definition of genius, which ever since Schopenhauer has been used and varied incessantly by artists anxious to describe and justify the 'extraordinary' character of art and their own estrangement from the world.   Once more we might ask what precisely it is that the 'pure contemplation' contemplates if it is not, in Schopenhauer's own terms, the spiritually so unre- warding Will objectified as World?   For only because the World for him is Will can Schopenhauer proclaim that the original purpose of mind is to be the Will's servant, a thesis almost Marxian in its metaphysical subordination of the spirit to a kind of cosmic greed.   However, be it enough here to say that this most radical separation of artistic vision from the 'real person', of aesthetic creativity from 'empirical living', is prompted by the suspicion that world and persons are in a sorry state indeed.

It is, perhaps, the state which Goethe, in a rare apocalyptic mood, prophesied as the 'Prosaic Age' [20] when all poetry would cease, and which Hegel, so vigorously despised by Schopen- hauer for turning metaphysics into historicism, declared a historical necessity that in his time had actually come to pass. 'The mode of prose', Hegel wrote, 'absorbs all the concepts of the mind, impressing them with its prosaic stamp', and so much so that 'art is, and will remain, a thing of the past' [21]—unless it miraculously rises above the historical hour, creating in pre- cariously intense isolation, and 'out of its own pure self', a supra-historical thing called 'absolute poetry'. [22]   If this diag- nosis may be decried as dangerous historicism, it is yet true as a statement of what poets did feel: Schiller, for instance, when in a letter to Herder (4 November 1795) he wrote: 'This supremacy of prose in the whole of our condition is, I believe, so strong and definite that the poetic mind, rather than conquering it, would unavoidably be infected with it and perish.   Therefore I know

no salvation for the spirit of poetry than to withdraw from the
real world, shun the dangerous coalition with reality, and aim at
the strictest separation.' It is the classical formula of that which
the English genius for understatement (so often merely the overstatement of the slightest touch of banality in a thought or an
experience) has termed 'escapism'; the programme too for a
poetical departure, as un-Schillerian as can be, which leads to
the purest distillation of poetic essences, and defies—in Rimbaud,
Mallarmé, Valéry—the slightest encroachment of prosaic reality. Theoretically and philosophically, the separation of
poetry from the condition of reality is most strictly prepared
by Schopenhauer's metaphysics of art, this fountain-head of a
current of aesthetic speculation which is at its mightiest in the
theory of French symbolism, is still powerful in the thought of
Rilke, Valéry, and T. S. Eliot, and comes to stagnate in all the
more whimsical absurdities of modern criticism.

Empirical reality, as conceived by Schopenhauer, is so
thoroughly estranged from all true inspiration that *every* true
inspiration must be sought in a region close to saintliness. And
Schopenhauer does not hesitate sublimely to embarrass the
artist by making him go to and fro between the world and the
ultimate place of lonely distinction: in his creative moments the
artist shares, according to the pessimistic philosophy, the vision
of the saints, but without gaining their '*lasting* freedom from
the Will'. 'Comforted only for a while', [23] he returns to the
world, suffering henceforward the pain of deprivation and the
embarrassment of knowing better—a Platonic cave-dweller who
for a moment stood in the light of the Ideas and lost to them the
eyesight meant for finding his way in the darker sphere.

The history of nineteenth-century literature reverberates with
the laments of poets and writers at the injuries their 'empirical
persons' have received in the exercise of 'pure vision', just as,
vice versa, the history of criticism abounds with diagnostic
findings of wounds taken to be the real provocations of artistic
practice. From Goethe's Tasso, who 'from his inmost being'
released the thread of poetry and spun 'the delicious cocoon'
in which to enclose himself 'as if in a coffin', through many a

romantic agony, through Flaubert, Rimbaud, Ibsen, to Valéry, Rilke and indeed Thomas Mann, the feud between art and life has never ceased, demanding great sacrifices of 'real entity' and 'identical self'. 'The Sun, the Moon, the Sea and Men and Women who are creatures of impulse'—Schopenhauer would have said: creatures of Will—'have about them an unchanging attribute—the poet has none', writes Keats in the celebrated letter to Richard Woodhouse (27 October 1818) and goes on to confess the 'wretched thing' 'that not one word I ever utter can be taken for granted as an opinion growing out of my identical nature—how can it, when I have no nature?' Here a poet experiences dejectedly the 'extinction of personality' which for Schopenhauer is the seal of the glorious brotherhood between artist and saint. Once again we witness the amazingly speedy shift of values attached to the same situation, changing in the twinkling of an eye, an eye now angelic and now evil; and once again it is in Nietzsche, that epochal manipulator of contradictions, that we may watch the *volte-face*.

In *The Birth of Tragedy* it is, in youthful obedience to Schopenhauer, the saints and angels who are by the side of the artist: 'In so far as the subject is an artist, he is liberated from his individual will and, as it were, transformed into a mere medium through which the one and only real subject (the Will) is redeemed in pure appearance.' [24] Yet, once again, the 'pure *appearance*' bodes ill for the stability of the redemption. And indeed, fourteen years later, in *Concerning the Origins of Morality*, the 'redeeming power' has passed into the hands of mocking demons who cynically seem to receive Keat's wretched confession and turn the 'medium of redemption' into 'manure': 'Certainly, one does well to separate artist and work, not taking *him* as seriously as one takes *it*. He is, after all, not more than a condition of his work, the womb, the soil, sometimes the mere manure, from which it grows. One must forget him if one wishes to enjoy his work. . . . Beware of the error . . . of mistaking him for that which he represents, imagines, and expresses. The truth is that if he were all this, he could not possibly represent, imagine, and express it. . . . The perfect artist is for ever and ever shut off from all "reality".' [25]   It might serve as a motto for *Tonio Kröger*.

Without the slightest change in the philosophical basis of the argument, and with a mere injection of psychology, the Schopenhauerian vessel of the glorious vision has become precisely the 'wretched thing' of Keats. And how well Nietzsche understands Keats's complaint and Tonio Kröger's distress! 'I tell you I am often sick to death of having to represent what is human without having myself a share in it', we have heard Tonio say, and: 'What a fate! That is, if you have enough heart-left, enough warmth of affections, to feel how frightful it is!' [26]   It might be by Keats; and as if commenting on both their outcries, Nietzsche continues: '. . . on the other hand, it is understandable that sometimes the artist should tire, to the point of desperation, of this eternal "non-reality" and falseness of his inner existence, and try to venture into the most forbidden territory—the real, try in fact to exist in earnest. How successfully? One may guess . . .' [27]   But there is no need to guess. We know the outcome of the dangerous experiment from Goethe's *Torquato Tasso*, Grillparzer's *Sappho*, from the lives of Novalis, Hölderlin, Nietzsche himself, indeed from what amounts to a whole library of nineteenth-century literary biographies. And among Thomas Mann's works, *Tonio Kröger* is only the idyllic prelude to the more violent encounters between the non-reality of the artist and the reality of life, tragically treated in *Death in Venice* and *Doctor Faustus*, and outrageously as high comedy in *Felix Krull*.

Rilke's '*Anschaun, das nichts begehrt, des grossen Künstlers Anschaun*', his artist's contemplative gaze which desires nothing, Proust's exiling himself from the actuality of life within the insulated cell of memories and words, Valéry's Monsieur Teste with his frozen feelings and the mind's crystalline constructions, all this is prompted by the presumed insight, the Tonio-Kröger-insight, into the aesthetic uselessness of the immediacy of life, and more often than not by horribly bungling it.

This state of affairs, with all its refinements and sophisticated eccentricities, has not only the sanction of Nietzsche's

F

psychology of art, but also of Schopenhauer's lofty metaphysics. Naturally, literary criticism had to adjust itself eventually to these persistent revelations of the poet's self-experience, their insistence on the essential 'otherness' of art and life. T. S. Eliot's essay 'Tradition and the Individual Talent' marks the moment of this critical awakening, and it is a little triumph of the *Zeitgeist* that some of its assertions read like the soberly Anglo-Saxon versions of philosophically and lyrically more exalted Germanisms. Thus Goethe's silkworm spinning himself to death for the sake of the 'delicious fabric' of poetry, and Schopenhauer's artist who 'disowns for some time his whole personality', become T. S. Eliot's 'continual surrender of himself as he is at the moment to something which is more valuable', namely to Schopenhauer's 'pure subject of knowledge, the medium of pure vision'. And when T. S. Eliot writes: 'The progress of an artist is a continual self-sacrifice, a continual extinction of personality', he means the same 'progress' which for Tonio Kröger lies in the discovery that he may only 'pluck a single leaf from the laurel tree of art by paying for it with his life'. And when Tonio Kröger says: 'It isn't so much a matter of the "redeeming power" of the "Word" as it is of storing your feelings on ice',[28] he uses almost the same metaphor as Eliot: 'The poet's mind is in fact a receptacle for seizing and storing up numberless feelings, phrases, images, which remain there until all the particles which can unite to form a new compound are present together.' Nor is there the slightest difference between Nietzsche's saying that the poet is a 'mere medium', 'mere soil', so that 'one must forget him if one wishes to enjoy his work', and Eliot's 'that the poet has not a "personality" to express, but a particular medium . . . in which impressions and experiences combine in peculiar and unexpected ways'.[29]

The historical truth of Tonio Kröger's vision of life, art, and artists seems indisputable. Would it also have struck artists of other ages as true? It is hardly thinkable that the builders of Greek temples or medieval cathedrals were haunted by a sense of non-being, or that Homer, or Aeschylus, or Dante, felt that their poetic pursuits entailed a loss of personality. But even much later this manner of interpreting the nature of artistic creation might have met with nothing but blank incomprehension even in the highest ranks: from Bach, for instance, or Mozart. Certainly, there is no doubt that the creation of a work of art has always been something other than the 'artistic' expression of subjective feelings and experiences; no doubt whatever that the vision of the artist must reach beyond the field hemmed in by the wilful purposes of the self. Certainly, genius consists in the gift, rare at all times, to surrender freely to a command issuing from a truth beyond appearances. But only a complete reversal of the order and hierarchy determined by the spiritual tradition of Europe could suggest the name of non-reality and nothingness for that which is comprehended in the saintly vision, and which is equated by Schopenhauer and his followers so liberally with the aesthetic imagination. And what a perverted doctrine of the human person had to be accepted by the world before artists could feel that they ceased to be persons precisely at the point where the real person should begin: in the act of submitting to an objective vision!

This, then, is yet another theme in modern literature, as new and as revealing as that of the demonic boredom and the sickly Eros. It postulates the obscurest of transcendental realms: the *aesthetic* transcendence. For where exactly grows the straw with which the bricks are made for the aesthetic edifice? Where is the point of vision from which the artist's mind observes the world as if from outside or above? What is the nature of the medium into which the creator 'depersonalizes' himself? And if Heidegger, very much in keeping with the spirit of the prevalent aesthetic theory, says that 'the artist is, in relation to his work, an irrelevancy, hardly more than a passage ... for the transit of the work' [30]—whence and whither does the passage lead? It is neither irreverence nor idle curiosity which asks these questions, but an anxiety inspired by the 'transcendent' satanic company which a still more 'depersonalized' Tonio Kröger, in his final incarnation as the composer Doctor Faustus, will one day seek and find. Amid all this aesthetic pother the suspicion grows that there must have been a time when the artist shared the reality of his fellow-men, and was distinguished from them not so much by a unique vision and agony as simply by the power to give surpassing form and shape to the common intimations of meaning. For a world in which the makers of beautiful and meaningful things are barred from 'real' existence is indeed a strangely inhuman and deeply disquieting world—a world immune from that idea of creation which, beside much sorrow and darkness, also knows the reality of grace. The aesthetic transcendence is then, perhaps, nothing but an optical delusion enforced upon the eye by the dark prospect of a historical period, and caused by a pathological narrowing of the common vision— by an insidious deficiency in the concept of what is real. When the sea recedes, many a strange creature of the ocean is left behind on the sands, dazzled and dazzling outcasts from another medium. At high tide they are in their own and need not transcend quite as much.

Schopenhauer's genius of art, transcending all self-centred purposes and coming face to face with the Absolute, Goethe's poet engaged in the self-annihilating service to his demon, Keats's surrender of all individual identity, the young Nietzsche's redemption of the empirical world in the aesthetic phenomenon, Rilke's pure contemplation, T. S. Eliot's doctrine of the continual self-sacrifice of the artist's personality, Thomas Mann's artist who pays with his life for a leaf of the laurel tree— it all appears to be spoken in the idiom of religion, in the language of '. . . but whosoever shall lose his life . . .' It is therefore less surprising than may appear at first glance that from *Tonio Kröger* Thomas Mann turns to Fra Girolamo Savonarola, contrasting and yet linking in *Fiorenza* the spirit of art with the spirit of religion—or at least with what at the time, instructed by Nietzsche, he took to be religious genius. This play—or 'dialectical *Novelle*', as he once called it—is an illuminating failure. What it illumines is the utter precariousness of that extreme spiritualization of art in an age dispossessed of any concrete notion of the 'spirit'.* Thomas Mann himself

---

* It is this lack which, in his essay on 'Tradition and the Individual Talent', induced T. S. Eliot not to pursue too far his argument concerning

says in a letter to his brother (18 February 1905)—and more or less repeats in *Meditations of a Non-Political Man*—that in *Tonio Kröger* he had gone too far 'in running into one the concepts of "spirit" and "art"'. *Fiorenza* was to show the 'hostile opposition' between them.[31] But the opposition, alas, is not maintained. They come together again. Both end in Nietzschean psychology.

3

The scene is Florence on an April day in 1492, the day on which Lorenzo de' Medici is to die. The stage seems to be occupied by the late Renaissance in person, or in persons: by philosophers, politicians, painters, and above all by Fiore, Lorenzo's beautiful mistress. Successions both to the throne and the Holy See are in the air. Bright pagan thoughts are uttered and intrigues are conducted. Upon the gross display of cynicism and decadence, with even the fashionable resurgence of moral and religious zeal savoured as an aesthetic *delicatesse* —'Let me whisper a little piece of news in your ear: morality is possible once more!' [32]—there fall two shadows: Lorenzo's imminent death and the religious mob hysteria stirred by Savonarola, Prior of San Marco. In the meeting between him and the dying Lorenzo the drama culminates and ends. Thomas Mann himself appears to have been much perplexed by it.

In the correspondence with his brother the plan to write it

the distinction between the empirical self of the artist and that 'something which is more valuable' (*Selected Essays*, London, 1948, p. 17). Stopping 'at the frontier of metaphysics' (p. 21), he resorts instead to the pseudo-empirical concept of 'tradition' which, so that it may at least resemble something metaphysical, it left in suitable vagueness. It is neither 'the past as a lump' nor 'one preferred period'; it is 'the main current', the more difficult to find because it 'does not at all flow invariably through the most distinguished reputations' (p. 16). Nevertheless, the poet must discover it in his own 'consciousness of the past' (p. 17). Obviously, Eliot uses 'tradition' as a historically-sounding makeshift for a pure value-judgment which would require, not a historical, but a metaphysical or religious definition.

is mentioned even before any hint appears of *Tonio Kröger*.
In a letter of 17 December 1900 he speaks of *The King of
Florence* of which 'so far exist only the psychological idea and
a shapeless dream'. 'The ambiguity of the title is intentional,'
he says: 'Christ and Fra Girolamo (Savonarola) are one and
the same: weakness, turned genius, gains power over life.' [33]
But in the completed work the 'ambiguous identity' exists,
more interestingly, between Savonarola and Lorenzo, and
becomes the main 'psychological idea', so much so that it
decisively interferes with the intended contrast between 'spirit'
and 'art'. As soon as Thomas Mann has finished the play, he
tells his brother that 'this effort to fill an intellectual construction with life' is a 'fiasco'.[34]   Despite the fiasco and the 'psychological idea', and contrary to his resolution, expressed in the
same letter, to remain firm in his self-criticism, he defends the
'failure' in 1908 against the reviewer of a Catholic journal.
For this dogmatic critic, he says, had not noticed that the drama
is about 'Christianity assuming political power through the hero
of San Marco, one of the most passionate and radical Christians
of all times'.[35]   But ten years later, in *Meditations of a Non-
Political Man*, the Savonarola of *Fiorenza* is no longer recommended to the benevolence of a Christian critic: he is described
as Nietzsche's 'ascetic priest'—who, in his turn, is equated with
the 'radical *littérateur* of the most recent type' [36]—that is to
say, with the *Zivilisationsliterat*, Thomas Mann's great
polemical creation of the First World War. Seldom has an
author had so varied uses for a product of his mind. The perplexity caused by *Fiorenza* is greater than one would expect
of an 'intellectual construction'.

The truth is that the intellectual construction did in fact fill
itself with a measure of life, and only failed because in a sense
it was not intellectual enough. For there can hardly be any
doubt that the theme has all the backing of the writer's emotions; what it lacks is the controlling power of an imaginative
intelligence mature enough, or naturally equipped, to do justice
to the situation invoked. In his hour of death, Lorenzo de'
Medici, having lived a life of power justified, as he thought,

by aesthetic glory, asks about the 'immortal self'. Misshapen, plagued by chaotic passions, born to be a misfit, he has become, through the ceaseless exercise of discipline, the 'Lord of Beauty', as they call him, and has, from 'the smouldering lust and misery within kindled the clear flame'.[37] But having knowingly willed not to be himself—who is he now? Can a man know what he knows and yet be himself? Who is that self that, unable to believe in himself, has come to despise all the world? And above all those who, deluded by an artifice of identity, submit to his power: the courtiers, philosophers, artists, and Fiore herself, an allegory of Florence and indeed of Life.

After *Tonio Kröger* it is difficult to believe that Lorenzo is merely an 'intellectual construction'. It is more likely that it is the emotions that have constructed him, emotions genuine enough and, alas, almost as 'genuine' as those which prompted, in *Tonio Kröger*, the Hamburg business man to wonder at the stars. The electrical illumination of these Renaissance scenes, the theatrical flamboyance of smouldering lusts and kindled flames, the strained eyesight and upward squint which seek to envisage Tonio Kröger's problem on the pinnacles of the quattrocento—all this speaks of a desire to resolve a perplexity of the spirit by thrusting dramatic greatness upon it. 'God performs miracles,' says Savonarola to Lorenzo, 'you see before you the miracle of innocence reborn.' It is the miracle that would assuage the burgher-artist's troubled conscience and miraculously give him the unattainable: the *knowing* spontaneity of authentic living, just as to Savonarola it seems to grant the power to do the deeds of faith despite his knowledge of its impure sources.[38] It is at this point that the miracle fails, condemning to failure the whole of *Fiorenza*. And it does so at the intervention of Nietzsche assisted by Sigmund Freud— or rather by the *Zeitgeist* itself, for Thomas Mann, when he wrote *Fiorenza*, knew as yet nothing of the new science, just as Freud, when he first conceived his theory of the psyche, did not know Schopenhauer's metaphysics of sex, or Nietzsche's psychological observations teeming with 'Freudian' insights.*

* Thomas Mann, in his essay, 'Freud and the Future' (1936), says that

The stage has been carefully arranged for a great climax. Lorenzo, on his deathbed, enquires of his court philosophers what is to be thought of the immortality of the soul. They are evasive, call it a tricky question, and tell him of Aristotle who, it is said, goes about the kingdom of shades still uttering equivocal ideas on the subject and refusing to commit himself. But Lorenzo, so they flatter, can at least be sure of immortal fame. 'That is poetry, my friend!' Lorenzo replies, 'beautiful poetry, but neither knowledge nor consolation!' And 'I am tired. I long to have something simple to hold fast to. Purgatory is simpler than Plato. . . . What I need is a father-confessor who would be as strong in faith as I have been in irony and sin.' [39]   It is clear that he wishes Savonarola to come to him, the monk who has inflamed the people of Florence with puritanical zeal against the luxurious ruler and has damned him from the pulpit of the *duomo*.   But even before the 'miracle of innocence reborn' appears before Lorenzo, the climax turns to anticlimax: Fiore gives away the secret of Savonarola's career in saintliness: in Ferrara once they were neighbours, she a pretty girl, he a boy ugly, shy, lonely, and studious.   He fell in love with her, she outrageously humiliated him.   He fled into a monastery, henceforward preaching the sinfulness of the flesh. 'You have made him great!' [40] exclaims Lorenzo, melodramatically confirming the psychological woman's findings.

This, of course, is the 'psychological idea' intended by Thomas Mann.   Nevertheless it brings about a literary collapse unique in Thomas Mann's writings.   While everything in the play that precedes the *dénouement* may pass as a questionable

he came to know Freud's work very late, 'much later than one might have expected, considering the connection between this science and the poetic and creative impulse in general and mine in particular' (*Essays of Three Decades*, p. 413).   Ernest Jones, in his *Sigmund Freud, Life and Work* (II, London, 1955, p. 385), reports Freud as saying that Nietzsche 'had in no way influenced his ideas', even though he later held that 'Nietzsche had a more penetrating knowledge of himself than any other man who ever lived or was ever likely to live'.   Schopenhauer is first mentioned by Freud as late as 1917 in the essay 'A Difficulty in the Path of Psychoanalysis'.

experiment in a medium alien to the writer's natural gifts, it is precisely at this calculated point that the writing breaks down. This embarrassing accident is caused by a total incongruity between problem and solution. The problem is one of living and dying, of souls in action and in defeat; and where this is the problem, Thomas Mann, even at his weakest, is artist enough not to leave his characters entirely at the mercy of an 'intellectual construction'. Yet the solution is provided not by minds articulate in the state of tragic contemplation, but clever in the state of ingenious theorizing. Therefore the pathos in which they indulge in order to honour their real situation becomes the pathetic subterfuge of psychology posing as poetry. Whatever his intention was, Thomas Mann could not help endowing with at least a measure of poetic sympathy a dying man calling for the priest. But this is as far as he goes; and as soon as the priest arrives, the vacuum of faith is invaded by melodramatic psychology.

The scene between Savonarola and Lorenzo is a series of variations on the theme of 'What is the meaning of ascetic ideals?' from Nietzsche's *Concerning the Origins of Morality*. For ascetic ideals are, according to Nietzsche, above all the priest's 'instrument of power and, at the same time, his highest authority to gain it'.[41] They are the subtlest revenge taken on life by those whom life has ill-treated, indeed their sublime trick to transform their own wretchedness into the guilt of the strong, and of weakening their adversaries by insinuating themselves into their conscience so that these will become ashamed of their happiness and say to one another: 'It is shameful to be happy. There is too much misery in the world.'[42] And this is indeed the essence of the confession which the dying Lorenzo, in a macabre exchange of roles, wrings from the Prior of San Marco who, as a youth, oppressed by his own privations and the insolence of power, was once, at the sight of an eagle rising from the castle of the rulers, overcome by 'the fervid wish, the tremendous resolve: could I but break those mighty wings'.[43] Lorenzo is intimately familiar with this psychology. For he himself is far from being Nietzsche's 'glorious Renaissance beast'.   He is an artist whose soul is cast in the same Nietzsche-Freudian mould, suffering from Savonarola's self-same wounds and only healing himself into another shape.   Nietzsche has described him in *Beyond Good and Evil*, and in doing so has anticipated many a later speculation on traumata and compensations, on lusts and sublimations, on wounds and bows:

> The world of historical values is dominated by forgery.   These great poets, like Byron, Musset, Poe, Leopardi, Kleist, Gogol (I dare not mention greater names but I mean them)—all endowed with souls wishing to conceal a break; often avenging themselves with their works upon some inner desecration, often seeking oblivion in their lofty flights from their all-too-faithful memories, often lost in mud and almost in love with it until they become like will-o'-the-wisps of the morasses and simulate the stars . . . what a torture are all these great artists and altogether these higher beings, what a torture to him who has guessed their true nature! [44]

Yet the extraordinary Nietzsche, incomprehensible in his contradictions except as the common strategist of two opposing armies who plans for the victory of a mysterious third, a few pages later self-insultingly takes back the guessing: 'From which follows that it is the mark of a finer humanity to respect "the mask" and not, in the wrong places, indulge in psychology and curiosity',[45] and still further on 'He who does not *wish* to see what is great in a man, has the sharpest eye for that which is low and superficial in him, and so gives away—himself.' [46] Indeed, very little respect for their respective masks is shown by Lorenzo and Savonarola in their ecstatic duet of guessing and confessing.   What might have been the administration of the Last Supper becomes a panegyric to the Will to Power, and reveals the meaning of the allegory: Lorenzo and Savonarola, each in his way, are the impure Spirit struggling from a position of seemingly pre-ordained defeat for mastery over Life, over Fiore, over Florence.   Much later, in 1929, Thomas Mann was to write yet another allegory of this kind, and it was to be incomparably more successful: *Mario and the Magician*, the story of the deformed hypnotist, using a freakish power of the spirit in order to set up, for an hour of cheap showman triumph, his hysterical dominion over the little world of a holiday audience, with life, healthy and innocent, in the end catastrophically rebelling against its abominable humiliation. In 1929, with the scene set in Mussolini's Italy and with Hitler's rising in Germany, the political meaning of the story will be obvious and intentional. But even in 1904, *Fiorenza*, by virtue of the inherited Nietzschean clairvoyance, has something of the *actualité* of *Mario*.

If Thomas Mann himself later believed that his Savonarola had much in common with the *Zivilisationsliterat*, it is even truer that he bears prophetically some of the features of the shrieking demagogue who was to impose his insanely jealous will and slum-begotten vision upon the German people. 'How laughable is the docility of the world!' exclaims the Prior with the contempt of the successful demagogue for those with whom he succeeds. And Lorenzo joins in: 'And laughing, one seizes the world as one seizes an instrument on which to play.' 'On which to play one's own self', concludes the monk.[47] They are truly brothers in the Will to Power, and Lorenzo even invites Savonarola into the brotherhood of artists: 'I perceive a remarkable perversion here: you zealously denounce art, and yet, Brother, you yourself—you too are an artist!' 'An artist who is at the same time a saint' [48]—this is how Savonarola promptly replies to the compliment. It is a strange parody of the 'pure vision' in which Schopenhauer joined artist and saint, as strange as the little essay Thomas Mann wrote in 1938, 'Brother Hitler', where the hateful madness of the dictator is diagnosed as a catastrophically neurotic perversion of the artistic impulse, and consequently: 'I quietly suspect that the frenzy which drove him into a certain capital was aimed at the old analyst who lived there, his true and most personal enemy, the philosophical man who has revealed the nature of neurosis, and administers sobriety and sobering knowledge even about "genius".' [49] Savonarola, on the other hand, has nothing to fear from psychoanalysis. He is his own Freud as he is his own Nietzsche. He has himself the soberest

insight into the springs of his 'genius'. He knows that Fiore
has driven him up to his pulpit, and knows that it is the malice
of his insulted libido that makes him preach the Cross, a crooked
cross indeed.—'What is the condition of grace?' Lorenzo asks.

> *The Prior:* That you set Florence free, at once, for ever, free
> from the lordship of your house.
> *Lorenzo:* Free—for you.
> *The Prior:* Free for the King who died on the Cross.
> *Lorenzo:* For you. For you! Why do you lie? We know each
> other. Fiorenza, my city! Do you love her, then? Say
> quickly! You love her?
> *The Prior:* Fool! Child! Take them to bed with you, to your
> grave, these playthings, these childish notions! Love indeed!
> A torrent of love, hatred, all-embracing and sweet! Con-
> suming chaos! I am this chaos, and this chaos wills that I be
> lord in Florence!
> *Lorenzo:* Monster! To what end? What can be your purpose?
> *The Prior:* Eternal peace. The triumph of the spirit. I will
> break them, those mighty wings.[50]

What is the meaning of the ascetic ideal, asks Nietzsche, why
should it have meant so much to man? It is the expression,
he answers, of 'the fundamental nature of the human will: its
horror vacui. Man needs a goal, and rather than not will, he
wills nothingness.' [51]   And Nietzsche has the last word in the
play. Lorenzo is dead. The people of Florence are in revolt.
Rumours have spread that Savonarola is a prisoner in Lorenzo's
palace. They come to liberate him. Fiore appears at
Lorenzo's deathbed, facing Savonarola. She warns the monk:
the fire he has fanned will consume him. 'Cease to will', she
implores him in Nietzsche's own words, 'cease to will, rather
than will the void.' But he loves the fire.[52]

It is not merely a 'psychological idea' and a literary failure
on which the curtain comes down. If it were, we should not
have done Thomas Mann the injustice of dealing at some
length with *Fiorenza* while we shall give no space to many
another minor work and major success, to *Tristan*, for instance,
or *Disorder and Early Sorrow*, or *Mario and the Magician*.

The failure of *Fiorenza* is momentous. What is at fault is not so much the power of the individual writer as the age to which he belongs: the age of 'psychology'; and this psychology cannot but render meaningless the great gestures of the human spirit. For it contemplates them in a spiritual vacuum. Yet at the same time the writer is engaged in the paradoxical business of extracting from it aesthetic significance: a work of literature. And *Fiorenza*, in its dealing with men of power and religion, is, of course, particularly endangered by this paradox. Indeed, the piece was written at a moment in the writer's career when the paradox proved insuperable, with the pathos of those great affirmations not even exploded but merely reduced to bathos.*

In the essay 'Freud and the Future' (1926) Thomas Mann confesses to his inclination to equate 'truth' with 'psychology', indeed to think of psychological truth as 'truth in the truest and bravest sense of the word' [53]—for it was psychology, that 'honest and courageous knowledge', which gave to the nineteenth century its pessimistically disillusioned and soberly heroic mind. But twelve years after *Fiorenza* and ten years before the essay on Freud, he denounced psychology as 'the cheapest and meanest' manner of knowing because there is 'nothing on earth, no belief, no feeling, no passion, which could not be reduced to worthlessness by psychological analysis'.[54] This is from *Meditations of a Non-Political Man*, and is one of the many boomerangs he uses in that strangest of literary civil wars. It certainly comes closer to the truth of *Fiorenza*. But both manners of speaking about 'psychology'—as if there

---

* Thomas Mann's first sketch for Savonarola is to be found in the story *Gladius Dei*, written in 1902. Its hero is a young religious fanatic with Savonarola's features who in a Munich art shop delivers a helpless tirade against the city's pagan artistic abandon and in particular against the exhibited portrayal of a very unholy-looking fashionable madonna. Avoiding the dangers both of the grandiose setting and the deep psychology, the anecdote succeeds in its modest way. The young zealot even anticipates something of *Tonio Kröger* and hints at the reason for the failure of *Fiorenza*: 'Is it possible to see through a thing and yet not be disgusted and pained by it?' (*Stories of Three Decades*, p. 191.)

were 'psychological truth' as such!—are as erroneous as they are historically relevant. The error of such assertions lies, strangely enough, in a psychological oversight. For they ignore the fact that there is no knowledge worth speaking about without a compelling urge to acquire it; and the knowledge acquired invariably reflects the nature of the impulse which has directed the mind. It is this impulse which creatively partakes in the making of the knowledge, and its share in it is truly immeasurable when the knowledge is about the very source of the impulse: the soul. Homer does not know less about heroes than does Stendhal, Flaubert does not know more about women than does Dante, and Shakespeare's knowledge of lovers is certainly as great as is Benjamin Constant's. To be sure, Achilles and Julien Sorel are different heroes, Beatrice and Emma Bovary are different women, Romeo and Adolphe are different lovers. But it would be naïve to believe that they simply differ in 'actual fact'. Actual facts hardly exist in either literature or psychology. All is interpretation. Those creatures of perceptive imaginations can indeed not be compared, but they are incommensurable above all by virtue of incommensurable wills to know the human person, to know the hero, the woman, the lover. It is not better and more knowing minds that have created the suspect hero, the unlovable woman, the disingenuous lover, but minds possessed by different affections for a different knowledge, affections other than the wonder and pride which know Achilles, the love which knows Beatrice, the passion and compassion which know Romeo. When Hamlet comes to know the frailty of women, he knows Ophelia not better than when he was 'unknowingly' in love with her; he knows her differently and knows her worse. The 'brave knowledge' may be brave; it is not necessarily greater knowledge.

Psychology is bad psychology if it disregards its own 'psychology', remaining unsuspicious of the impulse of suspicion that may be the father of its thought. Can it ever happen that the freely discovering mind says to the soul: 'This is what you are'? Must not the soul speak first? In the economy of the psyche the mind cannot know about the soul what the soul does not actively reveal: for here subject and object of knowledge are, if not identical, yet inextricably intertwined. The mind which has come to know the soul is no longer the same mind which did not know the soul; the soul which is known to the mind is no longer the same soul which was unknown. All *new* knowledge about the soul is therefore knowledge about a *different* soul; and the 'psychological mind', so strangely compelled to explain the life of the psyche always in terms of causes which are, in the order of traditional values, beneath the psychic phenomenon explained, may well be at the mercy of a soul 'feeling low', that is, a soul which has lowered its self-assessment and can therefore not help supplying the evidence it has itself suggested. The ensuing dialogue between the prompting soul and the theorizing mind would then go merely to confirm and strengthen what the soul already knew dimly of itself.

Tell an oyster that its pearl is the result of a pathological irritation. It will neither stop producing healthy pearls nor fall in love with pathology. The human soul, on being similarly enlightened, may do both, and must in fact have subtly done so before the mind could tell. Once it is told, the price of pearls drops in the exchanges of the spirit while the demand for pathological irritation soars. They are sold now as chances of winning a pearl, a poet, an artist—still desirable things even with their value reduced. It is this disturbing state of affairs which makes Nietzsche deplore the 'torture' of 'guessing the true nature of those higher beings', and at the same time recommend 'respect for the mask' as a condition of 'finer humanity'. For Thomas Mann, after having subjected himself, with *Fiorenza*, in frightful earnest to the tortures of the unmasked artist and the pathologically irritated saint, there is no escape except into what he himself has termed 'parody'; and he will raise the parodistic manner to a literary status nobody would have thought it could ever attain.*

* The word 'parody'—here and whenever it is used with reference to Thomas Mann's works—has to be dissociated from its usual connotations. It certainly does not mean simply 'travesty'. The English reader will do

Tonio Kröger ironically compares the artist to two other outcasts from the burgher world: first to a prince, then to a criminal; [55] and in 1905 there appears *Royal Highness*, in 1911 the first fragment of *Felix Krull*. Both heroes are parodistic versions of the artist: the one a duke, the other a confidence trickster. *Royal Highness*, written in the year of Thomas Mann's marriage, wittily and gracefully tells the fairy-tale of a prince who, asleep to the world in aristocratic isolation, is kissed into life by an extremely wakeful American millionairess. Whereupon Spirit and Life arrange for a wedding and are blessed ever after with love and money, and the all-but-bankrupt duchy with a sound economy.

Among the works of Thomas Mann this novel is like a gay little arrow shot off when 'the strain of knowing had become too great and the bow reached breaking point',[56] as the weird countess says in the book. She is one of a whole gallery of exquisitely drawn caricatures, the best of which are an exceedingly overbred collie and Doctor Ueberbein, the duke's tutor and friend, whose aristocratic persuasion is so aggressive that each time he hears *The Magic Flute* he feels like protesting against the humanitarian-democratic sentiment which sees in a prince 'more than a prince—a human being'. Also a farcical Tonio Kröger stalks into the story: the prize-winning poet Axel Martini whose poetry is full of the joy of living, and his living full of the miseries of ill-health and frustration. He looks a little like Nietzsche and talks not a little like Nietzsche: 'Renunciation', he says, 'is our compact with the

well to think of it in terms of James Joyce's *Ulysses* as a 'parody' of the classical epic. The word may be regarded as denoting a typical literary manner of the latecomer within a tradition of writing, of an artist whose spontaneity is inhibited by an unavoidable element of self-consciousness and self-irony—namely, the suspicion that he may be working in a medium the possibilities of which are exhausted. One of the main themes of *Meditations of a Non-Political Man* is that love of tradition which yet cannot help being 'the solvent of traditional forms'. In the autobiographical sketch of 1930 Thomas Mann uses the same words (*Die Neue Rundschau*, 1930, p. 752) for describing his literary 'mission', that is, for defining 'parody'.

Muse . . . and life is our forbidden garden, our great temptation, to which we yield sometimes, but never to our profit', and, with regard to the wine and the women of his dithyrambs: 'If I were the man to experience all that, I should not only not write such poems, but should also feel utter contempt for my present existence.' [57] Yet the light-hearted comedy with its skilfully constructed plot does not lack literary weight. This is provided not only by the unfailing eye for subtle detail combined with a cartoonist's talent for sketching a character in one rhythmically modulated line; it comes above all from a seriousness concealed, and yet not quite concealed, by laughter: the serious tension between the conservative zeal of Ueberbein (a forerunner, even in the manner of his death, of Naphta in *The Magic Mountain*) and the social-democratic virtues (Settembrini's domain in the later and greater novel) apparently affirmed through the very meaning of the story. Thomas Mann, in *Meditations*, hardly overstates the case by saying that the 'turn towards democracy', marked by *Royal Highness*, is taken not without the qualms of a heart going out in spontaneous sympathy to 'the aristocratic monstrosities, the impossible collie, and the not less impossible Doctor Ueberbein'.[58] There is indeed a touch of melancholy, a flicker of regret at a lost dream, in the duke's conversion to sober human happiness, and in the transformation of his country's relaxed decline into disciplined prosperity. It is this palpable hesitancy in welcoming the progressive happy ending, the sense of a blessing not undiminished by loss, which raises the literary quality of *Royal Highness* above that of a mere interlude. Yet interlude it is, sounding for the first time a theme which will be taken up later: in the turmoil of a personal crisis by *Meditations of a Non-Political Man*, and with the mature mastery of the novelist in *The Magic Mountain* and *Joseph and his Brothers*.

If *Royal Highness* is more in the nature of comedy than parody, then *Death in Venice*, written in 1911, is parody throughout, although parody of a particular and very unusual kind: tragic parody, produced when the experiment with the comic, *Felix Krull*, had to be temporarily abandoned. Thomas

G

Mann's failure to maintain the parodistic mood of high comedy led him to write his greatest *Novelle*, a work which is one of the very finest in the history of the genre. Although once again it is concerned with the psychology of the artist, it parodistically avoids the habitual psychological manner. The ruinous psychological cleverness of *Fiorenza* is now resolved in artistic wisdom.

4

Near the beginning of *Death in Venice* Thomas Mann describes the kind of works on which rests the literary reputation of its hero, the writer Gustav Aschenbach, or von Aschenbach, since he was knighted on the recent occasion of his fiftieth birthday. The description amounts to almost a list of Thomas Mann's own works, with their typical protagonists plainly discernible: it is without doubt Thomas Buddenbrook who 'with elegance and surpassing self-control conceals his inwardly undermined existence from the eyes of the world'. There is also the ugly and chaotic sensualist who sets up his 'dominion of beauty'—Lorenzo de' Medici; the physically weak man who 'from the depth of the mind' draws the strength to rally 'an arrogant people at the foot of the Cross'—Savonarola. His Royal Highness is easily recognized in 'the gracious bearing preserved in the empty yet rigorous service of form', and Felix Krull in 'the unreal and precarious life of the born impostor'. And of Aschenbach's other works, the epics of *Maia* and *Frederick the Great*, we know now that Thomas Mann had at least planned to write them. (The Prussian King was in fact made the subject of one of Thomas Mann's best and most controversial essays.) [59]

The secret of Gustav Aschenbach's art, we are told, lies in the defiant conquest of doubt and irony, in his aspiration to render possible a new kind of dignity. If as a young writer he had startled the world with his 'cynicisms about the questionable character of art and artists', the charm of such psychological initiation soon wore off. The style of his later works resulted from a determined rejection of all doubts concerning the validity of the moral law, the dismissal of all 'sympathy with the abyss', the denial of the moral flabbiness of '*tout comprendre c'est tout pardonner*'. Indeed, 'the miracle of innocence reborn' which, we gather, 'played a part in one of Aschenbach's earlier dialogues where it was treated not without some oracular emphasis', seems to have come to pass in his own literary life, bringing about the classical balance of the mature work. It is 'a moral resolution beyond all inhibiting and disintegrating knowledge' [60] which is reflected in his deliberate mastery of language and has recommended some of his exemplary pages to the editors of prescribed texts for his country's higher education.

Such deliberately exemplary language is the parodistic idiom of *Death in Venice* itself. Thomas Mann has spared no allusion to suggest that the hero of the story resembles its author at least with regard to his literary production. Yet Aschenbach is said to have achieved in earnest the classical style befitting a conqueror of the abyss—the very style which Thomas Mann parodies in telling the tragic story of Aschenbach's disillusion and downfall. With Thomas Mann then the miracle is certainly not one of innocence reborn, but of a literary intelligence superbly succeeding in this extreme experiment with parody; and he succeeds because he himself desires the foothold of innocence, and yet knows that it cannot be gained consciously. If nothing else, *Fiorenza* has taught him this lesson.

One of the tests of an artistic creation lies in its hold on the memory, in its manner of staying there. Works of art often provoke the memory to play the tricks of a child's mind: to abstract from the adult wholeness of the impression the random and mysteriously significant detail which with the passing of time assumes a monumental quality. Particularly with a minor work it may easily happen that, coming upon it again, we find to our dismay that the remembered monument is a mere trifle within the composition. This is less likely to occur in the case of a major work, for there every detail is infused with the meaning of the whole. In *Death in Venice* there is indeed hardly a detail which is not 'telling', which does not tell in its miniature way the entire story. Yet the total effect is not one of overloading, but of complete lucidity. In fact, what stays in the mind and absorbs every detail is a truly monumental vision: a man meeting his fate in beauty, a man on his own, whom we never see in the company of other people, and of whose past life we know next to nothing. But this monumental quality is achieved without the slightest deviation from strict realism. Everything is what it is: the tramp is a tramp, the street-musician is a street-musician, the hotel is a hotel, and Venice is Venice. No attempt is made—say, in the manner of Kafka—to unsteady our trust in the reliability of every-day experience. Nevertheless the ordinary world is under notice of dismissal. We feel that at any moment we may be left with the purest extract from reality: man, sea, sky, an empty beach—playthings in the hand of Fate. *Death in Venice*, alone among all the works of extreme psychological realism, achieves in all seriousness the parodistic semblance of mythic innocence. It is a triumph of deliberation and intuition, helped not a little by the limited scope of the chosen form.

The story is as well-known as it is simple: the writer Gustav von Aschenbach, fifty, living in Munich, tired by years of uninterrupted work, decides to travel. His journey, after a brief and unsatisfactory stay elsewhere, leads him to Venice. Guests at the same Lido hotel are a Polish family. The youngest child, a boy of about fourteen, called Tadzio, strikes Aschenbach as possessing perfect beauty. His admiration gradually grows into passion. As he keeps the secret of his love, so Venice seeks to guard its own: a spreading epidemic of Asiatic cholera. Yet Aschenbach discovers it. Instead of warning the Polish family and departing himself, he yields to the hypnosis of his passion. Staying on, he joins with his own the sinister secret of Venice. With his moral will broken and his soul deranged, he dies on the beach in the sight of Tadzio, who stands Hermes-like on the fringe of the sea, silhouetted against the blue horizon.

This may be the place to show in some detail the working

and great efficiency of Thomas Mann's literary technique, for *Death in Venice* is the quintessential proof of its power. However, close analysis calls first for a word of caution. In the case of a translation it obviously has but the minutest scope. But it is on all occasions the critical method of 'close reading' itself which requires wary handling. Although regarded with such fervent favour by modern criticism that it threatens to become one with it in sterile and jealous matrimony, it is yet only moderately helpful, and positively mischievous in the hands of a critic who presumes on its modesty. In any event, it is good to realize that 'close reading' is merely the virtue of a vice: of that lettered illiteracy which is the ruinous price paid for universal education. Where reading means the reading of the daily papers, the reading of literature must perhaps be given another name. But another name is not necessarily a new method; and indeed, the closer the reading practised by trivial minds, the more oppressive will be the yield of triviality. In more propitious times 'close reading' is not a method, but simply the civilized habit of thoughtful readers; and elevated to the status of a technique, it is more often than not a strenuously elaborate manner of special pleading. For literary analysis, however close, can neither assess, nor explain or prove, the *quality* of a literary work. It can do so as little as astronomical calculation can prove or disprove the harmony, as distinct from the symmetry, of the spheres; or as little as chemical analysis can account for the charm, as distinct from the chemistry, of the aroma of jasmin. There is not one objective symptom ever adduced by a stylistic analyst to demonstrate literary eminence which cannot be found with equal frequency in worthless literature. All the paraphernalia of the close reader's laboratory, all those key-words and key-phrases, rhythmic idiosyncracies and purposefully arranged clusters of vowels, complexes and complexities, patterns, structures and textures, ambiguities and ambivalencies, moral seriosities and cultivated ironies— why, they have a place in any deliberate accumulation of words. They may be excellent in an excellent work, and very, very bad in a bad one. They are worth examining if the work is good, but they do not necessarily *make* it good; and their examination may indeed increase our understanding, but it may also fortify the intelligence in a state of misapprehension. In literature as elsewhere there is no wisdom in *making* sure. There are only wise or unwise ways of being sure and not quite so sure, useful or useless ways of debating convictions and uncertainties.

An overture which contains *in nuce* the whole drama and is yet the beginning of the story proper—this is what Thomas Mann achieves on the first pages of *Death in Venice*. Being made explicit, this condensation may appear over-deliberate and obtrusive. It is not. Such are the literary tact and economy of the author, that only repeated readings will reveal the technique. What then, it may well be asked, is its point and immediate effect? To work the first and decisive spell of seduction. The reader's imagination is made to accept, unknowingly yet, the final consummation, just as the hero of the story is set on a road which looks harmless enough and is yet paved with the intentions of doom. What these first pages describe is a dramatically very modest situation: Aschenbach, his mind overstrained by repeated and repeatedly vain attempts to manœuvre his work over an obstinate difficulty, has been out for a lengthy walk. Having returned to the outskirts of the city, he is now waiting for the tram to take him back. The stopping-place is in front of a stone-mason's yard and opposite the entrance to a cemetery, At the gates of the cemetery stands a tramp-like figure with rucksack and walking-stick. The sight awakens in Aschenbach the strong desire to travel. He decided that he will do so.

Most of the powerful insinuations of the scene are brought out even in a translation which, however, cannot help adding a note of slightly clumsy portentousness. This is the literary drawback, almost unavoidable, of all English renderings of Thomas Mann, and so often his undoing in the eyes of English critics. What the translation invariably misses is the ironical elegance and the overtone of mockery, subtly ridiculing the habitual posturing of the German language. In English, alas, the ironically draped velvet and silk often look like solemnly donned corduroy and tweed.

The neighbourhood happened to be quite empty. No vehicle was in sight, either on the Ungererstrasse, with its deserted and glistening tramlines stretching off towards Schwabing, or on the Föhring highway. Nothing stirred behind the railing of the stone-mason's yard where crosses, tablets and monuments, exhibited for sale, made yet another, unreal and untenanted graveyard. The mortuary chapel opposite, a structure in Byzantine style, caught and threw back into the silence the gleam of the ebbing day. Its façade, adorned with Greek crosses and hieratic designs in light colours, displayed symmetrically arranged inscriptions in gilded letters, select scriptural texts concerning the future life, such as 'They are entering into the House of the Lord', or 'May the Light Everlasting shine upon them'. Aschenbach passed a few minutes of his waiting immersed in the transparent mystical meaning of those words, until his attention was diverted by the sight of a man standing in the portico, above the two apocalyptic beasts that guarded the flight of steps. Something not quite usual in this man's appearance gave his thoughts a fresh turn.[61]

This is how both death and Venice make their first appearance at the Munich opening of *Death in Venice*. For it is, of course, already Venice which is present in the glistening desertion, the gleam of the departing day, the Byzantine structure, the ornate façade, the hieratic designs, and the apocalyptic beasts, while the untenanted graveyard may somehow belong to the domain of the stranger of whom it is impossible to tell 'whether he had come out of the chapel through the bronze doors or mounted unnoticed from outside', as suddenly as he will soon vanish again out of Aschenbach's sight. What is unusual about him? Only if we impress the details of his appearance upon our memories shall we recognize him, as Aschenbach will not, in three future disguises. He is 'of medium height, thin, beardless, and strikingly snub-nosed', and 'obviously not Bavarian'. His 'broad, straight-brimmed straw hat makes him look distinctly exotic'.

True, he had the indigenous rucksack buckled on his back, wore a belted suit of yellowish woollen stuff, and carried a grey mackintosh cape across his left forearm, which was propped against his waist.   In his right hand, slantwise to the ground, he held an iron-shod stick, and braced himself against its crook, with his legs crossed.   His chin was raised, so that the Adam's apple protruded conspicuously and baldly from the lean neck above the open shirt.   He stood there sharply peering into the distance out of colourless, red-lashed eyes, while two energetic, perpendicular furrows showed on his forehead in curious contrast to his little turned-up nose.   Perhaps it was his heightened position which strengthened the impression he conveyed of domineering superiority, boldness, even wildness, for his lips seemed to curl back, either by reason of some facial deformity, or else because he grimaced, blinded by the setting sun, laying bare his long, white teeth.[62]

If we add the bare teeth to the description of his physical attitude, as he supports himself with the iron-shod stick resting slantwise on the ground, then a mere extension of stick and iron, and a mere disregard of the meagre flesh, bring before our eyes a Dürer image of Death, the first in a little procession which will accompany Aschenbach on his journey. And journey he must, for at the sight of the journeyman the urge to do so comes upon him with hallucinatory violence; and his imagination, not quite at rest yet after the hours of work, seizes upon 'a model of the marvels and terrors of the manifold earth'.   He sees

a landscape, a tropical marshland, beneath a heavy sky, steaming, and of monstrous luxuriance—a kind of primeval wilderness-world of islands, morasses, and alluvial rivers.   Hairy palm-trunks rose near and far out of a tangled profusion of fern, out of fat and swollen plants with fantastic bloom.   There were other trees, distorted as a dream, which sent their naked roots straight through the air into the ground or into water that was stagnant, shallow, and glassy-green, where giant milk-white flowers floated and high-shouldered birds with misshapen bills stood gazing sideways without sound or stir.   Among the knotted joints of a bamboo thicket the eyes of a crouching tiger gleamed—and Aschenbach felt his heart throb with terror and an inexplicable desire.   Then the vision vanished.   Shaking his head, he resumed his walking up and down along the railing of the stone-mason's yard.[63]

This hallucination of the jungle completes, in anticipation, the story of Gustav Aschenbach. He, the classical writer of his age and country, who has 'rejected the abyss' and entered into a covenant with Apollo, determined as he is to let his art do service in the humanization of man, unwittingly goes out in search of Dionysus and dies in his embrace. As the messenger of Death will come back, so the vision of the fertile chaos will recur, and each time death will be in an ever-closer alliance with the chaotically brooding sources of life, an alliance irresistibly strong in its attack upon the disciplined forms of the human spirit. But as the disciplined forms of art require for their being the most intimate association with the dark ground of creativity, *Death in Venice* is Thomas Mann's first tragic allegory of art.

Aschenbach travels. He first goes to a fashionable island in the Adriatic. Soon discovering that he has chosen wrongly, he suddenly knows where he must go, where in fact he had wished to go from the outset. Perhaps he had tried to avoid Venice because many years ago it happened that he felt unwell there and had to leave. Yet Venice it has to be now. As soon as he enters the boat, the subtle inner compulsion which drives him becomes personified in the figure of the man who, below decks, in 'a cavernous, lamplit cabin', sells him the ticket. With his 'beard like a goat's', his routine vivacity and commercial flourishes, he reminds Aschenbach of an old-fashioned circus director. 'Venice!' he cries, 'an excellent choice . . . What a glorious city!', and 'his copious gesturing and empty phrases gave the odd impression that he feared the traveller might change his mind'.[64] On deck Aschenbach finds a vulgarly boisterous party of youths. One of them, in a 'yellowish suit' —the suit of the stranger at the cemetery was of the same colour—'a rakish panama', and 'a red cravat', outdoes the rest in noisy exuberance. But he is, as Aschenbach recognizes, no youth at all. He is an old man, with wrinkles and crows'-feet round eyes and mouth; there is rouge on his cheeks and dye on his hair. 'The unbroken rows of yellow teeth that he shows' are false. The sight of this character, obviously accepted

as their equal by his company, fills Aschenbach with a feeling
of horror and nausea, and indeed with a sensation 'as if a
dream-like uncanny distortion of the world had set in'.[65]   The
perfect objective equivalent of such a sensation is, of course,
Venice, capital of the realm of ambiguity, vast pigeon-hole of
the romantic spirit.

If Gustav Aschenbach had no choice, neither had Thomas
Mann.   He could not have chosen another scene for Aschenbach's doom.   Venice is its inevitable location.   For it seems
a city built by the very Will to Power in honour of Death.
Teeming with Life, it is yet entirely Art, the residence of Eros
Thanatos, the *Liebestod*, the music of which it has inspired,
just as it has inspired Nietzsche's one almost perfect lyrical
poem.   Venice is to Nietzsche 'another word' for both music
and the South, of that happiness of which he was unable to
think without a 'shudder of fear'.[66]   It is the city too of Platen's
poetry—and 'Tristan' is the prophetic title of the poem which
begins with the best line he ever wrote: '*Wer die Schönheit
angeschaut mit Augen, ist dem Tode schon anheimgegeben*',
handing over to death him who has set eyes on beauty.   And,
indeed, it is Death himself who rows Gustav Aschenbach to this
consummation.   Having left the boat, complimented down
with lascivious jokes by the then inebriated elderly youth with
the false teeth showing, he hires a gondola to cross over to the
landing-stage of the vaporetto for the Lido.   But he soon
notices that the gondolier, disregarding his orders, makes for
the open sea.   He is a man 'with an unpleasing, even brutish
face', wearing 'blue clothes like a sailor's, with a yellow sash'
and 'a shapeless straw hat, with the braid torn at the brim,
perched boldly on his head'.   He looks non-Italian, with his
'curling blond moustache under the short snub nose'.   The
effort of rowing makes his 'lips draw back and bare his white
teeth'.   He is determined to take Aschenbach the whole way
to the Lido.   Aschenbach resigns himself to the will of the
despotic boatman, indolently relaxed as he feels in the incomparable comfort of his 'gently-rocked, black-upholstered seat'.
'How much do you ask?' he enquires.   'You will pay', comes

the reply. 'I will pay nothing if you don't take me where I want to go.' 'You want to go to the Lido.' 'But not with you!' 'I am a good rower, sir, I will row you well.' And Aschenbach relaxes again, thinking, 'So much is true. You row me well.' On arrival, Aschenbach bids him wait and goes to change some money. When he returns, the gondola has gone. The gondolier, 'a man without a licence', has only just escaped arrest. Aschenbach has had 'a ride for nothing'.[67]

That very evening Aschenbach sees Tadzio for the first time —and Charon may be sure of his obol. Thomas Mann now tells the history of a passion with an economy and intensity unsurpassed in all his work. It is as if the art of writing tried to gather into itself some of the resources of architecture and music in order to produce transparent clarity of form by means of ceaseless musical allusiveness—a parody of the classical manner achieved with Wagnerian methods. Tristan in hexameters—the obvious absurdity of the suggestion is the measure of the startling success of *Death in Venice*.

It is 'with astonishment' that Aschenbach notices Tadzio's beauty when he first sees him in the hall of the hotel. There seems to be no more in his reaction than the artist's surprise at meeting in reality a perfection of form held to be the prerogative of art. With no more than 'a slight stirring of regret' he notices that his table in the dining-room is at some distance from the Polish family. Yet there is already a subtle hint that, to use Tonio Kröger's phrase, 'his heart is alive'. He passes the time of dinner with abstract speculations about form, beauty, art, only to find at the end that his thoughts and conclusions have the quality of those seemingly exciting discoveries, made in a dream, which on waking one has to dismiss as stale and worthless. (Tonio Kröger had said the same of the verses that formed in his mind when he 'felt alive' on the boat which took him to Denmark.) Next morning, when Aschenbach comes to breakfast, the Poles have almost finished their meal, all except the boy, who has not yet arrived. Aschenbach smiles, pleased as he is in his aristocratic heart to see privileges bestowed upon 'natural merit': 'Ah, little Phaeax, you seem to have the right to sleep as long as you wish', and he quotes to himself an appropriate classical hexameter. Hexameters are soon to recur: the description we are given of Tadzio, as he finally arrives, gradually and unnoticeably rises to the old metrical form—'. . . *ruhte die Blüte des Hauptes in unvergleichlichem Liebreiz*', the head of Eros in incomparable loveliness. 'Good, very good indeed!' thinks Aschenbach with the seemingly detached approval of the connoisseur.

For the time being, the classical mood dominates Aschenbach's mind as well as the style of the narrative. In the beach scene that follows, however, another ingredient is faintly added to it: the soft, melodious sound of Polish. Aschenbach, not without curiosity to learn the boy's name, tries to catch the word by which he is called. First, he can only make out 'two musical syllables, something like Adgio—or, more often still, Adjiu, with a long-drawn-out *u* at the end'. But even before he has found out the full name—Tadzio, a shortened form of Thaddeus, with its vocative Tadziu—we are back again in classical antiquity: Tadzio has a playmate on the beach, another Polish boy, most affectionately devoted to him; once he even embraces and kisses Tadzio. 'But you, Critobulus,' Aschenbach socratically quotes to himself with a smile, 'you I advise to take a year's leave. That long, at least, you will need for complete recovery.' Meanwhile Tadzio is bathing far out in the sea; and at once the Dionysian flute breaks in. Mother and governess anxiously call out to him, and his name 'with its soft consonants and long-drawn *u*-sound, seems to possess the beach like a rallying cry; the cadence had a quality at once sweet and wild: Tadziu! Tadziu!' [68]

This would suffice to show the extraordinary and yet unforced consistency of Thomas Mann's composition. There is hardly a moment in the narrative which is not reached by an echo at least of the war which is its subject—the war between form and chaos, serenity of mind and consuming passion, articulate names and enticingly melodious syllables, hexameters and long-drawn *u*-sounds, with Death presiding over it as judge and ultimate conqueror. What happened at a Munich tram-stop, where an upholder of the classical virtues of writing was momentarily lost in a vision of the jungle, is tentatively repeated on the Lido beach where the Apolline contemplation of beauty is ever so slightly disturbed by the first quiver of the Dionysian carnival. Aschenbach is still in high spirits as from his deck-chair he delights in the sight of Tadzio while tasting fresh strawberries he has purchased from a vendor. Yet this piling of deliciousness upon delight already savours of excess, and before too long it will be strawberries again, but then overripe and soft, possible carriers of the deadly infection, bought in an unclean corner of the plague-infested city to quench an intolerable thirst. Aschenbach will greedily swallow them, almost fainting with exhaustion after a mad and vain pursuit of his idol through the sirocco-sultry maze of Venetian alleys.[69]

But before the story of Aschenbach reaches this dissolute climax, Thomas Mann traces with consummate skill all the stages of passion: how the aesthetic enjoyment changes to infatuation, infatuation to love, love to degrading abandon, abandon to death. And Venice joins in: the temperature on the beach rises from day to day, the blue sky turns leaden, a sirocco sets in, the streets begin to smell of carbolic acid, nothing can any longer stop the spreading disease. At one point, before he has acknowledged to himself the nature and power of his passion, Aschenbach, suffering badly from the sirocco, determines to leave. It is the last exercise of his moral will; and it fails. The virtuosity of the narrator is at its highest in the delineation of this incident: how Aschenbach, resentful at being hurried over breakfast, but in fact only desirous of seeing Tadzio once more, allows his luggage to be taken to the station ahead of him on the hotel's private motor-boat, while he himself will follow later—for there is plenty of time—on the public vaporetto; how his sadness mounts, sadness at losing Venice for ever, as he travels along the palaces of the *Canal Grande*; how he curses his rash decision as the weather seems to improve; how at the station he finds that his luggage has gone on the wrong train; how he is easily persuaded to await its return on the Lido; how his innermost soul rejoices at the accident as if secretly celebrating the successful conclusion of a subtle manœuvre; and how, as he settles down again in the hotel, he realizes that he will be in no haste to leave again, for it is Tadzio to whom he has come back. And indeed, the weather changes, the sky is clear, and the prose itself seems now to worship the sun god with Homeric metaphors and rhythms which are yet disquietingly upset by adjectives and inflections announcing the wilder deity.[70]

As he lies by the sea, Aschenbach's mind weaves image after image from the glitter and haze of sun and water; and one is of the ancient plane-tree where Socrates holds forth to young Phaedrus. 'For beauty, my Phaedrus, beauty alone is lovely and visible at once. Mark you, it is the sole aspect of the spiritual which we can perceive through our senses, or bear to perceive. . . . So beauty, then, is the lover's way to the spirit —but only the way, only the means, my little Phaedrus.' [71] Soon, however, this wanderer will miss his way and arrive at another destination. It happens one evening when the Polish family are absent from dinner. Aschenbach, restless after his meal, walks up and down in front of the hotel. Suddenly, in the light of the arc-lamp, he sees them approach and, caught unawares, his face may perhaps express more than he normally permits it to show in the sight of Tadzio. And Tadzio responds, and smiles at him. 'Such must have been the smile of Narcissus as he bent over the mirroring pool, a smile, profound, infatuated, lingering, as he put out his arms to the reflection of his own beauty; the lips just slightly strained, strained perhaps by the vanity of his desire to touch the lips of his shadow—with a mingling of coquetry and curiosity and a faint unease, enthralling and enthralled.' 'And he who had received that smile turned away with it as though entrusted with a fatal gift.' As Aschenbach flees into the darkness of the garden, words strangely mixed of tenderness and reproach burst from him: 'Listen, one must not smile like that at anyone! How dare you smile like that!' And Aschenbach knows that he is lost in love.[72]

'Mirror and image',[73] these are the names which Aschenbach once gave to the beauty embodied in a work of art. Mirror;

and now Narcissus. Addressed to Narcissus, Aschenbach's
declaration of love is at the same time his declaration of defeat.
For Narcissus is in love with himself, and no passion is more
disastrous than the love he calls forth from others. From this
intense moment in Aschenbach's story light falls on past and
future preoccupations of Thomas Mann's, and indeed on much
in modern literature itself which, from the romantics onwards,
is again and again irresistibly drawn to the motif of the mirror,
the *Doppelgänger*, and their erotic concomitants: homosexual
and incestuous love. It is a complex of themes which is
certainly never absent for long from Thomas Mann's writings:
Tonio Kröger and Hans Hansen, Aschenbach and Tadzio,
Hans Castorp and Przibislav Hippe, *The Blood of the Walsungs*
and *The Holy Sinner*, Adrian Leverkühn and Rudi Schwerdtfeger. The young Joseph is first shown to the reader, and not
without the author's forethought, in all the loveliness of a
Narcissus at the well, and the story of Felix Krull, himself so
unshakable in his fondness for his own person that he easily
gets the better of all his amorous rivals, is the wittiest exploration of the domain of Narcissus. Beauty that loves itself and
destroys its lovers, and the lover who is centred upon himself,
his own sex or his nearest kin—these must become forceful
themes in a world which is felt to be an unfit partner for receiving the confidences of spirit and passion. In such a world
both art and love will be pursued in the strained self-sufficiency
of Narcissus—art for art's sake, and love for love's sake.
Thomas Mann, from beginning to end, from Hanno Buddenbrook and Tonio Kröger to Adrian Leverkühn and Felix Krull,
is both fascinated and agonized by the spirit and passion in their
lonely pursuit of themselves, exiled as they feel from the world
in its determined otherness. This is why he burst out with the
dictum 'Literature is death' in that early letter to his brother,
why he 'saves' Tonio Kröger through 'the love of the ordinary',
and why he achieves such mastery in a story which offers the
exactly appropriate scope to both his sympathy with, and his
moral critique of, that love which is death.*

* It is, in this context, not without interest that at about the time of

Death himself makes yet another, his last, appearance in the story, this time in the shape of a musical buffoon, a guitarist, leader of a band of street-musicians. Aschenbach watches them, with Tadzio nearby, from the terrace of the hotel. The leader, 'scarcely a Venetian type, half pimp and half comedian', with his garments giving off the smell of the disinfectant now lavishly used all over Venice, is 'a man of slight build, with a thin, under-nourished face; his stubby felt hat rested on the back of his neck, a great mop of red hair sticking out in front. . . . The words of his song were trivial and silly, but on his lips, accompanied . . . with leers and winks and the loose play of the tongue in the corner of his mouth, they took on meaning: an equivocal meaning, and vaguely offensive.' Above his open shirt protrudes a 'strikingly large Adam's apple'. 'From the pale, snub-nosed face it was hard to judge his age; vice showed in it, and in strange contrast to the grin of his mobile mouth there stood two deep furrows, as if of defiance and self-will, between the red brows.' After the performance, he collects money, 'gliding between the tables, bowing and scraping, and showing his strong white teeth in a servile smile'; and then he sings an encore with a refrain of hysterical laughter, infecting the whole dignified company of the hotel with uncontrollable mirth. It is in this street-musician that the various features distributed among the previous messengers of Death are merged and enriched: the thin, snub-nosed face, and teeth showing, vagrancy—they all appear to come from another place—poverty oddly combined with the signs of a despotic will, an existence unconventional to the point of the illicit, lasciviousness and the power to bring about the relaxation of all rules of discipline, and, added now, the odour of disease and a rather dubious association with the art of music. Also, Tadzio is now part of the scene; and as if to hint at his having a place among the images of death, Thomas Mann makes him

Death in Venice Narcissus is received into the mythological order of psychoanalysis. 'Narcissism' plays its first part in Sigmund Freud's book on Leonardo (1910) and is systematically treated in his essay 'On Narcissism' in 1914.

stand at the balustrade of the terrace in a position reminiscent of the stranger in Munich: 'with his legs crossed' and one of his arms 'propped against his waist'.[74]

Aschenbach tries in vain to extract from the guitarist the secret behind the smell of disinfectant. He comes to know it on the following day. The English clerk of a travel bureau tells him the truth 'in his honest and comfortable language'. Asiatic cholera has made its way into Venice, that pestilence which has its source 'in the hot, moist swamps of the Ganges delta, breeding in the mephitic air of the primeval jungle where the tiger crouches in the bamboo thickets'.[75] Aschenbach's mind goes back to those cemetery gates in Munich, but the very thought of return, sobriety, labour and mastery appals him beyond endurance. No, he will not warn Tadzio's mother, he will keep the secret; and indeed, his sharing in it fills him with a sense of wild conspiracy, with giddy and unreasoning hopes. Virtue and art count for nothing compared to the 'advantages of chaos', and Aschenbach's feverish brain seizes upon the abominably sweet prospect of a deserted island, emptied by death and panic, and his remaining there alone with Tadzio. That night Aschenbach has his dream of the jungle again; this time it is of an outrageous orgy in honour of the 'strange god', a dance of obscene mythological creatures around the vast obscene symbol, all stirred and accompanied by the dark, enticing tone of the flute, the apotheosis of the *u*-sound. He awakes with his moral existence annihilated. Day after day now, cosmetically rejuvenated like that monstrous man on the boat and, like him, wearing a red cravat and around his straw hat a gay striped band, he either follows Tadzio on his walks through Venice or watches him on the beach in helpless fascination.

For one moment, shortly before his death, the vision of Socrates under the plane-tree comes back into this world of long-drawn *u*-sounds: 'For mark you, Phaedrus,' his lazy mind articulates, 'beauty alone is both divine and visible, and so it is the way of the senses, the artist's way, to the spirit.' To the spirit? *Must* this way not lead astray? Is not Eros the inevitable guide and companion along this path? 'We poets

H

must needs go astray, must be adventurers in the realm of feeling. Our magisterial style is all folly and pretence, our fame, and all honours bestowed upon us, are a farce. . . . And to teach youth, or the people, by means of art is a dangerous practice and ought to be forbidden . . .' And Socrates-Aschenbach instructs his Phaedrus still further: once upon a time, he tells him, he foreswore the moral laxity of knowing and understanding, because it led to 'sympathy with the abyss'. He devoted himself henceforward to the achievement of simplicity, the pursuit of innocence, the discipline of form. But form—and Aschenbach now, approaching his end, dreamily repeats what was said more tidily at the beginning of his story —'form has two aspects. It is at once moral and immoral: moral in so far as it is the expression and result of discipline, immoral—and indeed hostile to morality—in that it is by its very nature indifferent to good and evil.' And so it too heads for the abyss.[76]

Death in Venice is not only 'parody', it is also paradox: a work of art embodying so radical a critique of art that it amounts to its moral rejection. Aschenbach's scruples read like that letter, already quoted, which Keats wrote to Richard Woodhouse (27 October 1818): 'The poetical character . . . has no character', and 'what shocks the virtuous philosopher delights the chameleon Poet'—a deficiency of character which Keats views with equanimity: 'It does no harm from its relish of the dark side of things any more than from its taste for the bright one; because they both end in speculation.' But Thomas Mann—perhaps because he has in him less of the poet and more of the virtuous philosopher—fears harm. His, or at least Aschenbach's, Platonic speculations lead straight into the Platonic Republic from which the poet is banned for the sake of civic order and moral dependability. In this respect, too, Schopenhauer is left behind. For Schopenhauer accepted, transforming it into a metaphysical psychology of art, Kant's definition of beauty as something that pleases without appealing to any self-interest in the beholder, something that gives pure, disinterested pleasure.[77] Nietzsche, however, mocks so saintly a conception. Quoting Stendhal's definition of beauty as *'une promesse de bonheur'*, he asks: 'Who is right, Kant or Stendhal?—When our aesthetic philosophers never tire of protesting, in support of Kant, that under the spell of beauty one may *even* behold statues of female nudes "without interest", one may well laugh at their expense. The experience of *artists* is, with regard to this delicate point, more "interesting", and, surely, Pygmalion was not a man without "aesthetic judgment".' [78] Neither is Gustav Aschenbach, whose fate places *Death in Venice* at an extreme point in the endless debate about the moral significance of art.

It may, of course, be asked whether so paradoxically *artistic* a presentation of the case against art deserves to be taken seriously. The answer may be found in the fact that the 'speculation' in which *Death in Venice* ends has none of the Keatsean 'harmlessness'. It is the speculation of a radical moralist who ironically asserts his moralism in a subject of seemingly modish morbidity. With *Death in Venice* Thomas Mann has closed the circle of doubts besetting his moral existence as a writer. In *Buddenbrooks* art emerges as the destroyer of life. The artist Tonio Kröger, on the other side of life, can only justify himself by holding on to his love for the artless world. The artist's love for the artless world is psychologically scrutinized and monstrously suspected in *Fiorenza*. And Gustav Aschenbach, having seemingly risen beyond suspicion in the disciplined service of art, is brought down by the revengeful forces of life. The circle seems to be as vicious as can be, and so firmly drawn that it is hard to break. To be sure, no book of Thomas Mann's, apart from the essay of Frederick the Great, was written between 1911— the year of *Death in Venice*—and 1918; and what did appear in 1918, *Meditations of a Non-Political Man*, was no work of art. It was a vast volume of speculations, all bearing the mark of deep and passionate concern, about the moral state and possible self-defence of writer and writing in a world which, not unlike Aschenbach, had upheld the virtues of moral discipline and civilized achievement only to sink into chaos and war.

IV

The Conservative Imagination

1

THE 'epic in prose about the life of Frederick the Great',
which in *Death in Venice* Thomas Mann ascribes to his
writer-hero Aschenbach, he himself had planned to write
several years before.[1] He did not leave it at such vicarious
fulfilment. Reduced to the modest dimensions of an essay,
Frederick and the Great Coalition was published in 1915 as a
small book which also contained reprints of two patriotic
pieces, 'Thoughts in War' and 'Letter to the *Svenska Dag-
bladet*'. Like these, the essay was inspired by the First World
War and caused the painful break, lasting longer than the war
itself, in Thomas Mann's hitherto closest personal and literary
relationship. For his brother Heinrich responded with the
celebrated essay on Zola (which first appeared in November
1915 in the periodical *Die weissen Blätter* and was later included
in the volume *Macht und Mensch*).[2] This essay was Heinrich
Mann's *J'accuse*. Zola's attack upon the perversion of truth
in the name of ill-conceived patriotic ideals, his denunciation
of the political powers in the land who had contrived, and
their intellectual supporters who had condoned, a miscarriage
of justice in the trial for espionage of the Jewish officer Dreyfus,
served Heinrich Mann as the historical disguise for his own
condemnation of the German war and all those German writers
who espoused the national cause.

There can be little doubt that many of Heinrich Mann's
obvious allusions to the contemporary intellectual scene in
Germany were aimed at the conservative and patriotic author

of *Frederick the Great*. The polemic brought into the open an old discrepancy of temperaments, attitudes, and views, an intimate tension not quite free from rivalry and jealousy, which until then had been a hardly acknowledged element in the friendship of the two brothers. Yet the ensuing crisis in the life of Thomas Mann was far in excess even of the momentous occasion. The war and the conflict with his brother only precipitated it. It had been in the making over a long period. All the problems which Thomas Mann had succeeded in resolving aesthetically through works of literature suddenly broke through the barrier of irony and imaginative objectivity which had kept them at a distance from the core of the person. Now they demanded a personal answer. Thomas Mann spent three years in the attempt to give it in the six hundred pages of *Meditations of a Non-Political Man*. The conventions of nineteenth-century biography would suggest the words 'religious crisis' to name the state of mind and soul reflected by a book of which the author himself says in the Preface that it is 'not a work of art, but the work of an artist whose existence was shaken to its foundations, whose self-respect was brought into question, and whose troubled condition was such that he was completely unable to produce anything else'.[3] Nevertheless it is not a mistakenly published private document which tact and wisdom would do better to ignore.

Its claim to publicity rests not only on the fact that, as Thomas Mann puts it, 'to the best of my knowledge, it shows the intellectual foundation of my literary work'.[4] It shows still more. Being the intellectual autobiography of a highly intelligent writer, written at a time when his confidently 'non-political' frame of mind was shattered in a vast political conflagration, it offers in all its laborious excitement an indisputably authentic insight into the tangled relations between literature and politics. The particular national worries of this non-political man may by now be of merely historical interest. What is left is nevertheless, and surprisingly enough, almost the whole book. For its argument, conducted with passionate pedantry and in a mood of obstinate fascination and moral hypochondria, never loses sight of questions which are still in season and are at no time likely to remain unasked for long. The questions are about individual ethics and moralistic politics, traditional loyalties and intellectual radicalism, and above all about art and political commitment.

Meditations of a Non-Political Man would be an essay in conservative philosophy equal in rank to that of Burke (who was unknown to Thomas Mann) were it not marred by the author's self-consciously hopeless attempt to interpret the opposition between conservative pessimism and republican optimism, between the ironical, contemplative mode of living and the facile earnestness of literary politics, even between 'music' and 'literature', in terms of the state of war between Germany and the West. This was his tribute to the folly of time and place, a tribute so expensive that it left him for the rest of his life with the awkward sensation of being in political debt; and more often than not he tried to pay them off in exceedingly papery currency. The exception is, of course, his denunciations of Hitler's Germany. They were inspired by genuine hatred and contempt, emotions as deep as, in reverse, the national attachment of *Meditations,* and by a grief as poignant as the agony of *Doctor Faustus*—a book which could only have been written by one who felt for Germany what Thomas Mann felt in 1914. But all the forward-looking political exhortations of his later years have, embarrassingly, an ingredient of deliberate well-meaningness and studied simple-mindedness: from the Berlin oration of 1922 (*Von deutscher Republik*) in which he surprised the German social democrats and trade unionists with a literary bouquet made up of Novalis and Walt Whitman, and with all but the offer of the inheritance of the Romantic Movement, to the Chicago address of 1950 (*Meine Zeit*), which, on the margin of what is otherwise a moving piece of autobiographical reflection, counselled the two 'good-natured colossi in East and West' to be as good to each other as their soldiering 'Vanyas and Sams' in occupied Germany, united as these were by 'a certain kinship in temperament' and a certain 'gay primitivity of drinking and love-making'. Indeed, the appeals of a Hamlet who, upon discovering that the time was out of joint, was to found a society for the prevention of royal assassinations could not ring more incongruously. After *Meditations* it was again and again the guilty conscience of the non-political man (related, of course, to the moral scruples of the young artist Tonio Kröger) which persuaded Thomas Mann that he should occasionally play the part of a Lübeck senator reminding, in a voice not unlike brother Heinrich's, the citizens of a ruined city to fulfil their municipal duties.

In *Meditations*, however, the voice of Heinrich Mann is the unloved voice of the enemy, the *Zivilisationsliterat*, the literary champion of 'civilization', a word into which the German language had managed to gather the combined distaste felt by Nature, and Rousseau, and Herder, and D. H. Lawrence, for the rationalistic, high-minded and shallow-spirited planners and levellers of existence, long before Spengler came to use the term as meaning the death of *Kultur*. Although Thomas Mann never mentions the *Zivilisationsliterat* by name, his identity is not in doubt. 'A little more than kin, and less than kind'—even if the quotation did not occur, even if the address '*Bruder*' and '*du*' were not used now and then, with the accent intriguingly hovering between the rhetorical and the intimate, and even if passages from Heinrich Mann's essays were not—anonymously but profusely—quoted, the reader of *Meditations* would soon notice that its author was a man talking not quite to himself and not quite to his audience, but to himself in front of an audience so that *one* should hear who no longer shared his privacy. It is this tone of voice which makes the book so compelling. Longwinded, meandering, resolutely confused, boldly self-centred, it yet exerts the fascination of a private feud conducted by a finely enraged, hurt, proud, and civilized mind almost pretending to be unaware of the presence of others. And in the end the feud turns out to have been still more private than the public of eavesdroppers suspected—not so much a quarrel between brothers as an interior dialogue between the Germanically traditional two souls in the one breast, and thus truly of universal interest in an age full of private dilemmas and divided loyalties. There can be few books in the world like *Meditations*, books in which the noisiest public concern of an age is treated as a matter of the most intimate urgency. In this lies its value but also the reason for its neglect. For many of the ideas, with which Thomas Mann showed himself so personally involved, afterwards embarked on an extremely compromising career. Therefore the work has long remained a stumbling-block for the author himself as well as for his critics. It is perhaps time that critical thought should take the place of stumbling.*

It all began with the essay on *Frederick and the Great Coalition*.† We need not know its strange history—a subject

* The confusion which the political vocabulary is liable to cause is shown by the fact that *Meditations* has been squarely classified, by the vague political consciousness of the age, as a book in sympathy with 'fascist' tendencies. This is nonsense. While a totalitarian conception of the State is fundamental to Fascism, *Meditations* is truly 'non-political' at least in the sense of being an impassioned plea for individualistic privacy and against the invasion of its sphere by 'total politics', a danger Thomas Mann believed to be inherent in *all* radical political ideologies. Although he later, of course, revoked the jealous distinction between 'private' and 'political' concerns, he would yet write in the same breath a sentence which could have its place in *Meditations*: 'Absolute politics . . . is the end of freedom' (*Das Problem der Freiheit*, Stockholm, 1939, p. 26).

† Almost forty years after its first publication Thomas Mann decided, 'not without some reluctance', to include this 'document of a conservative-nationalistic and "militaristic" period' (*Stimmungsperiode* is the word he characteristically uses) in a new collection (1953) of 'minor prose of five decades', entitled *Altes und Neues*. The Preface to this volume says with regard to the Frederick essay: 'Even today I cannot help feeling a certain affection for the little historical fabrication, this strange mixture of critical prudence and hotly patriotic allusions. Time and history have deservedly neglected it; yet literary criticism has not quite followed suit. A French journal, *Les Langues Modernes*, wrote recently: "*S'il fallait nommer les trois chefs-d'oeuvre de T.M. dans le genre bref, nous n'hésiterions pas à y ranger, à coté de* Tonio Kröger *et de l'étude sur Schopenhauer, la dissertation sur Frédéric II de Prusse.*"—I must say, a judgment of astonishing liberality!' (p. 12). This, however, is preceded by a typical example

long considered, superseded by other works, and apparently abandoned by letting the imaginary Aschenbach have it—in order to feel that it is the fruit of long gestation, suddenly forced into the open by a day of exceptional heat. Despite some damage done to this cool and northern product by the tropical outburst, the French critic who praised it is right: it deserves a place by the side of Thomas Mann's best essays. Nevertheless it is regrettable that it never became what it was meant to be: the kind of long book that *Lotte in Weimar* is. By the nature of his genius, instinctively drawn to the psychological exploration of the heroic, the grim and tragic humour of the quixotic madness, as well as by his intellectual upbringing in the schools of Schopenhauer's metaphysics of the Will and Nietzsche's metaphysics of Power, Thomas Mann seemed predestined imaginatively to recreate the King of Prussia rather than the Majesty of Weimar. And indeed, the essay is a condensed 'epic in prose', with the voluminous imagination of the born maker of characters grumbling, as it were, between the lines at the limited space available to the essayist. Quite apart from Frederick himself, every figure mentioned is a sketch for a portrait to be painted, a rehearsal for a performance to be given: Menzel, for instance, Frederick's spy with Brühl's government in Dresden, or Brühl, the dandy politician with, in Frederick's words, 'fifteen hundred wigs

of that singing out of tune to which Thomas Mann became so prone whenever the song was a political one: 'The democractic powers, until they were forced to make war, had connived at Fascism for so long, and even today, full of remorse at their own victory, assist it so much all over the world, that their sins somewhat mitigate my shame at remembering my own political folly—the polemical incomprehension with which I opposed Democracy in a certain period of my life, at the time of the First World War' (ibid.). Whether or not one sympathizes with this political sentiment, as an opinion about what passes between 'Fascism' and 'Democracy' it is, in its blue-eyed innocence and robust dilettantism, more appropriate to the Hans Hansens of this world than to the Tonio Krögers ; not to mention the absurdity, however playfully advanced, of allowing the present 'sins of Democracy' to affect in any way the moral judgment on things one has written forty years ago; and again not to mention the persistent need for justification, 'the awkward sensation of being in political debt', which the passage betrays.

and no head', or Kaunitz in Vienna, or the three female
rulers of Europe, Madame de Pompadour, Elizabeth of Russia,
and Maria Theresa, against whom the misogynist King, who
habitually called them sexually abusive names, fought his
Seven Years' War, perhaps in some respects, as the essay
suggests, a catastrophically literal variant of the war of the
sexes. Of Maria Theresa, above all, Thomas Mann paints an
exquisite miniature, forceful, humorous, and tender. But it is
not only the palpable drive of the imagination which throughout
the essay seems to call for the ampler dimensions of a novel;
it is also the all-pervasive sense of broad epic justice which is
ill at ease within the limitations of sketch or essay, and gratingly
at odds with the fragments of patriotic homily thrown in here
and there for the benefit of 'the day and the hour'. Without
them—and they could be detached, not only without any hurt
to the fabric but almost as if to free it from foreign bodies—
the essay might well have struck, as Thomas Mann later suggested it actually did, the chauvinists of 1914 as a diatribe
against the national legend of the Great King.

Among Germans the Frederick theme had never before been
treated in such pessimistic humour. Not the faintest echo of
the customary Hohenfriedberg trumpets is discernible in
Thomas Mann's orchestration. Its dominant tone is irony,
the tragic irony of a heroism which rises defiantly above the
felt meaninglessness of human achievement. It is an essay
in the heroic activities of spiritual desperation, and if it justifies
anything, anything at all, without having recourse to this
paradoxical way of affirming, then it is Maria Theresa's
judgment of Frederick: for the Emperor-Queen, with whom
Thomas Mann cannot help sympathizing, would not mention
the King's name, always referring to him as *der böse Mensch*,
the wicked man. And wickedness, a kind of ruthless and
amoral obedience to his historical instinct, a grandiosely
cynical betrayal of all his earlier beliefs in the moral principles
of government as set out in his *Antimachiavell*, is certainly a
quality with which the Frederick of the essay is abundantly
endowed. Indeed, it provides the best possible object-lesson

in the impossibility of writing history free of moral judgments. For while nothing could be further from Thomas Mann's timely patriotic intentions than to condemn the King, he nevertheless emerges as a moral monstrosity somewhat jarringly recommended by his author to the untender mercies of History. Yet one need not be an analyst of style to feel how alien to the intellectual nature of Thomas Mann are these appeals to historical grace. We may be sure that no furtive intimacies with the destiny and mission of a 'great people' would have distracted his attention, had he written his book on Frederick immediately after *Buddenbrooks* or *Tonio Kröger*. For even the enthusiastic seductiveness of the patriotic occasion could tempt Thomas Mann only into rather half-hearted and rather grimly flirtatious compliments to the national cause. His intellectual passion is engaged elsewhere: in the psychology of the hero whose heroism is wrung from weakness and unbelief.

Of the imaginary, and yet not quite so imaginary, Gustav Aschenbach, author of the book on Frederick the Great, Thomas Mann had said that all his main characters shared precisely this quality: 'the heroism born of weakness'. For it was Aschenbach's conviction that 'almost all greatness was great in despite: had come about despite affliction and pain, poverty, destitution, infirmity of the body, vice, passion, and a thousand other obstacles'.* And Aschenbach's literary

---

* To this idea (we read in *Death in Venice*) Aschenbach 'had once given direct expression—though in an inconspicuous place' (*Stories of Three Decades*, p. 384). The passage provides a characteristic example of the autobiographical hide-and-seek that Thomas Mann is fond of playing even in the most serious context; and the uncalled-for information about the 'inconspicuous place' merely satisfied the author's urge teasingly to confess the identity, in essential respects, between himself and Aschenbach. For it was indeed in an inconspicuous place, namely in response to a newspaper enquiry (in 1906) concerning alcohol as a creative stimulant, that Thomas Mann himself used these very same words. The short piece was later reprinted in *Rede und Antwort* (Berlin, 1922, p. 376). And there 'Aschenbach's pronouncement' was spotted by Hermann J. Weigand, the most learned and perceptive student of Thomas Mann, to whose book *Thomas Mann's Novel Der Zauberberg* (New York and London, 1933) I am indebted for much more than this little *trouvaille* of literary detection.

success, we learn, was due to the timeliness of this heroic type: for many were those who in this age exerted themselves on the verge of exhaustion and were sustained not by a living faith, but by the sheer 'morality of achievement'. All these saw themselves vindicated by his works 'and thanked and praised him'.[5]

Thomas Mann's Frederick is certainly such an Aschenbach hero, just as before him Thomas Buddenbrook and Savonarola were. Despised and maltreated by his father for being a good-for-nothing, a dandy, a bohemian, an effeminate highbrow, he disciplines himself, as soon as he is King, into an ascetic of power politics, the idol of his soldiers and terror of Europe. He wages hopeless wars as if it were his aim merely to test his tenacity in not losing them, wins battles without gaining anything except the proof that he cannot be defeated. If his lands are laid waste, he almost welcomes the chance to build them up again, and exerts himself, as if he loved his people, to restore the fields and houses of the '*canaille*' for whom he feels nothing but scorn. Proclaiming the rationalism of Voltaire (and he once kissed the hand that wrote: 'I detest all heroes'), he leads a life as insensibly heroic as Don Quixote's, and believes that his body is bullet-proof. Although all his triumphs are triumphs of his will, he yet sees himself as a mere tool of fate. 'The ox must drag the plough,' he says, 'the nightingale must sing, the dolphin must swim, and I must fight battles.' As Thomas Mann paints him, his will is a stranger to his intelligence, and both are torn apart from his sentiments: the world is a plaything for his passions, ideas are toys for his mind, and for days on end he weeps at the death of his favourite dog. 'Heroic foibles' he calls his performance in the Seven Years' War, and despite all his philosophical enlightenment he resorts to a 'mysterious instinct' to account for his politics, which are incomprehensible to himself. And as if quoting Aschenbach, Thomas Mann speaks at the end of Frederick's 'nihilistic fanaticism of accomplishment' and of a 'sovereignty as vicious as it is melancholy'.[6]

If this portrait of the King of Prussia was meant to fire

the nation with patriotic zeal, than surely no gloomier placard has ever been displayed for national edification. True, there are the scattered allusions to contemporary events—for instance, to Germany's invasion of Belgium—where the author seems all on the side of his hero's 'vicious and melancholy sovereignty' and mockingly all against his morally outraged enemies: 'Frederick gave the order to cross the frontier of Saxony. But was Saxony not neutral? Indeed, Saxony was no party to the game. Never mind! On the twenty-ninth of August Frederick invaded Saxony with sixty-thousand moustached warriors. Nobody can imagine the noisy indignation caused in Europe by this unspeakable offence against peace and international law. Nobody can imagine it? Of course, one can; indeed, just now it is quite easy to imagine. But if we want to listen to Frederick before listening to Europe, he will tell us that his breaking of the law was the result of the following considerations. . . .' [7] And what follows reads substantially like Germany's official explanation in 1914 of her attack on neutral Belgium. Nevertheless, we need only compare the mood of the Frederick essay with the massive literary hysteria that broke out in 1914 all over Europe (for instance, with Rilke's panegyrics to the god of war) to get the measure of the pessimistic sanity which tempered Thomas Mann's patriotism, and to be amazed at the violence of the ensuing fraternal feud.

There is a passage in Heinrich Mann's essay on Zola which is the first Thomas Mann anonymously quotes in *Meditations*, feeling sure that it is directed at him. No doubt he is right. For it is an intimate observation, sharpened by political anger, which Heinrich expresses, an invective confidently aimed at the very centre of his brother's problematical position. In this passage Heinrich Mann speaks of the treason of those intellectuals who believe they 'know', but in spite of what they know, in disloyalty, as it were, to their intellects, supply the intellectual justification for everything that is not 'mind', and even glorify the power and violence of 'infamous rulers'.[8] The 'glorification' of power and violence is, of course, sheer immoderate polemic. What is left is a grain of truth: the truth of the 'Will' being pessimistically acclaimed by Thomas Mann as ultimately superior to all 'ideas'. The essay on Frederick certainly does not glorify the King; it merely equips Tonio Kröger with royal energies, soldiers and gunpowder. *'Il pense en philosophe et se conduit en roi'*—Thomas Mann approves of Rousseau's epigram and adds that the dualistic formula sums up Frederick's vexatious character. What he means is, of course, the old Tonio Kröger dualism of 'spirit' and 'life', and promptly quotes the King, the ex-*littérateur* and admirer of Voltaire, as saying that if he wished to punish a province very severely, he would let it be governed by men of letters [9]— a thought which might easily have occurred to Tonio Kröger.

What occurs to Thomas Mann at this point in his polemical exchanges with his brother, is Kant and Nietzsche, and— ingeniously and daringly—he interprets Kant in almost Nietzschean terms, thus trying to meet Heinrich's charge of intellectual treason on the highest level of ethical speculation. Was Kant himself, he asks, not such a 'traitor'? Was he not prepared to sacrifice Mind for the sake of Life? For Kant's *Critique of Practical Reason*, he asserts, gives to Life precisely that which his *Critique of Pure Reason* had taken away from Mind: absolute certainty; only as an active and 'practical' being, involved in practical life and answering its moral demands, can man become sure of that which for ever eludes his reflective faculties: reality. And Thomas Mann reveals what, he thinks, has prompted that particular polemical turn of Heinrich's: in one of his war-inspired utterances he, Thomas Mann, had said that the Categorical Imperative, upheld beyond the profoundest intellectual scepticism, was the most characteristically German contribution to thought—to political thought in particular. Even now, at the time of *Meditations*, he protests that such dicta, although 'they have acquired a somewhat stale taste' for himself, contain some truth. Of course, they do—despite the outrageously cavalier manner in which they treat Kant as a philosopher of Life and his Categorical Imperative as almost sanctioning the invariable element of intellectual dishonesty to be found in all politics. But at least Thomas Mann knows that the body politic wilts if fed on a diet of purely intellectual prescription, and that it cannot survive without the occasional reckless disregard of even the uncommonest sense offered by political theories and ideologies. Such an offer is Heinrich Mann's essay on Zola, enlisting in its turn Nietzsche among the promoters of progressive and progressively rationalistic politics, and determined to put 'Geist', Mind, Reason, 'on the throne of the world', a piece of political furniture which the author surrounds with aggressively sentimental sincerities. Their pretty frenzy called forth Thomas Mann's rejoinder: 'Strindberg once said to Björnson: "Speak the truth, Björnson! You are as untruthful as a platform orator." '10

This, then, is how the two brothers face each other: the one, nobly enraged by the ignominy of the ruling powers, courageously proclaiming with catastrophic platitudes his belief in a better future; the other, indignant at the untruth of high-minded and highfalutin rhetoric, supporting with many a true insight into the human condition an insupportable cause. It is the exact picture that Thomas Mann himself was later to draw of the struggle, with Naphta and Settembrini fighting it out in *The Magic Mountain*, paradigmatic victims, perhaps, of one of the most disturbing perversions of an age in which all profundities tend to be sinister, and shallow all the friendlier thoughts about man.

2

The confused and confusing history of Thomas Mann's political sympathies must exasperate all those who wish their politics to be the simple good neighbour of their friendliest moral ideas and their largest human generosities. For the irritating truth is that he was an incomparably profounder political thinker when he was a 'non-political' man, a political 'obscurantist' and 'reactionary', than ever as the advocate of democracy, progress and, more recently, 'co-existence' (that tiresome word which seems to claim for a harsh political necessity some sort of ideological and sentimental value). This is not surprising. For a creative writer's politics cannot be detached, without loss of authenticity, from the nature of his imagination, and Thomas Mann's imagination must needs incline him towards an ironical, and even a tragic and aristocratic, reading of history, and towards the utmost scepticism concerning all possibilities of politically engineering a higher degree of human happiness and dignity. This is true not only of Thomas Mann. It applies to most, and certainly the most poetic, imaginations. The blessings bestowed by great works of literature upon forward-looking causes are rare and never unmixed. Lionel Trilling, in *The Liberal Imagination*, rightly remarks on the scarcity of support to be drawn for the liberal virtues from the greatest literary reputations, and quotes Hazlitt, who in his time, and certainly without political rejoicing, observed that 'the language of poetry naturally falls in with the language of power': for 'the cause of the people is indeed but little calculated as a subject for poetry'.[11]

Although Hazlitt's belief that poetry is spontaneously attracted to the majestic and glorious, and repelled by the drab and wretched, is hardly relevant to modern literature, it is yet true to say that the poetic imagination is naturally more a glorifier of memories than a designer of utopias, more loyal to origins than enamoured of causes, more rooted in the past than allured by the future. If it rebels, it rebels not against 'systems' but against the meanness of heart, the dullness of vision, and the·perversion of truth on a level deeper than that reached by the designs of organized political opinion. The creative mind has its communal life in a society of creators whose historical distribution over the ages makes nonsense, in their sphere, of the idea of progress. As art looks upon nature not as the scientist does, so it looks upon man not with the eyes of a social planner. On the contrary, its image of man remains more 'natural' and 'chthonic' than 'social', even where the imaginative discourse is about man in society, so much so that often the artist's imagination makes a mockery of his declared political intentions; and this not by means of logical inconsistencies creeping into his work but, far worse, through the imaginatively implied refutation of all far-reaching political hopes. For there is about the characters, for instance, of Balzac, or Tolstoy, or, at his best, even of the 'literary scientist' and political reformer Zola, or indeed of the revolutionary Bertolt Brecht, a quality of natural destiny and monumental inevitability which reduces to all but irrelevance any expectation of radically affecting their good or evil by changing their social functions. Indeed, a writer's wish may well be to show his characters as pawns in a social game the abominable rules of which he desires to overthrow; yet the greater he is as a writer, the more likely it is that his imagination will defeat his purpose by setting these figures in their course more like heavenly bodies whose revolutions appear indifferent to anything except their own centre of gravity. If in 1914 Thomas Mann chose to be a conservative, he made a disputable political choice which was yet indisputably in character; and although he knew only too well that the conservative character of the artistic imagination is not smoothly translatable into the language of politics, he nevertheless believed that there was one idiom into which it was positively untranslatable: the political idiom of the *Zivilisationsliterat*; and so he called himself a non-political man in Germany, a patriot of the 'non-political country'.

There are words that have fallen on evil days, words like 'fatherland' and 'tradition' and 'patriotism'. Awful echoes cling to them and make them reverberate with the strident voices of political counterfeiters. Thomas Mann knew this when he wrote *Meditations*, and yet used them in self-conscious defiance of the enlightened liberators, whose manner of disavowing them was, he felt, fraught with spiritual and political disasters still greater than those which had come about in the name of the suspect phrases. He was alarmed by the irresponsible idealism and opinionated cynicism at work in the dismissal of 'antiquated patriotic values', stimulants which nevertheless made their detractors quiver with liberal emotion

I

whenever somewhere in foreign lands backward fatherlands were liberated, national traditions excavated and aggressive patriotisms stirred. The pupil of Nietzsche feared the terrible negativity of the intellectual banner-bearers of freedom, the unconsciously nihilistic self-destructiveness of those 'modern men', demolition squads insensibly busy to create empty spaces, not, as they believed, for the free society to enter in, but as a home, swept and garnished, for the worst tyranny. 'The negativity of their idea of freedom', Thomas Mann writes, 'is essentially nihilistic, and wholesome only in the smallest doses, as a homeopathic poison; and is it really indicated at a time when the innermost desire of the world, the whole world, is not for still more anarchy through liberty, but for a new binding faith, and when the belief in belief has already reached the point of a psychological readiness to accept a new obscurantism?' [12] This, of course, anticipates not only the terrible failure of German liberalism in effectively opposing Hitler's 'new binding faith', but explicitly something else: the proletarian tyranny which 'after this war will be boundless and shattering; all rebellious zeal and all satirical anger will be needed to oppose it'.[13] He certainly needed the zeal and the anger in the case of Hitler; but it was one of the minor historical misdeeds of Hitler that he also exhausted them. Later German tyrants, however shattering, were spared the satire. Yet the imagination remained fundamentally 'conservative' even then. The creative writer, as distinct from the occasional orator, gave no quarter to earnest revolutionary ideologies. And it is a comic turn worthy of Felix Krull that a German ministry of proletarian culture, in its *parvenu* hunger for literary prestige, was, by the not unfriendly conduct of the author, blinded to the persistently 'reactionary' behaviour of his Muse.

Such dissociation of political beliefs from the promptings of the imaginative vision deserves serious attention. It is so widespread a phenomenon that it may suggest one of two things: either the artistic imagination is, as Hegel taught, an archaic survival, or politics, severed from the fullness of the imaginative life, has become sham. The latter is more likely.

For the political consciousness is by no means *necessarily* shut off from the profounder realizations of the human lot. It is even possible to assume that it can and should have something in common with art and literature (and by literature we do not mean those fanciful reports about imaginary people and events which, innocent of all poetic comprehension but delivered with the skill, wit, and resourcefulness of artistically ambitious columnists, so often pass for 'imaginative writing'). Ideally speaking, art shares with politics precisely that which distinguishes both from the deliberate rationality of science and the blue-prints of ideological programmes: that it springs from the elemental human need to discipline into articulate form and communicable convention the inarticulate and rationally incommunicable forces of life, the chthonic ground of existence; and a rationality cut off from those roots leads to the corruption of the arts and the degradation of politics. Then both art and politics are exposed in hysterical impotence to the revenge of Nature which, betrayed by the Reason, and indeed as the crowning paradox of Reason's own manœuvres, mockingly regains its primeval and unmanageable demonic powers, condemning the speech of the political animal to hectic trivialities in the face of brainwashers, scientifically equipped sadists, and radioactive cataclysms, and the artistic productions of the creative creature to banal anger or desperate distraction and abstraction. It is in this sense, which is not necessarily a German one, that Thomas Mann was one day to bring together again the destinies of art and politics in *Doctor Faustus*, a resurrection, after all the forswearing of reactionary politics had been done, of the exact mood of *Meditations*—this time at the gates of Hell, and with a depth of perception which shows all his later waving and bowing to the Press cameras of the 'People's Democracy' to be a caricature of tragic knowledge flirting with optimistic ignorance—the melancholy farce of Tonio Kröger's last amorous entanglement with Life at its most 'ruthless' and 'stupid'.

Meditations of a Non-Political Man is not only a source book of Thomas Mann's creative life, a reservoir from which he was to draw, often to the point of literal quotation, in *The Magic Mountain*, in *Lotte in Weimar*, and even as late as in *Felix Krull*; it is also an invaluable record of a certain stage of European intellectual history. There is, for instance, at the opening of the essay 'Burgherdom', the citation of Georg Lukacs ('von Lukacs', as he was called then) who was at the time an aesthetic philosopher not too far removed from those aristocratic-idealist thoughts cultivated in the neighbourhood of Stefan George, and who later became one of the very few readable Marxist interpreters of literature, still later a university professor in communist Budapest, and finally one of the intellectual leaders in the 1956 Hungarian revolt against Moscow. In *Meditations* Thomas Mann quotes Lukacs's early book *Die Seele und die Formen* in support of his own artistic creed, the 'typically Germanic' conjunction of aesthetics and ethics which makes for the particular dignity of the 'burgher artists', of Stifter, Storm, Keller, Mörike, who fulfilled their literary vocations as one fulfils the duties of a profession, and often during the leisure left by a 'real' one. This means, in the words of Lukacs's quoted by Thomas Mann, 'the primacy of order over enthusiasm, of routine over the momentary, of quiet work over the sensational inspiration of genius'. For such writers the bourgeois form of existence is not, as it was for Flaubert, a 'nihilistic mask' but the lived belief that aesthetic sensations which are not 'contained' by life as its organic refinements are ethically utterly dubious and a debasement of life and art alike.

The *Zivilisationsliterat*, on the other hand, would appear to be a libertine. His literature has this in common with his politics that both aim at a chimerical aesthetic glory the condition of which is not only the conquest of the humdrum and the remedy of social shortcomings: its ultimate condition is chaos and its political consequences, therefore, tyranny. For it is to chaos that the pure and glorious ideal will in the end assign everything which does not conform with its demands —and that is, in the last resort, life itself in its native impurity; and the political answer to chaos is tyranny. It was, says

Thomas Mann, the art and ruinous designs of the 'aesthetic politician' which *Buddenbrooks* and *Tonio Kröger* opposed with bourgeois ethics, pessimism, and irony. And although this interpretation of his earlier works is not quite free from special pleading, it yet expresses Thomas Mann's desire to practise his art as a peaceful citizen of his society, contributing to its spiritual well-being and realizing himself ethically through his work, rather than be a *citoyen* delivering artistic invitations to radical political action for the sake of the ideal common-wealth of the future. And if Tonio Kröger saw things differ-ently, if he imagined that he sacrificed his life to art and had to die in order 'to be entirely a creator', then, his author now protests, it was a 'youthfully romantic illusion and affectation': 'My work . . . is not the product . . . of an ascetic-orgiastic denial of life but the ethical aspect of my existence.' [14] It is Lukacs's conservative text and Heinrich's republican rhetoric that have inspired this re-valuation.

Even then Thomas Mann knows only too well—and how could the creator of Hanno Buddenbrook and Tonio Kröger not know it?—that in actual fact the artist he has in mind exists in painful isolation from his society. What he as yet refuses to envisage is the possibility that the divorce may be due more to the misdemeanour of society than to the unfaith-fulness of art; and it is, notwithstanding the 'ethical aspect of my existence', his ineradicable moral distrust of the artist that prevents him from indulging such suspicions. In this he is as radical as Kierkegaard, and remarkably close, in his manner of argument and even turn of phrase, to the great moral hypochondriac (whose writings, according to his own testi-mony, he had not read at the time of *Meditations*). Thomas Mann believes that the artist, or at least the prevalent type of artist (and he acknowledges that there are artists to whom the following does not apply, austere, proud, and 'holy' artists), is condemned to a subtle kind of insincerity in his proclaimed opposition to the 'world' as represented by the society of his time. There is, above all, his inescapable 'aesthetic oppor-tunism'. He wishes to please. What ultimately matters to

him is success—not necessarily, of course, in the crudest but
certainly in the most fastidious sense of the word: success as
that delicious contentment achieved in the perfection of a
sentence, the happy appropriateness of a cadence, the finality
of a metaphor. Beliefs and opinions—what are they to him
if not the material for the grand aesthetic artifice, 'matter to
be consumed by form', as Schiller once defined the aesthetic
process. What pleases him more than the goodness of one
conviction is the splendid clash of two. For, as Keats said,
'the poetical Character . . . has no character. . . . It has as
much delight in conceiving an Iago as an Imogen. What
shocks the virtuous philosopher delights the chameleon Poet.' [15]
The artist is concerned to move men through beauty, not to
convince them of truth. He woos even with his aggression,
seduces even with his chastity, seeks the admiration of those
he dooms in his apocalyptic visions, and the applause of those
he damns with his last judgments.*

When Thomas Mann speaks of the ambiguous character of
the artist, of his ascetic dedication to his art and his metaphysical aspirations existing side by side with the most worldly
appetite for the luxuries of success, we may be sure that he
thinks of Richard Wagner; and some of the best pages in
Meditations are given to the critique of Wagner's genius. In
his work, Thomas Mann says on one occasion, we find a
passage 'which sums him up in every respect: it is the recurrence
of the *Sehnsuchtsmotiv* (the motif of longing) upon the word
"world" ("*Selbst dann bin ich die Welt*") in the second act of
Tristan'. It is the very passage which Thomas Mann once
before, in 1902, had used to great, and even witty, effect in an
artist's story: in *Tristan*.[16] Now it becomes a sublime symbol
not only of Wagner's deepest ambition, but of the artistic
character itself: the artist, however convinced he may be of
the essential 'otherness' of his medium, is a conqueror set
upon overpowering the world. Wagner's rich demagogy, with

---

* The exceedingly problematical nature of this conception of artistic
truth I have discussed in the essay 'Rilke and Nietzsche' in *The Dis-
inherited Mind*, Cambridge, 1952, and New York, 1957.

its robust exploitation of subtleties, its vigorous handling of
fragile profundities, and its wicked appeals for goodness, is
merely an extreme, and extremely successful, expression of
propensities almost always present in the artistic constitution.
In thus speaking of Richard Wagner, Thomas Mann speaks,
of course, also of himself: who would not recognize in this
interpretation of the *Sehnsuchtsmotiv* Tonio Kröger's craving
for the world? Or, much later, Joseph's 'Yes, it is I!', the
words with which he reveals himself to his humbled brothers
as the one who has risen from the pit, his punishment for
offensively haughty dreams of glory, to the highest power
wisely wielded in the land of Egypt? Or the Holy Sinner's
triumphant journey from sin and degradation to the papal
throne? What Thomas Mann says of Richard Wagner and
the artistic character is as much self-confession as it is critique
of the *Zivilisationsliterat*. Where then is the difference between
him and his brother, where the justification for his attack?
The answer is: in the fact that he knows and confesses whereas
the enemy pretends to be unaware; that, knowing himself, he
himself abrogates the right to be a leader of men, while the
other, deceiving himself and his public, pursues, in the guise
of a true believer, aesthetic power-politics. If the artist's
dealings with thoughts, convictions, or opinions must needs be
dubious, responsive as he is not to their 'truth' but to their
aesthetic equivalent, then all his political 'commitments' must
be flawed by irresponsibility: the responsible artist is a political
sceptic; and political scepticism is, according to *Meditations*,
the characteristic attitude of the conservative mind.

   '*Bellezza* radicalism' is Thomas Mann's name for the irresponsible politics of the aesthete seized by political enthusiasm.
In the denunciation of this *bellezza* radicalism his political
inspiration is at its most formidable: 'It is a common error to
mistake radicalism for depth. . . . Radicalism is a pretty
superficiality, a cult of the generous gesture which at times
assumes an almost choreographic quality, as a word of the
Zivilisationsliterat proves: ' "Liberty" he exclaimed one day,
"liberty—that is the Dionysian dance of Reason!" ' . . . This

is ballerina politics, demonized Dalcroze.'   And Thomas Mann
quotes Goethe who, in his *Italian Journey*, said: 'Liberty and
equality can only be enjoyed in a state of giddy lunacy.'   What
the *bellezza* radical lacks—and lacks 'to the most generous
degree'—is conscience.   For his doctrine 'that art must now
have *consequences*', political consequences, is merely his disingenuous manner of saying that now he expects to score
new and topically sensational aesthetic *effects*.   'The political
artist is of all artists the one most anxious to be *effective*' [17]—
above all artistically effective, even with his revolutionary
manifestos.   And he *knows* it; knows that opinions count
for nothing in the aesthetic sphere, and knows that he will
be most readily forgiven his political blunders.   'What does
it matter that he was wrong?' people will ask, and add: 'He
said it so beautifully.   Let him sing once again!'

Lacking conscience, is he an artist at all? asks Thomas
Mann.   No, he is a mere aesthete.   Yet 'aestheticism' is also
the fate of the true artist, and Thomas Mann's struggles with
the problems of the aesthetic existence is the most absorbing
and bewildering aspect of his *Meditations*.   This will hardly
surprise us if we think of the troubles and dooms he had decreed
for his artists Hanno Buddenbrook, Tonio Kröger, and Gustav
Aschenbach.   Nor is it inconsistent that 'aestheticism' now
fulfils a double task: it vindicates, on the one hand, the artist's
conservatism, and vitiates, on the other, the aesthete's radicalism.   For the political aesthete fraudulently aspires to a moral
status above his native moral means.   If only he had the
conscience of the artist, he would know that his 'radical beliefs'
must needs lack authenticity, and that it was his moral duty
to observe the utmost tact and restraint in dealing with the
'real' world.   What Thomas Mann says of the aesthetic politician, Kierkegaard, before him, had said of the 'aesthetic
priest'.   The poet, Kierkegaard wrote, is by his very nature a
spiritual menace—and he saw the poet with all but the eyes of
Aschenbach; yet a far greater danger (for the poet, after all,
does not want to be more than a poet) is a priest who is at
heart only a little artist advertising as 'belief' what is in fact

a mere play of the imagination with 'imaginative truths'.
'This is hypocrisy raised to the second power.' [18] It is exactly
such hypocrisy with which Thomas Mann charges the *Zivilisationsliterat*, the political aesthete, the writer who is so much
in earnest because he is not seriously concerned with the
hazards of the aesthetic existence.

Thomas Mann himself is untiringly concerned. He has
ransacked whole libraries and filled page after page of *Meditations* with the most apposite extracts from the literature of the
world, to make the case for aestheticism.   He quotes Goethe,
Schiller, Flaubert, Tolstoy, Strindberg, and to particularly good
effect Turgenev, who once confessed that he felt always a little
lost when asked to give his own opinion on this or that, and
deprived of the chance of hiding behind the exchanges of
imaginary characters: 'Then it always seems to me that one
might just as well and with equal right assert the opposite of
what I am saying.   But if I talk about a red nose or fair hair,
well, then the hair is fair and the nose is red, and no amount of
reflection will reflect it away.'   But Thomas Mann's chief witness is, of course, Schopenhauer, who said of the aesthetic
imagination that it works on the principle of Nature herself;
and 'Nature does not do as the bad writers do, who, when
they show a knave or a fool, set about it so full of clumsy purpose that behind every such figure we glimpse, as it were, the
writer himself, disavowing their minds and words, and warning
us with a raised finger: "This is a knave, this is a fool; do not
listen to what he says!"   No, Nature does as Shakespeare and
Goethe do, in whose work every person, and be it the Devil
himself, is, while he speaks, in the right; because he is conceived so objectively that we are compelled to sympathize with
him: for, like a product of Nature, he has grown from an inner
principle by virtue of which everything he says and does
appears natural and therefore necessary.'

This, then, is Thomas Mann's highly respectable (and highly
unorthodox) definition of aestheticism: it is the contemplation
of the world *sub specie necessitatis*, a definition which not
only seeks to establish the profoundly 'conservative' and

'non-political' character of art (and throughout *Meditations* this 'non-political man' equates the political mind with the radical mind, convinced as he is that it is an inescapable contemporary equation). It is a definition which implies even more: it raises art to the level of religion. For under this ambitious aspect art, like religion, is concerned with an ultimate affirmation. As religion affirms the ultimate goodness of what is truly necessary, so art affirms its ultimate beauty. The opposite of necessity, thus understood, is contrivance. Hence there is neither goodness nor beauty in what is contrived, and the aesthete differs from the artist in that he is, as a practitioner of his craft, a contriver of aesthetic sensations and, as a political enthusiast, a contriver of unauthentic moral satisfactions. For the morality of what Thomas Mann calls aestheticism lies in the conscientious contemplation of what is, not of what might be enjoyed or might be done; and he quotes Goethe's saying that only the contemplative man has a conscience: the active man is always without it. Only in the creations of the artist, Thomas Mann adds, is the dilemma resolved: his work is active contemplation, not contemplated action. And as the *Zivilisationsliterat* has accused the 'non-political man' of irresponsible relativism and scepticism, he replies that he is not guilty of such intellectual frivolities; what he has is respect —respect for that which is; and doubt—doubt of those magniloquent abstractions from reality to which the aesthetic politician is 'committed'. 'Respect *and* doubt,' he asks, 'to be conscientious *and* uncommitted—does this combination exist? Indeed it does, and it is the essence of the aesthetic philosophy.' [19]

3

If only this were the whole truth! The non-political man could then conclude his meditations at this point, return to his business, and produce another work of art. Yet, like the war itself, the desperate self-defence seems to go on for ever— for many hundreds of pages. Why? Kierkegaard, in his critique of the aesthetic philosophy, knew one of the answers when he wrote (as if he had read *Tonio Kröger* and *Death in Venice*): 'I know very well that an artist, who simply follows his talent without asking himself what it means to be a man, commands much admiration. But the admirers of his work forget *him*. For I also know that he leads a tragic life. His tragedy is that ethically he remains unrealized, a non-entity.' [20] And Kierkegaard knows still more: that even the most ardent ethical aspiration of the aesthetic man will be halted by his very aestheticism at the stage of 'living ironically'. What condemns *Meditations* to their agonizingly sustained inconclusiveness is precisely this: that their author is caught in the paradoxical enterprise of *establishing irony as a mode of ethical and even religious existence*. He is, as Tonio Kröger protested, 'no nihilist', nor has he, as *Meditations* make clear, any time for such 'intellectual frivolities' as relativism and scepticism. If he is not 'committed', it is due to his respect for the truth of life and his conscientious doubt of the 'truths' offered by believers. Yet what is it that he himself believes in? In conscientious aesthetic contemplation—in Art. But is not Art precisely the thing which *Buddenbrooks*, *Tonio Kröger*, and *Death in Venice* have besieged with hosts of moral questions? Is not the artist precisely the man whom *Tonio Kröger* and the fragment *Felix Krull* have made into a relation of the criminal and the impostor, and of whom Gustav Aschenbach has learned that, moralist or not, he 'heads for the abyss'? And what about his separation from life, his being exiled, by a law of the spirit, from the community of morally sound and healthy people? It is obviously no simple task to bring *Meditations* to an end.

Even if the precarious aesthetic play on the verge of 'nihilism' and moral catastrophe is now dismissed as a 'youthfully romantic affectation'—an act of grave injustice Thomas Mann does not only to the seriousness of his past work but also to the future *Doctor Faustus*—there still remains the artist's isolation, the supreme *moral* problem about which all his literary ancestors have been in a perpetual state of dynamic worry. For one of the obsessive themes of German literature

is the conversion of souls from their self-consuming inwardness to a redeeming concern with the community. The great
Faust himself is carried into Heaven as soon as he conquers
the devilish pride of his lonely pursuits, diverting his 'eternal
striving' to the common good. Tasso is snatched from the
poetic abyss by the statesman in his common sense. And
Wilhelm Meister has set the whole genre *Bildungsroman* on
that course which invariably leads from the solitary excesses
of sensibility to the nobly restraining acceptance of social
purpose. Will Thomas Mann defy the hereditary national
pattern, deteriorated as it has in the hands of contemporary
designers—the political aesthetes? The answer is, as is so
often with him, yes and no; but his manner of eating and
having the national cake in *Meditations* merits closer inspection,
not only because all his future work reflects the insoluble
dilemma, but also because a whole hungry epoch would seem
to assist in the paradoxical procedure.

Against the social moralism of the *Zivilisationsliterat*,
Thomas Mann indeed insists upon the unconquerable 'isolation'
and even fundamental 'self-centredness' of the aesthetic man;
but despite all his moral scruples, he now, in a kind of religious
bravado, attributes superior ethical value to this morally questionable state. For if the aesthetic man is isolated, if he refuses
to play the game of people who all 'know what they want'
and unproblematically 'take sides', this is not a matter of
choice. He is under compulsion. What compels him is the
aesthetic vision of that which necessarily is, of a wholeness
of being in which all the moral clashes and contradictions of
individual men are both contained and surpassed. His ethics,
therefore, are the ethics of 'being', not the morals of 'doing'.
He may appear—to others as well as to himself—as one concerned with himself alone. But this is an illusion caused by
the fact that he cannot have any seriously felt concern for the
arbitrary fluctuations of the social dispute. Instead, his
isolation has an opening into religion. And he quotes
Nietzsche's saying: 'A religious man thinks only of himself.' [21]
As the *Zeitgeist* is an incorrigible plagiarist, he could, had he

known him, have still more appropriately quoted Kierkegaard, who said of the truly ethical state (which in his order
of spiritual growth precedes the religious state) that 'as soon
as a person reflects upon himself ethically, and demands of
himself that he should exist ethically, he is instantaneously
isolated. Then he does not bluster about millions of generations and, at random, mankind—as little as the police ever
arrests the essence of humanity. Ethics is concerned with the
particular human being.' [22] For Kierkegaard too knew the
literary champion of civilization: 'Well informed as he is, he
knows his orders. His orders are: the complete transformation
of the world. But he has got it wrong. The order is: complete transformation of himself.' [23]

It is the very order with which Thomas Mann counters the
civilizing transformers of society: whole pages of *Meditations*
might have been prompted by Kierkegaard's brilliant scorn for
the unregenerate believers in regeneration through revolutionary politics. For to Thomas Mann too, 'the people' is opium
for the man without religion. 'No social religiosity', Thomas
Mann writes, 'can bring conciliation to the life of society.
Only true religion could do that . . . Institutions matter little;
what matters is states of mind. Become better yourself!
And everything will improve.' This is either a truth known
and felt by a religious man, or else one of those half-truths
which so easily pass as true because they are indisputably the
better half of the whole truth. Is it then Thomas Mann's
religious truth? Alas, not quite. For no sooner have the
ominous words 'true religion' found their way on to the
paper than he is constrained sincerely to subtract from them:
'Or let him who does not wish to speak of religion put another word in its place . . . goodness, or humanity, or freedom.' [24] And the better half-truth is instantly changed into
a sentimental platitude worthy of the *Zivilisationsliterat* himself.
Compare it with Kierkegaard's definition of religious faith:
'The object of faith is the reality of the Other, and the relationship of faith to its object is an infinite interest' [25]—and Thomas
Mann's essay in religion which seems to have set out in the

direction of Kierkegaard ends at the doorsteps of a rationalist church.

Or does it? When the champion of civilization shows the same magnanimity towards the word 'religion', this is Thomas Mann's reaction: 'Religion! Yes, I once heard the literary champion of civilization hold forth on religion. It was at the graveside of a poet of whom it was said that his last hours had been filled with religious scruples. He had cried out for God and perhaps died believing in Him. How did the *Zivilisationsliterat* set about apologizing on his behalf, how did he solve his own embarrassment? *"Our duty towards the spirit,"* he said, *"which we call religion"*—of that duty the deceased had been most vividly aware. Well, we know what the *Zivilisationsliterat* means when he says "spirit". He means literature, he means politics, he means both together, namely Democracy. And that he calls religion! When I heard these solemnities of a counterfeiter of ideas, of a "liberally religious" Sunday preacher who claimed for that sort of "spirit" a soul which in its extremity had longed for salvation—when I heard it, I put on my hat and went home.' [26] And so, enraged by the subterfuge of one who, like himself elsewhere, 'does not wish to speak of religion' and 'puts another word in its place', he leads us back again to the Kierkegaardian starting-point, that is, to the religious 'ethics of being', paradoxically propounded here by an artist whose foremost concern has been with the uncommitted existence and the inescapable non-entity of the true practitioner of art. His own only honest, intellectually sanctioned, possession is still the aesthetic philosophy; and, as a German saying puts it, he is 'a rogue who gives more than he has'. Yet much more, he fears, is demanded from him. By some devilish design he seems to have been tricked into responsibilities he cannot meet; and *Meditations* is nothing more than the diary of the rogue who desperately tries to hand out more than he possesses. For such, he feels (and he feels it deeply and sincerely), are the demands of the age that 'there seems hardly anything I can afford not to take seriously, hardly anything my conscience will not hold me responsible for—although I do not know who it is to whom I am responsible.' [27] Thus the sense of responsibility, as vague in direction as it is boundless in conception (and so boundless *because* it is so vague) continues to overstrain his religious resources.

Such are the generous gifts of the *Zeitgeist*, and the logically often perverse relations between its children, that Thomas Mann found in Schopenhauer, the philosopher who had supplied him with the comforting metaphysical sanction of the artist's non-entity, the very doctrine Kierkegaard could have taught him with greater logical consistency: the ethical superiority of 'being' over all the moral intentions of 'doing'—the exact doctrine the non-political man now needs in his fight against the aesthetic politician and 'activist'. Of course, he might have found it in the Gospels, had not the *Zeitgeist* made it easier for him to discover it in the pessimistic philosopher's *The Foundations of Morality*. It is, says Thomas Mann, 'the profoundest thought that I have ever been able sympathetically to understand, indeed, it is one of those thoughts which I had understood before I read it. For if one loves a writer, one knows his ideas even if they are expressed on pages as yet unread.' [28] In these pages Schopenhauer offers his solution to the most vexing philosophical problem which age has been unable to mellow: the problem of freedom and determinism. If we assume the role of a spectator, Schopenhauer writes, and look upon the *operari* of a man, upon his doing and functioning, we cannot but conclude that everything he does is determined from without by his circumstances and from within by his character. Yet he is also free and absolutely right in behaving as if he were free: pondering his actions, rejoicing at their merits and regretting their wrong. But this freedom resides not in his doing, as it may seem to him, but in his *esse*, in what he is. Man is only ostensibly responsible, Schopenhauer teaches, for what he does; his real moral responsibility concerns the nature of his being; and however determined every one of his actions may appear, he yet knows in his heart of hearts that he could have acted otherwise. For hidden in his heart of hearts is the knowledge that he could have *been* other. And thus Schopenhauer, basing himself upon Kant's moral philosophy, corrects 'the radical error which sees determinism in *esse* and freedom in *operari*', and recognizes 'that the opposite is true'.[29]

Nowhere does Schopenhauer, the philosopher of aesthetic contemplation, come closer than here to Kierkegaard, the anti-aesthetic philosopher of Christian existence, because nowhere is he as faithful as here in philosophically paraphrasing a Christian doctrine. For the thought which strikes Thomas Mann as the profoundest he ever understood is the very same which appalled the law-abiding Pharisees: that grace is better than righteousness, the love of God not bounded by the Commandments, and that there is more rejoicing in Heaven at one man made new in repenting his sin than at ten grown old in righteous obedience. It was Jesus, not Kant or Schopenhauer, who first attached freedom to *esse*, and the moral order to a state of heart, not to the laws of *operari*. Whatever its origin, it is a thought keenly comprehended by the non-political man, and, according to him, abominably betrayed by the *Zivilisationsliterat* who, in his blindness to the religious truths of human existence, invests his zeal for social re-arrangements and progressive operations with the spiritual pathos of a saviour. What he achieves is the rhetorical effect of 'moral *kitsch*', what he conjures up is the deplorable prospect of a 'morally castrated life', a life 'robbed of all its tragic accents'.[30] Satiated with aesthetic excess, he has discovered, like the aesthetes of Savonarola's Florence, the thrill of morality and the fascination of social virtue. Virtue! Righteousness! Belief! But is not even sin, disturbing and possibly re-casting a man's innermost being, more moral than that righteousness with which the social enthusiast manipulates the moral order? Is not doubt, Thomas Mann asks, more religious than belief— the belief in the virtuous society? Madame Chauchat, in *The Magic Mountain*, will speak the part which, in *Meditations*, the non-political man wrote for himself, and will speak it more successfully than he, and ironically enough, in French, a

language so dear to the *Zivilisationsliterat* on account of its
civilized rationality. '*La morale?*' she will ask, just as Thomas
Mann's Schiller was made to ask, a little incongruously perhaps,
in the early sketch *A Weary Hour*, and just as he himself
does ask again and again in *Meditations*, satirically indignant
at the moralism of the political moralist:

> *La morale? Cela t'intéresse? Eh bien, il nous semble, qu'il*
> *faudrait chercher la morale non dans la vertu, c'est à dire dans*
> *la raison, la discipline, les bonnes moeurs, l'honnêteté, mais plutôt*
> *dans le contraire, je veux dire: dans le péché, en s' abandonnant*
> *au danger, à ce qui est nuisible, à ce qui nous consume. Il nous*
> *semble qu'il est plus moral de se perdre et même de se laisser dépérir,*
> *que de se conserver. Les grands moralistes n'étaient point de*
> *vertueux, mais des aventuriers dans le mal, des vicieux, des grands*
> *pécheurs qui nous enseignent à nous incliner chrétiennement devant*
> *la misère.*[31]

It is a composite quotation from *Meditations*, and is said in
The Magic Mountain by the Russian woman in that long-
delayed first *tête-à-tête* with Hans Castorp, during that 'Wal-
purgis-Night', in which the education of the hero is so
considerably furthered, very much against the will of his
mentor Settembrini, the great comedy version of the *Zivilisationsliterat*. As Hans breaks away from his party and advances
towards his enchantress, Settembrini raises his arm in rhetorical
despair and, as if to make it impossible for us not to remember
his eloquently Francophile model from *Meditations*, cries
'euphonious words, in a foreign tongue', well-meant warnings
of Western Reason against the lures of passion and sin, the
traps of the 'ethics of being'.[32] But in *Meditations* no trace
is yet discernible of the ironic freedom gained on the Magic
Mountain. The *Zivilisationsliterat* is not yet the amiably
comic, paternally rational and shabbily elegant man of illuminating letters, tubercular advocate of health, sick conspirator
against darkness and death, and deliberately sane inmate of
the sanatorium. For the time being, he is still the operator
against the author's spiritual being, and a menace to Germany.
To Germany—and this is the point at which the 'ethically

K

isolated individual', the 'aesthetic sensibility exiled from society' conquers, in accordance with the Faustian pattern, its isolation and its exile, yet without having to surrender its proud miseries and glories. It has found its—appropriately interpreted—community: the ethically isolated country exiled, by virtue of its aesthetic sensibility, from the society of nations. Yet this is also the point at which the anguished attempt to make the aesthetic philosophy into a form of religious existence breaks down in anguish—that anguish which years later, and after the consolations of *The Magic Mountain* and *Joseph*, was to assume its final literary form in *Doctor Faustus*, and be confessed once more when Thomas Mann, a little shy with age and a little rambling, and as if talking to himself about himself, breathed it, one year before his death, into his essay on Chekhov.

4

At the troubled heart of *Meditations of a Non-Political Man* is a religious imagination and religious conscience in conflict with a sceptical mind—the deepest source of Thomas Mann's irony. This is a state of spiritual affairs radically different from that to which so many a Victorian sage had to attend 'with terrible earnestness', like, for instance, George Eliot on that solemn Cambridge occasion in the Fellows' Garden of Trinity when, according to F. W. H. Myers's report, she pronounced that God was inconceivable, Immortality unbelievable, but Duty peremptory and absolute, and left her companion gazing 'on a sanctuary with no Presence to hallow it, and Heaven left lonely of God'.[33]   This is the pronouncement of a mind formed by religion and now earnestly embattled with a sceptical imagination and a rational conscience. The difference lies in that which appeals to the imagination and engages the passion of the mind. The course which the intellectual history of Europe has taken since those Victorians fought their battles of conscience makes it difficult to grasp the true nature of their dilemma. But of many of them it is true to say that the idea of rationality wielded an *imaginative* spell stronger than that of the religion which had formed their minds, and that their moral conscience was employed by a vaguely conceived ideal of scientific truth. Not since the days of the Enlightenment had the passions been so enamoured of Reason, and the sense of rational truth been so tyrannical in its dealings with the conscience.

The writer of *Meditations*, on the other hand, would in perfect moral gladness part company with his sceptical mind, if only he could bargain for its rationality the undisturbed possession of the religious truth which his imagination woos. Conscience forbade George Eliot to believe in God. Belief, for her, was the 'natural', the unregenerate condition. To Thomas Mann unbelief comes 'naturally' and is almost the guilty stage, while Duty tells him that the sanctuary should be hallowed by the Presence, and conscience, that the imagination should be right: and to his imagination God is not inconceivable, and Immortality not unbelievable. Both inconceivable and unbelievable to him is, on the contrary, the attachment of 'belief' to the rational virtues—as if 'belief' could be the proper attitude of mind towards that which is self-evident or knowable. And what he dreads is the 'rational belief' in its state of degeneracy: the faith of the metropolitan backwoodsmen in the redeeming power of political ideologies, the hankering for salvation diverted to that which can be 'reasonably' attained—and will, on the strength of this spiritual derangement, be most unreasonably bungled. He calls it 'the betrayal of the Cross', a distasteful substitute for true belief.[34] But what is the true belief? Certainly, it is not to be found in 'the obstinate and rhetorical advocacy' of just any 'doctrine' such as that of 'Liberty, Equality, Democracy, Civilization, and Progress'. What is it then?

The answer comes as a shock: 'It is the belief in God.' And does he himself believe in God? For the second time he engages in the kind of evasive manœuvre which, without weakening his religious appetite, does nothing to increase his religious resources. The passage continues: 'Yet what is God? Is it not the comprehensive vision, the principle of form, the omniscient justice, the love affirming everything that is?' These are words lifted from another context and rhetorically adjusted to the religious purpose. They come from the exposition of the aesthetic philosophy which, as we have seen, holds that the artist is barred from any particular belief by that comprehensive vision, the passion for affirming whatever can be made to yield to the principle of form, and by that boundless justice which gives its assent to everyone who in the drama of the imagination speaks his own particular truth—'and be it the Devil himself'. And promptly Thomas Mann concludes his theological discourse with the words: 'Belief in God is the belief in love, in life, and in art.' [35] Held against the tenets of the aesthetic philosophy, this amounts to saying that faith in God is the faith in unbelief, while belief is 'the betrayal of the Cross'.

And he does say it. 'I cannot say that I believe in God, and even if I did believe, it would be a long time before I said so.' [36] He doubts, and even believes in doubt, for doubt is better than a false belief. He even believes in despair, for 'despair is a more religious condition than the mellifluous religiosity of the revolutionary optimist'.[37] Thus, from the depth of his unbelief, Thomas Mann religiously denounces the heretical believer. For belief is belief in the wrong thing. And morality and social virtue? To the profounder inner life, sin is a more moral experience than the virtuousness contrived and secured by a virtuous organization of society. Thus, from the depth of his inwardness, he religiously denounces the propagandist of virtue. For virtue is a stupid and feeble goodness if it is unexercised and unenlightened by evil. Such is the conscientious irony begotten by the sceptical mind in the religious imagination: the irony of a religious conscience without spiritual employment, and the irony of an intense inwardness without moral direction.

Both ironies we have seen destructively at work in the life of Gustav Aschenbach. His labour was inspired by a moral determination unaided and unmellowed by faith, and this was also the favourite theme of his books, in particular of his *magnum opus* about Frederick the Great.   Not only has Thomas Mann taken Frederick's melancholy triumphs out of Aschenbach's pen, but identified himself, in *Meditations*, entirely with Aschenbach's foremost literary fascination. 'If I have', he writes, 'understood anything of my time sympathetically, then it is its particular kind of heroism, the form of existence . . . proper to the moralist of accomplishment who, overstrained and overexercised, works on the verge of exhaustion.'[38]   And beyond this marginal morality there lurks the other irony, the morally undirected inwardness, which unscrupulously invaded and destroyed Aschenbach's life, just as it had brought about the downfall of Thomas Buddenbrook who, having exhausted the ethos of achievement, surrendered to the raptures of Schopenhauer's metaphysics of death. Also the young shipbuilding engineer Hans Castorp will come to know the same story, as he absents himself from the moral steamships of Hamburg, from a life which 'opposes with a hollow silence the questions which a man asks, consciously or unconsciously, concerning some ultimate, some more than private, some absolute meaning in all his efforts and activities';[39] and allows himself to be detained in the Magic Mountain by Clavdia Chauchat, the irresponsible siren of the inner life. It is, however, in *Meditations of a Non-Political Man* that Thomas Mann has created the largest hero in whom to embody the soul divided in itself between the faith-less ethos and the amoral inwardness: Germany, the country of the unquestioning discipline and the undisciplined ecstasies, of soldiers and mystics, of the desire to possess the world and the urge to withdraw from it into lyrical privacy, of engineering and romantic music, of aggressive energy and metaphysical excess.

5

The writer of *Meditations* is a latecomer in the procession of illustrious minds wedded in spiritual and unhappy marriage to Germany. If ever the history of Germany and her lovers comes to be written, it will be as full of passion, intrigue, disinheritance, adultery, jealousy, and murder, as the history of fiction. And fiction is what it will be about, good fiction and very bad fiction. No other Western secular society, in the late eighteenth and nineteenth centuries, suffered so much from the traumatic craving for the vanished Holy Empire, and took so badly to that rational-legalistic conception of the State which has found its extreme formulation in the *contrat social*. Not contract but sacrament, not *commune* but communion— this remained the vain aspiration. The German mind clung obstinately to the idea of the State as an incarnation of the religious spirit, and when the religious spirit had irretrievably lost its concrete Christian articulation, its luminous fragments were assembled in a mosaic displaying all the mythologies accessible to historical fiction, above all the Greek and Teuton mythologies. Their mysterious essence, poetically distilled, had to supply the spiritual flavour which was to make social existence acceptable to souls intent upon religious meaning. Hölderlin's *Hyperion* is the noblest expression of the agony of minds in search of a nation ready to house the genii, and Hegel's philosophy the grandest intellectual design to bestow the luminosity of the spirit upon the secular history of man.

It is perhaps impossible satisfactorily to account for this striking German disposition. One of its causes (which, of course, is again 'caused') may be, as has often been suggested and not least by Thomas Mann, the Reformation, which rekindled, more so in Germany than anywhere else, medieval religious passions, and at the same time thwarted, through its radical emphasis upon the inward faith of the individual, man's sense of a meaningful worldly society: so that the faithful inwardness, when it began to lose its hold upon the divine partner, turned to 'the people' in quest of new spiritual company and of deliverance from the lonely religious plight. This is the way Hölderlin went. Kleist knew the temptation. The very tone of voice in which Fichte addressed the German Nation betrays this state of mind, which almost found its systematic theology in the political theories of the Romantics. Sought after by such sublime desire, 'the people', of course,

had to be found wanting. But the indignation at its shortcomings hardly ever took the form of social criticism; it was
almost always uttered with the wrath and pathos of prophecy—
at times even by the ironical Heine. Not since the Old Testament has there been a national record so full of messianic hope
and apocalyptic despair engendered by the state and conduct
of the nation.

It is well-nigh impossible to read what, throughout the nineteenth century, articulate Germans have to say about Germany,
without forming the impression that it is a country which,
inhabited entirely by problems, lives in a state of constant
expectancy, waiting for their transcendent solution. From
Friedrich Schlegel's seeing in Germany's present 'only the
germ of a great future age' when 'things will come to pass
among our people such as never did in human history',[40] to
the young Nietzsche's discovering, 'hidden beneath the unquiet
life of our culture, a glorious power' which 'will burst into the
open in a tremendous moment',[41] the voice of Germany pro-
nounces incessantly its ominous 'Not yet'. Even a much later
Nietzsche, the Nietzsche of *Beyond Good and Evil*, is prompted
by Wagner's music—'once again, and yet as if for the first time'
he has heard the overture to *Meistersinger*—to observe: 'This
kind of music expresses best what I think of the Germans:
they are of the day before yesterday and of the day after to-
morrow. Today has not yet come.'[42] The suggestion of this
strange national destiny must indeed be compelling if also
Karl Marx, so little given to generalizations of this sort, remarks:
'As the ancient peoples experienced their past through their
imagination, their mythology, so we Germans experience our
future through our thought, our philosophy. We are philosophical contemporaries of the present without being its historical contemporaries. German philosophy is the ideal
extension into the future of German history.'[43]

Of course, he was a Hegelian, and 'we Germans', says
Nietzsche, 'would be Hegelians even if there had never been a
Hegel, in so far as we (different in this from the Latin nations)
instinctively attribute to "becoming", to "developing", a

deeper meaning and a richer value than to that which "is"— we can hardly believe that the notion "being" is justified.' [44] And elsewhere he says: 'A German *is* not, he *becomes*, he "develops".' *[45] The German language itself seems to play into the hands of Hegelianism, meeting Hegelian thoughts, as it were, half-way. Some of these, from Hegel to Heidegger, could certainly not have been conceived in a less obliging language, particularly not those bearing upon the profoundly bothersome dialectical or existential entanglements between 'being' and 'becoming'. German, in its vocabulary as well as in its syntax, is a restless idiom, better suited to expressing, it seems, the mobile confusions and dynamic exasperations of the mind than its stability and equipoise.   It is not for nothing that its greatest poetic triumph is the poetry of *Faust,* the drama of the mind's disquiet, and one of its most sublime lyrical moments Goethe's poem of the mystery of 'becoming': *Selige Sehnsucht.* This is also why the rare moments of peace and repose into which German poets now and then charm their restless medium, with, for instance, '*Der Mond ist aufgegangen*' or '*Ueber allen Gipfeln ist Ruh*', overwhelm us with such a shock of poignant delight, and why the prophet of the 'gentle law', Stifter, had to invent the most tortuously complex style in order to proclaim the message of the simple life and of the stillness of the world: commotion comes more naturally to the German tongue.   Even the anti-Hegelian Schopenhauer once remarked (and earned, of course, Nietzsche's applause for the observation) how much more satisfactory than 'reality' the German word '*Wirklichkeit*' is as a name for the fidgety thing it means, and how much more appropriately it expresses the eternal agility of that which is and yet can hardly ever be said to 'be' in its untiring movement from cause to effect (*Wirkung*) with not a moment's rest.[46]   And does not '*Gegenwart*' too differ in the same Germanic manner from 'present', expressive as it is, verbally and even philologically, of opposition and

---

* Ernst Bertram (*Nietzsche,* Berlin, 1920, pp. 64 et seq.) has assembled a whole anthology of similar sayings from German literature.

expectation, of enmity, perhaps, to what happens to be now, and of waiting for what is to '*werden*', to become?

This national lack of 'reality' and 'present', lamented or messianically interpreted by so many a German writer and thinker, including Karl Marx, and sanctioned, it seems, by the language itself, can of course be derived from numerous historical causes. But whatever these are, the fact remains that ever since the Reformation and the Thirty Years' War the history of the German people has been felt, inside and outside Germany, to be disquietingly out of step with the rest of Europe. Intellectually, this may be due to the peculiar absence of any clearly articulate transition from the Middle Ages to 'modern' Germany. In the second half of the eighteenth century, Germany, during its 'classical' epoch, acquires a highly sophisticated intellectual culture with a suddenness which bodes ill for its broad efficacy and pervasive vitality, and which, in its abrupt efflorescence, may have caused the chronic 'indigestion of the German mind' which Nietzsche diagnosed, and before him Friedrich Hebbel when he confided to his diary (19 December 1843) that 'we Germans, unlike the English or French, cannot look upon ourselves as an organic continuation of the past: for that which, after all, we must call our history, is more in the nature of a case-history. . . .'

A country the very language of which suggests a deficient sense of 'reality': there could not possibly be a more suitable country for the aesthetic philosopher to be a patriot in, providing as it does a spacious local habitation for his problematical relations with the 'real'. Infinitely malleable as it must appear in its emphatic state of 'becoming', withholding, in its indefinitely sustained 'not yet', the sobering finality of the 'Here and Now', the eternal adolescent among the nations, it is the predestined recipient of the Pygmalion love roused by that which is as clay in the hands of the Imagination. A people sick at heart and full of music—like Hanno Buddenbrook, scrupulous in accomplishment and consumed by unscrupulous passions—like Gustav Aschenbach, religiously aspiring to 'being' and unable to be—like the non-political man: such a people, surely, can be embraced without the slightest risk to one's aesthetic loneliness. It is the ideal object of religious devotion for the religiously undevoted, and the ideal 'other' for the unrealized 'self'. It is a spiritual fiction which is so powerfully persuasive because it is occasioned by a real presence in the flesh: the multitudes are indisputably there. This distinction it shares with the great romantic fictions of love, with which it has something else in common: the illusion of community created by being lonely together. What Nietzsche, in the Preface to *Human, All-too-Human*, says of his past allegiances also fits the nationalism of *Meditations*:

> What time and again I needed most for my own cure and recovery was the belief that I was not quite so isolated . . . a charmed suspicion of kinship and sameness of vision. . . . Maybe I am guilty in this respect of a great deal of 'art', a great deal of subtle forgery: for instance, about Richard Wagner's incurable romanticism, as if it were a beginning and not an end, or about the Greeks, or about the Germans and their future. . . .[47]

But why, it may be asked, did Thomas Mann choose the nationalist attachment to Germany as his 'artful' escape from loneliness? Why not the other 'subtle forgery', practised to more timely effect by his many fellow-escapists from intellectual isolation—for instance, by the *Zivilisationsliterat*? Why not the flight into the international brotherhood of man to be inaugurated by the revolutionary proletariat? The answer has, of course, been already given: it lies in his conservative imagination. 'Who am I?' he asks in *Meditations*, 'whence do I come so that I am as I am, and am neither able nor willing to be anything else?' He is a citizen, he says, and (despite or even because of Tonio Kröger) a burgher, a child of the German burgherdom. And how does he see the German burgher? 'It is not by accident', he writes, 'that, when I search for the image of the burgher, it is a face from medieval Nuremberg that appears before my eyes'[48]—the very image of his idea of German burgher *Kultur*, the face as it was painted in its pessimistic dignity and non-political inwardness by Dürer or Holbein. Thomas Mann's forbears on his father's side came from Nuremberg, and the idea of culture associated with them has a hold upon his imagination against which, for the time being, the new and very different bourgeois reality has no chance of prevailing.

To this memory, some time even after it had made its precarious peace with the demands of the new age, some exquisite pages of *The Magic Mountain* were to be devoted. They are about Hans Castorp's boyhood life in the house of his grandfather, Senator Castorp of the Hansa city, whose 'real image' was impressed upon the boy's mind not so much by 'life' as by 'art' and death: by his portrait on the wall, which was 'an excellent painting in an old-master style that suited the subject', showing the Councillor in his official medieval garments, both resplendent and austere; and the boy could not help feeling that this was the authentic and real grandfather, while the grandfather with whom he dined every day at the table was 'an interim person, adjusted to the ordinary in only a provisional and imperfect manner'. And so young Castorp 'from the depth of his heart agreed that it should be the authentic and perfect grandfather who lay in medieval state when the day came to take leave of him'.[49] In the grandfather's keeping is the baptismal bowl of the family, which in Thomas Mann's description becomes the very vessel of the conservative imagination. From time to time Hans would ask his grandfather to show him the dignified object resting on its silver plate, on the back of which were engraved the names of its successive owners, and the grandfather would recite them: father, grandfather, *Urgrossvater*, with the untranslatable sonorous prefix *'ur'*, which was doubled, tripled, quadrupled, in the course of the recitation. Listening to this repetitive *'ur—ur—ur'*, 'this sombre echo of the tomb and the falling away of time, which yet expressed a devoutly cherished link between this present life of his and the buried past', the boy would experience a sensation both exciting and strangely soothing, and 'it may well have been for the sake of hearing this sound that he so often begged to see the baptismal bowl'—the very bowl, it seems, from which Thomas Mann's imagination received its christening, making it respond for ever, approvingly like young Hans Castorp and like him 'from the depth of his being', to the ethos of conservation.[50]

Thomas Mann never ceased to see Germany with the eyes of this conservative love.   Doctor Faustus is the fruit of its despairing passion.   His development from *Meditations* to *Doctor Faustus*, from the patriotism of the First World War to his implacable national indignation during the second, from the indictment of his 'westernizing' brother to his first angry refusal to visit Germany in 1946, is uncannily reminiscent of Nietzsche's way from *The Birth of Tragedy*, still vibrant with the hope that the spirit would elect Germany for its new incarnation, to his violent onslaughts on the hateful people in *Ecce Homo*, tirades unequalled in their fury by any foreign enemy.   And it is ironical indeed—ironical in its absolute consistency—that on the occasion of Thomas Mann's seventieth birthday his brother Heinrich, who once enraged him not so much by his 'political opposition to Germany' as by 'being un-German in his soul',[51] should be able to say: 'He wanted to believe in Germany. . . .   Hence his unforgiving anger. A man, thus disillusioned, must beware of rejecting a whole nation together with its guilty men. . . .   When we talk about it now . . . then it is rather I who refuse to see the unhappy country of our origin as a unique monster.'[52]   And indeed, in that seventieth year of his, Thomas Mann published an essay, *Germany and the Germans*, a by-product of *Doctor Faustus*, which cunningly quotes, without of course giving chapter and verse, whole passages from *Meditations*, the only difference being that the new context reverses the accents of approval and disapproval.   But as in *Meditations*, the Germans are still 'the people of the romantic counter-revolution against the rationalism of the Enlightenment—of the musical rebellion against literature, the mystical uprising against intellectual clarity'.[53]

No doubt, this strange *Volk*, which has haunted the souls of its sons with the uncontrollable persistence of a ghost, has denied itself the 'present' not only for the sake of its 'becoming' and its messianic future, but also in its archaic faithfulness to the mythological past. What a European anachronism, for instance, Richard Wagner is! Where else in Europe, at that time, could a primitive national mythology have been revived on such a scale (Yeats is a miniaturist in comparison) and, fed on the resources of a most advanced artistic inventiveness, not have produced the effect of sheer travesty? While France and England and even Russia, in their great novels, created the image of mythless modern man, a conductor from Dresden conquered the world with the Nibelungs and a bass-baritone cobbler from Nuremberg. There is an astounding measure of national authenticity in such success, which could not have been achieved without a genuine liveliness of the archaic imagination.

Early in *Meditations* there is an autobiographical reflection concerning Wagner which, in its portentous and deliberate confusion, sums up the final problem of this problem-riddled book: the writer divided in himself between his conservative imagination and his exceedingly disruptive, 'modern', and even 'decadent' literary talent. It is one of his oldest and most fruitful problems—one of those he has by unimpeachable right inherited from the early German Romantics, in particular from Friedrich Schlegel. Its other name is 'myth and psychology', and Thomas Mann mentions it for the first time in 1910, in his affectionate essay on the old Fontane. 'Myth and psychology,' he says there, 'these are opposites, and where they live together in one and the same mind, where the "poetic" is joined together with the "literary", there will be contradictions'; for 'the poet is conservative in his role as guardian of the myth, while psychology corrodes and undermines, and is the most effective tool of democratic enlightenment'.[54] This will fit Fontane only at a stretch, but it certainly fits Thomas Mann (who in nothing is more like God than in the irresistible urge to create all great men a little in his own image). Myth and psychology—it is this quarrelsome pair which is almost omnipresent in Thomas Mann's works, sometimes with ruinous effect, as in *Fiorenza* and *The Tables of the Law*, sometimes humorously fighting on the edge of disaster, as in *The Holy Sinner*, sometimes splendidly reconciled in long aesthetic peace, as in *Joseph and his Brothers*.

In *Meditations*, in the passage we have in mind, Thomas Mann protests that it was his youthful devotion to Wagner's music to which he owes almost everything of whatever artistic mastery he may have acquired; for Wagner affected him not as the musician or dramatist of myth, but as 'the modern artist *par excellence*, as Nietzsche has taught me to see him', just as Nietzsche himself was to him not what he was to the fashionable intellectuals, not the prophet of a vaguely visualized Super-man, but 'incomparably the greatest and most thoroughly initi-ated psychologist of decadence'. Having made these points, Thomas Mann goes straight on to make another, which ill accords with the unmythological modernity of his taste for Wagner. He remembers Italy, where, 'a youth for whom there was no room at home', he lived 'in a kind of voluntary exile'; and in Rome, 'the unloved city', Wagner's music was 'literally the home of my soul'. He would listen to it on the Pincio, at a concert, standing, 'poorly dressed amid a welter of inter-national elegance', at the foot of the platform, 'under a thickly blue sky which never ceased to get on his nerves, under palm-trees which he despised', and would, 'feeling weak in his knees with enthusiasm, receive the romantic message of the overture to *Lohengrin*. Did he remember those hours when, twenty years later, there was war between the spirit of the *Lohen-grin* overture and the elegant international world?' If so, then 'the modern artist *par excellence*' has inspired rather antique passions.

Wagner was also played on the Piazza Colonna whenever the Wagnerite maestro Vessella conducted the concerts of the municipal orchestra. And each time there were nationalist and conservative demonstrations against the new and foreign music. One day Vessella put the Funeral March from *Götter-dämmerung* on the programme:

> Everybody knew there would be an uproar. The piazza was crowded, all balconies were occupied. The fragment was played

through without interruptions. Then all around war broke out, with ostentatious applause and nationalist protest. Some shouted 'encore' and clapped, some shouted 'boo' and whistled. It looked as if the opposition would win; but Vessella encored. This time they ruthlessly demonstrated during the music. Whistling, and cries for home-grown music, drowned the *piano* passages; during the *forte* the acclamations of the enthusiasts gained the upper hand. I shall never forget how, amid *evivas* and *abbassos*, the Nothung-motif emerged for the second time, how it unfolded its powerful rhythms above the tumult of opinions, and how at its climax, at that shattering dissonance before the two thunderous C-Major chords, there rose a triumphal yell which drove the shaken opposition back and reduced it to silence for quite a while. The stranger, twenty years old—as strange here as this music—stood wedged there on the pavement. He took no part in the shouting because he was choking. Staring at the platform which furious *Italianissimi* tried to storm and the players defended with their instruments, he smiled, pale though he felt his face to be, and his heart beat in tempestuous pride and youthfully morbid emotion . . . Pride in what? Love of what? Only of a disputed musical taste?—Likely, more than likely, that twenty years later, in August 1914, he would remember Piazza Colonna and the nervous tears which had filled his eyes at the victory of the Nothung-motif, and streamed down his cold face because, hemmed in by a foreign crowd, he was unable to lift his arm.

This lengthy quotation could be used for many a critical purpose, not least for that of showing that the non-political man is as expert as the *Zivilisationsliterat* at turning 'commitments' to the purplest of 'aesthetic effect'. But its importance in our context lies elsewhere: in what it suggests—and in how it is followed up. For it is only too obvious that the pride and love of the enraptured young man are not roused merely by the uproarious triumph of an artistic conviction. More even is involved than simple patriotism or a romantic message: the Nothung-motif is the thing, the lure of the archaic past, and the enchantment of vistas stretching far beyond baptismal bowls and senatorially clad grandfathers into regions where the '*ur*' rules supreme. It is there that the imagination has its roots. Sever it from them—and it is lost, as lost as life itself,

its music, its poetry, its truth, and its love. Beware of civilization and its literary champions! Thus speaks the conservative
artist and non-political man, or thus would he like to speak,
and might, if he spoke more moderately, speak a truth, just
as he has spoken many others in the course of his meditations.
Yet *is* he what he speaks? The question haunts every page
of the book, and will, being faced and answered, seal the
destiny of a great ironical writer, a fate which the works to
come will, in many shapes and ever richer constellations, now
serenely accept, now tragically contemplate, now comically
exploit—but never transcend; and least of all will it be affected
by the political man's occasional unfaithfulness to the ironical
aesthetic philosophy.—The quoted passage continues:

> Yet I do not deceive myself. Even if the young man then
> experienced Wagner's art as a source of patriotic sentiments, it
> was in truth an intellectual experience which I shared with
> Europe. . . . For this German composer was not a ' German
> composer' in the old, intimate, genuine sense of the word. . . .
> What entranced me had nothing to do with the nationally German,
> poetically German or romantically German in his art—or only
> in so far as all this appears in it in an intellectualized, decorative
> and self-conscious manner. . . . No, I was not German enough
> to overlook the profound similarity between his effects and those
> of Zola and Ibsen, who are both, like him, above all deliberate
> manipulators of symbols and of tyrannically schematic inventions;
> the French novelist in particular, a naturalist and romanticist also,
> is his true brother in the will and the power to intoxicate and
> overwhelm the masses . . . The Rougon-Macquart and the Ring
> of the Nibelung—the Wagnerite cannot think of them together.
> Yet they *belong* together: for the critical observer, if not for the
> loving admirer.[55]

Thus the archaic shudders of the Nothung-motif are instantly
outgrown, while the war between the spirit of the Lohengrin
overture and the literary taste of the elegant international
world, between the conservative imagination and the disruptive
psychological modernism, between the non-political man and
the champion of civilization (whose essay on Zola, it will be
remembered, was largely responsible for *Meditations*) is trans-

ferred to its predestined battlefield: the writer's own soul and mind.   Dear silly Tony Buddenbrook could have warned him. Her brother Thomas had flown into a rage when, at the instigation of friends, she suggested to him a highly 'unconserv-ative' and recklessly 'modern' business deal.   She countered his anger by saying: 'I may be only a stupid woman, but I know, from myself and others, that we get so cross only when we are not quite sure of ourselves, and really feel like doing the thing which makes us angry.' [56]   And Thomas Mann takes the words out of her mouth when in *Meditations* he says:

> Why all this labour?   Why the prolonged and humiliating servitude in which I am kept by this book?   No one demands or expects it of me, and neither gratitude nor honour shall I earn with it.   It is obvious, is it not, that nobody would concern him-self to such an extent with something which *need* not affect him, because he understands nothing of it and has nothing of it in himself, in his own blood. . . .   Could it be that what I am . . . does not correspond exactly to what I think and believe, and that I am destined to further precisely that which on these pages I have called 'Progress' through the very act of conservatively opposing it—opposing it by means of 'literature'? [57]

And again: 'A writer who, when this war broke out, was on the point of writing a parody of the German *Bildungsroman* in the form of memoirs of a confidence-trickster, has a share in the intellectual disruption of German culture'.[58]   And again: 'What else is this long monologue if not a review of what I was —what for a while I was legitimately and honourably—and what clearly I shall no longer be able to be without feeling old?' [59]   And finally: 'Literature is analysis, intelligence, cepticism, psychology; it is "Democracy", it is the "West". And where it is joined in one person to conservative convictions, there will be inner conflict.   Conservative?   Of course, this is not what I *am*; for even if I wished to believe it, my nature would refute me.' [60]

The 'ethics of being' can hardly be more persistently used as an instrument of self-critique.   Yet the problematical exist-ence revealed by the critique is strangely determined not to

L

part with its problems but to remain in the 'ironical state'; and most of the works to come will have their central inspiration in the unresolved dilemma. *The Magic Mountain* would never have been written without the ironical vision of a Germany undecided, and perhaps mediating, between 'East' and 'West', between the baptismal bowl and the unchristened intelligence, between the time incalculably registered by the inward soul and the time reliably measured by minds knowing which hour has struck. The hero of *Joseph and his Brothers* is the apotheosis of the ironical life, blessed as he is 'from the heavens above and from the depths that lie beneath, blessed with blitheness and with destiny, with wit and with dreams',[61] the ideal synthesis of myth and psychology, 'music' and 'literature', 'culture' and 'civilization', non-political conservatism and political New Deal. And the Goethe of *Lotte in Weimar* also exists ironically; sustained by the chthonic darkness, the sphere of the 'Mothers', he becomes, like Joseph, a provider of light and sobriety, remaining loyal, nevertheless, to the mysterious deep in his ironical superiority to the emancipated follies of mankind: he too, like Joseph, a 'disciplined dreamer', an artist and a statesman, a destiny and an intelligence, uniquely succeeding at the precise point where the Adrian Leverkühn of *Doctor Faustus* fails—the point where the genius of artistic communication meets the demon of loneliness, and archaic terrors the supremely detached intellect.

6

Somewhere between the ideal synthesis and the tragic outcome Thomas Mann has lived his life as a writer. The war and his wartime meditations left him, at first, despondent and exhausted. 'Estranged and distant, essentially different from the father I knew before and after those years of struggle and bitterness'— this is how his son Klaus remembers the author of *Meditations*, the man whose face seemed then 'devoid of the kindness and irony which both inseparably belong to his character'.[62]   At Christmas 1917 the *Berliner Tageblatt* asked a number of writers what they thought of the 'prospects of world peace'. Heinrich Mann answered with generous and didactic expectations, all of a piece with his essay on Zola, and Thomas as sceptically and pessimistically as ever: not for him 'Rousseau's doctrine of "the good people" ' or any sort of 'revolutionary optimism'—the faith of the man who loves mankind but 'hates his brother'. The phrase moved Heinrich to write to him. It was the first letter after three years, and was a mixture of conciliation and polemic. Thomas Mann replied on 3 January 1918. He obviously was not ready yet for peace and friendship. The shadow of despair is unmistakable. His letter ends: 'I have not asked for this life. I detest it. I shall live it to the end as well as I can.'[63] This mood, however, happily passed. In the long run (and a long one it was) the intense confession of *Meditations* had a liberating effect. Proof is *The Magic Mountain*. None of his books before had so much of the quality—and against what odds!—of that 'mountain springtime' which in the novel momentarily reconciles even the rationalist grumbler Settembrini to the horrors of sanatorium life: 'Not here the confusions and agitations of spring in the valley! No seething depths, no steaming air, no sultry vapours! But dryness, clarity, a serene and piercing charm!'[64]

Yet the mood of *Meditations* was to return—and not only as the literary mood of *Doctor Faustus*. As his nature had once 'refuted' his conservative beliefs, so it did with the comforts he later sought in mild bouts of 'revolutionary optimism'. One of the last pieces he wrote, his essay on Chekhov, which, with the customary irony of his political fate, first appeared in 1954 in the German Democratic Republic, holds up the mirror to *Meditations*, reflecting in the gentler light of old age their sadness, their contradictions, and their strenuous groping for a social and political habitation. He quotes with cautious sympathy even one of the sillier remarks of the not often silly Chekhov, a remark directed at the old Tolstoy's 'reactionary morality': 'Sober reflection and a sense of justice tell me that there is more love for mankind in steam and electricity than in chastity and fasting.'[65] He quotes the 'positivist doctor's'

dreams of the future when 'no stone of your city will remain in
its place and everything will be changed as if by magic.   Gigan-
tic, marvellous houses will go up, beautiful gardens with foun-
tains in them will be laid out, a new type of men will dwell in
them, and everyone will know why he lives. . . .   Life will be
good fifty years hence.'   Yet at this point Thomas Mann
cannot help breaking in: 'Will it?' he asks: 'Alas, it seems
certain that man is a flawed creature.   His conscience, which
is of the spirit, is unlikely ever to be in complete harmony with
his real nature and social state.'   He even calls Chekhov's
prophecies 'slightly hectic', like 'fantasies induced by a phthisic
condition'.   Nevertheless he adds that these visions, phthisic
or not, may anticipate 'something of the socialist impetus of re-
construction with which modern Russia, despite the terror and
hostility she excites, impresses the West'.[66]   Does this take back
the sceptical 'Will it?'?   By no means: of all the words of
Chekhov's he has read, none has moved him more deeply than
those which express the utmost scepticism concerning his literary
fame: 'As I have no answer to the really important questions,
am I not bamboozling the reader?' [67]

What are these really important questions?   With all its
bewildering changes from resolution to hesitation, from sally
to withdrawal, the essay yet reveals that they are the very
questions which, at one extreme end of *Meditations*, the
Zivilisationsliterat asked, and, at the other, the non-political
man.   And jerkingly and haltingly, they are now run into
one, just as once upon a time they were pertinaciously kept
apart.   For the words Thomas Mann quotes from Chekhov,
with their emphasis upon the political miseries of society, could
have been said by the *Zivilisationsliterat* in a bleak hour: 'As
things are, the life of an artist is meaningless, and the more
gifted he is, the stranger and more incomprehensible is the
part he plays; for there is no doubt that he works for the
amusement of an unclean beast of prey and by doing so helps
to maintain the existing order.'   And although 'the existing
order' is, for Chekhov, the state of affairs in the Russia of the
'nineties, Thomas Mann now expressly identifies himself with

the writer's predicament: 'Chekhov has brothers in suffering today, writers whose fame makes them feel uneasy because they "are amusing a doomed world without offering it as much as the glimpse of a saving truth" . . . and who, just like him, can all too easily feel what the hero of *A Tedious Tale* felt, the old man with no answer to the question "What shall I do?". They too are unable to say what the meaning of their work is, and yet go on, in despite, working to the bitter end.' 'In despite'—these words remind the reader of past despondencies far deeper than all political discontents. For with this most persistent *leit-motif* of Thomas Mann's life and work we seem to have returned from 1954 to 1911 or 1914, and are back at Gustav Aschenbach's 'moralism of achievement', Frederick's 'nihilistic fanaticism of accomplishment', and the 'faith-less ethos' of *Meditations*.

Yet perhaps not quite. For this 'in despite', or so we read in the essay on Chekhov, 'must have a meaning after all, and thus give meaning to the work produced'. And this 'meaning' too takes us back to 1914 when it was most urgently proposed by the 'champion of civilization' and most indignantly rejected by the non-political man. It is as if a long-standing invitation were at last accepted—not, however, without a question-mark: 'Can it be that there resides in a work of literature, however much it looks like mere entertainment, something ethical, socially useful, which finally may even lead to that "saving truth" towards which mankind stretches out its hands?' And Thomas Mann goes on to reflect upon the connection there is, or may be, in Chekhov's work between its increasing mastery of *form* and its increasing *moral and political* awareness, that is, 'the ever clearer discrimination between that which is socially doomed and dying and that which belongs to the future'. And is it not such awareness and discrimination 'which gives to the ceaseless industry of the artist its peculiar dignity, its meaning, and its usefulness, and which explains Chekhov's high regard for work as such, and his condemnation of all idle drones and parasites, his ever firmer rejection of a life that, as he said, is "based upon slavery"?' [68]

'The *Zivilisationsliterat* has never heard more flattering things in Germany.' This was said by the non-political man in *Meditations* and referred to an essay he himself had once published in *März* (March—'a name filled with sweet intimations of political spring'). Its subject was 'philanthropy *and* the art of writing as the dominant passions of one man', was, in fact, the connection between a writer's increasing mastery of form and his increasing moral and political awareness. 'It is most significant', he wrote in *März*, 'that those philanthropical publicists of the Enlightenment who taught their contemporaries to abominate all social iniquities . . . distinguished themselves also through didactic books about language and style. . . . The social and moral progress of the human race is inspired by the spirit of literature.' Yes, the non-political man, in *Meditations*, confessed defiantly to having written this, and withdrew it with equal defiance. 'What a sermon!' he exclaimed, 'one might think it was Woodrow Wilson speaking, that lofty benefactor of humanity, who—I have it on good authority—is not a little proud of the style of his notes.' And while he confessed and withdrew, he revealed something else (unnecessarily, perhaps, coming as it did from the writer of *Tonio Kröger*): 'Yet my papers tell me that at the same time I was quite capable of thinking the reverse. "The error of the man of letters", I read there, "is his belief that the spirit of literature makes for greater decency. The very opposite is true: decency is only where the spirit of literature is not." ' [69] What he published in *März*, he later, in *The Magic Mountain*, put verbatim into the mouth of Settembrini, the amiably shallow 'organ-grinder' of Progress and Enlightenment —'Well, you see,' Hans Castorp would say to his cousin after Settembrini's effusion, 'you see, what matters in literature is beautiful words. I have always dimly felt that myself.' [70] What he wrote at the same time and did not publish, was given, equally verbatim, to Settembrini's deadly enemy, the rebellious conservative Naphta. [71] Such are the ways of the aesthetic philosopher. He will for ever experiment with beliefs which he may, or may not, hold himself.

To come back to Chekhov: the old man from *A Tedious Tale* who has no answer to the question 'What shall I do?' is of course not, though it may seem so from the context of Thomas Mann's quotation, despairing at the difficult business of abolishing an objectionable political regime. Far from it. The question is put to him by an unhappy young woman who despairs of the meaning of her life; and to this woman, his ward, the one human being he still loves, he is forced to say: 'I don't know, Katya; upon my honour, I don't know.' It is a non-political question and a non-political answer, the answer of a man who says of himself: 'Every feeling and every thought has an isolated existence in my mind; and the most experienced analyst will not find in my views what one could call a central idea or the God of the living man. And if that is lacking, then there is nothing at all.' [72] This too is quoted by Thomas Mann, and with a sympathy so deep that it can hardly be reached by the philanthropical answer with the question-mark.

What, then, is 'the really important question'? The God of the living man or the good life fifty years hence? In *Meditations* the fear that there might be 'nothing at all'—the besetting anxiety of the aesthetic philosophy—sought refuge and reassurance in a quasi-political fantasy of the conservative imagination, in a spiritual image of Germany. But the radical self-critique of the literary man eventually overtook the imaginative flight. In the essay on Chekhov the politically enlightened intelligence turns towards a social utopia only to be arrested in its progress by the conservative imagination. It is with a scene from Chekhov's *The Bride* that Thomas Mann concludes his piece: the 'bride' stands at the deathbed of the man whose revolutionary ideas have changed her way of living: 'and there arose before her eyes the vision of a new life, grand and free; and this new life, nebulous still, and mysterious, called and allured her'. And Thomas Mann adds: 'It was a dying man who wrote this just before the end, and perhaps it was only the mystery of death which called and allured. Or shall we believe that the dreams of a poet have the power really to transform life?' [73]

What is left is an 'obscure hope' and 'almost a faith'—and all the grave confusions and tormenting doubts of *Meditations* are re-affirmed in touching tenderness; what is left is echoes from the tumultuous burial of Goethe's Faust somewhere between the Mephistophelian 'eternal void' and the liberated ground of a happy human future.   Faith and salvation, however, remain in suspense.   The progress of an artist is not like a pilgrim's.   Even less is it like 'the progress of history'. Thomas Mann knew it when he wrote *Meditations of a Non-Political Man*, and knew it still when he wrote about Chekhov. For the conservative imagination is not easily persuaded of the progressive happiness of the human race, nor the aesthetic philosophy of any meaning to be found beyond the labour of conscientious creation.

V

Conversation on the Magic Mountain

THE dialogue as a form of critique stands in need of only
one apology; not, as it may appear at first glance, for
frivolity and playfulness but, on the contrary, for the semblance
of presumption: it seems disastrously immodest to provoke
memories of Plato or Dryden or even Friedrich Schlegel. But
it is with no thought of emulating them that I have decided
to break the monotony of a monologue which has all the time,
and no doubt noticeably, been a disguised conversation—
a conversation with myself, with fellow-critics, and not least
with Thomas Mann. In a letter written exactly one year
before his death he said that 'Thou com'st in such a questionable shape' had been 'only too familiar to me as a manner of
addressing myself'. It seems appropriate, then, that questions
should be asked.

A critic is well advised to heed Goethe's impatient words:
'If I am to listen to the opinion of another, then it must be
expressed positively; I have enough problems in myself.' Yet
we may be allowed a few experiments with contraries when the
subject of the discourse is an author who has given so positive
expression to the belief that everything is problematical. It
might be helpful then to clear the ground for affirmation by
letting someone else gather up the questions. The performers
of the following dialogue are Q, standing for the questionable
and the questioner, and A, standing for an answer and an
affirmation.*

* Many friends and colleagues have, without knowing it or perhaps
even, mercifully, without recognizing their shares, contributed to this

Q: At the end of his essay 'Dostoevsky—within Limits',
Thomas Mann tells us that a friend, who knew of his plan to
write a short introduction to the Russian writer, had warned
him: 'Be on your guard! You will write a book about him.'
And half apologizing for the brevity of the essay, half pleased
with himself for having been brief at last, Thomas Mann
adds: 'I have been on my guard.' [1] Admirable warning,
admirable obedience! I wish he had listened more often to
the voice of caution. Am I not right in thinking that both
The Magic Mountain and *Joseph* grew from very modest
conceptions?

A: Yes. *The Magic Mountain* was to be no more than a sequel
to *Death in Venice*, a caricature of the fascination with death
so seriously treated in that *Novelle*, and *Joseph* merely the
biblical section in a triptych of religious stories of which the
second would have been about Luther, and the third about a
Spanish theme from the Counter-Reformation. [2] We may
even add *Buddenbrooks* to your list of mountains magically
made out of mole-hills. Originally Thomas Mann thought

dialogue. Q in particular is a highly complex personality. For his
existence I have certainly to thank more critics than I can with certainty
relate to the troublesome Questioner. I should, however, be very much
surprised if some of the more recent books on Thomas Mann have not
helped to form Q's, and no doubt also A's, critical opinions: for instance,
Bernhard Blume's *Thomas Mann and Goethe* (Bern, 1949), Louis Lei-
brich's *Thomas Mann* (Paris, 1950), E. M. Butler's *The Fortunes of Faust*
(Cambridge, 1952), Henry Hatfield's *Thomas Mann* (London, 1952),
Jonas Lesser's *Thomas Mann in der Epoche seiner Vollendung* (München,
1952), Hans Eichner's *Thomas Mann* (Bern, 1953), Roy Pascal's *The
German Novel* (Manchester, 1956), R. Hinton Thomas's *Thomas Mann*
(Oxford, 1956) or, of course, Hermann J. Weigand's several recent articles.
But for particular, and to me particularly interesting, points Q is indebted
to H. E. Holthusen's *Die Welt ohne Transzendenz* (Hamburg, 1949),
Peter Heller's 'Versuch über Thomas Mann' in *Forum* (Vienna, May 1957),
and to a very relevant aside in Harry Levin's altogether very relevant
essay *Symbolism and Fiction* (Charlottesville, 1956).

I should like to repeat here the warning that the references, maintained
even in this conversation for scholarly (or perhaps pedantic) reasons,
merely locate quotations. Unless he wishes to make sure of these, the
reader is asked not to let the numbers trouble him.

only of the short life of Hanno. The attempt to 'sketch in'
the boy's ancestry led to a novel of two volumes. The author
himself tells us that he found some comfort in remembering a
tetralogy which had once grown from the plan for one opera,
The Death of Siegfried. It became *The Ring of the Nibelung*.[3]

Q: Six massive volumes instead of three short stories! Germanic thoroughness indeed! It is a thin line which divides
conscientiousness from pedantry. For me it is often rendered
invisible by Thomas Mann's work.

A: He himself once said that only that which is thorough is
truly entertaining. In that he is the very opposite of
Nietzsche, whose ambition it was to say in three sentences
what others say in a book—'and yet do not say'. But is
there not also high intellectual pleasure, almost a fairy-tale
pleasure, in discovering the inner riches of a modest-looking
idea? Or in exploring the potential range of a thought?
And how rare are truly expansive thoughts in an age whose
ideas, if they move at all, move usually by a series of
mechanical   explosions—jet-propelled.   Thomas   Mann's
ideas grow smoothly and 'organically', like seeds into trees.
They need no pushing or kicking. There is pedantry and
pedantry. The one is the tedious conscientiousness of a
trivial mind, the other——

Q: —the not necessarily less tedious conscientiousness of a
sophisticated mind. I think I have good reason not to be
entertained by Thomas Mann's excesses in thoroughness.
Pedantry is incompatible with form. Therefore it is the
enemy of art. A sculptor's workshop is strewn with chips
—matter lightheartedly sacrificed to shape. Thomas Mann's
aesthetic sin is a sin of non-omission. He spoils his shapes
by working the chips back into them. His workshop needs
no dusting. His works do. You have talked at some length
about his irony. He himself once defined it as the inability
to make up his mind. 'Maybe', he said, 'it is good to be
resolute. But the really fruitful principle, the principle of
art, is . . . reserve', namely 'that irony which plays subtly
and undecidedly . . . among the opposites, and is in no

great hurry to join issue . . .'⁴ As a 'principle of art'
this strikes me as calamitous, indeed as the very calamity
of his writing. If I were in a mood to evolve principles
of art, I should opt for resolve. Aesthetic decisions are
resolute. Things are either formed or left in abeyance.
They cannot be both. You will, of course, protest that the
'reserve' he means is an intellectual attitude towards the
material of his art, and need not affect its *aesthetic* form.
You will, of course, accuse me of confusing content and
form—

A: Of course?

Q: I say 'of course' because this is what you are bound to say
at some point, just as at another you are bound to say that
there is no such distinction. Not because this is you, but
because this is a discussion about literature; and in a discussion about literature someone simply *must* be told that
he confuses content and form, and *must* be told a little later
that the two are really one. I like literary debates. They
are full of such magic. If then I may for a moment avoid
the confusion of what at all costs must be kept apart, and
cannot possibly be confused because it is the same, let me
quickly say that Thomas Mann's irony brings into question
the very possibility of art. I admit that his pedantry is the
conscientiousness of a highly ironical and highly sophisticated
mind. He dare not leave out anything because anything
may be of unsuspected importance and therefore any choice
and decision premature. Hence the inordinate length of
his works. I once heard you describe the artist's mind as
occupying some kind of halfway house between the saint's
and the anarchist's. The saint, you said, sacrifices most
human potentialities to one supreme idea of truth, while the
anarchist is reluctant to pay with any of the riches of life
for the advantage of order. The artist, between the two,
desires both: profusion *and* order, abundance *and* form; and
so he goes out at night, equipped with his workshop lantern,
picking up every particle which has been thrown out for the
sake of order and tidiness, inspecting it carefully and com-

passionately, and asking: 'Poor thing, have you really got
to be abandoned for the sake of form, order and artifice?'
Through such salvage the great conquests of art come about,
such as Shakespeare's poetry or Renaissance painting.
Imagine, you exclaimed, how much of the hitherto unruly
world they have brought under their artistic rules! The
seemingly impossible is attained: form is enriched and yet
the chaos outside diminished; the tribe speaks more clearly
and more courteously without increasing the sphere of the
unsayable and of the menacing silence. This is what you
said, and it may be so. But surely, your salvager artist
must stop somewhere. He must not pick up too much.
The constant suspicion that *anything* may be important will
in the end persuade us that *nothing* is. Irony? It is the irony
of 'everything' on the verge of 'nothing', and of art on the
verge of its own impossibility. This is what I meant.

A: This is what *he* means too and has never ceased meaning
since he wrote *The Magic Mountain.* You remember he
once said that there was nothing left for art to do except
become its own parody? 'Art on the verge of its own impossibility'—it is the main theme of *Doctor Faustus*, and in
the diary he kept while writing the novel, he quotes Harry
Levin's observation that Joyce's *Ulysses* is 'a novel to end
all novels'; and himself adds: 'This is no less true of *The
Magic Mountain, Joseph,* and *Doctor Faustus.* . . . Would
it not seem that only such novels can still be written which,
strictly speaking, are no longer novels?' [5] And as for form
—'the form of the novel'! Dear me! The air thickens with
tedium at the mere approach of the question, and all about
us is the dry rustle of papers written for literary societies.
A great Viennese satirist and poet confessed that he was
unable to read novels: 'I once opened a book', he said, 'which
they had told me was a great work of art, and I saw the
following sentence "Had Napoleon not ridden out to the
village on the evening of the 24th, and had he not then
ordered an immediate attack on the redoubt but begun
the attack next morning, no one would have doubted that

the redoubt was the left flank of our position, and the battle would have taken place where we expected it." I closed the book again wondering what sort of art it was in which such a sentence could find a place.' This may strike you as capricious, but is it not perhaps true to say that the novel, as a literary medium, is the great concession art has made to the age of spiritual informality?

Q: Flaubert. What about him?

A: Yes, Flaubert: the aesthetic frenzy against the heaviest odds ever. And what remains in the end is the unconquerable odds: *Bouvard et Pécuchet.* How to make prose yield to an aesthetic rigour as exacting as that of the traditional forms of art—this is the besetting problem of the artists among novelists. And by 'prose' I mean not only a manner of writing. I mean life experienced in the mode of prose— prosaically. Our salvager artist with his lantern has certainly had rather troubled nights of late. The world, littered with utterly prosaic stuff, has sorely tempted him either to leave out everything—everything except the purest words cleansed of their prosaic meaning, and the purest forms abstracted from their content—or else shamelessly take in everything, lock, stock, and barrel, blotches, scratches, freckles, obscenities, muddy streams of consciousness. Thomas Mann is one of the very few who has neither given in nor given up. And *à propos* form, do you know that the most thorough reviewer of *The Magic Mountain*, Hermann J. Weigand, in his book on the novel, comes to the conclusion—after a very close scrutiny—that it is 'the most highly integrated' of all novels conceived on a large scale? [6] Everything I said about the strict organization of *Death in Venice* is true of the much, much longer work. And the irony of it all is that the danger of formlessness of which we spoke is not only one of the main themes of the book, but is actually 'used' as a means of enriching its form. May I read to you a conversation from *The Magic Mountain*? It is between Hans Castorp, the 'simple young man', the 'problem child of life', who has by then travelled a considerable distance towards becoming 'educated', and Hofrat Behrens, the jovially melancholy and medically straightforward ruler of the sanatorium. It is a lesson in physiology. Hans Castorp, seized by a rapture of curiosity, rhapsodically bursts forth: 'What is the flesh! What is the human body! Tell us, Herr Hofrat, tell us this afternoon, tell us exactly, so that we know once and for all!' 'Mainly water,' says Behrens, and then goes into scientific detail. 'And what is death?' 'Dissolution.'

'Dissolution, putrefaction?' said Hans Castorp. 'They are the same as combustion: combination with oxygen—am I right?'

'I couldn't agree more. Oxidization.'

'And life?'

'The same. Indeed, the same, young man. Life is principally oxidization of the cellular albumen. That's where the agreeable animal warmth comes from, of which we have sometimes more than we need. Yes, living is dying, no use mincing the matter—*une déstruction organique*, as some Frenchman has called it with his native levity. It smells like that, too. Whenever it affects us differently, our judgment is corrupted.'

'And if one is interested in life, one must be interested above all in death, mustn't one?'

'Oh, well, after all, there is some sort of difference. Life is where form is maintained throughout all changes of substance.'

'Why maintain form?' said Hans Castorp.

'Why? Now listen, young man! What you are saying sounds far from humanistic.'

'Oh, but form is so finicky.' [7]

May I bore you with a little exegesis?

Q: You may. But not too much. For I fear you might stretch the meaning of the passage beyond its natural elasticity. I have yet to meet a literary analyst who is not a stretcher. Certainly, the passage contains the very theme of *The Magic Mountain*: the juxtaposition of 'dissolution' and 'form'. I should say there is hardly more in it than this: Hans Castorp, whose newly awakened intellectual curiosity is a kind of inflammation of the mind caused by his passion for Clavdia Chauchat—his judgment concerning the human body is indeed 'corrupted'—is in danger of abandoning himself to disease, death, Dionysian chaos. Form is sobriety, discipline, clarity, and is 'so finicky' because it somehow goes together with being restrained, polite, and industrious—in short, with being a shipbuilding engineer in Hamburg, a rather unattractive career for young Tannhäuser if the alternative is life with Madame Venus in her mountain. Is it not just the old story again of Aschenbach's Greek hexameters unsteadied by the long-drawn-out *u*-sounds of the Venetian beach?

A: Not quite. It would be entirely as you say if *The Magic Mountain* were, as was originally planned, the mere foil to *Death in Venice.* As it is, it has moved on to yet another level of irony: the Dionysian intoxication is, as you have correctly observed, productive of learning. Hanno Buddenbrook, similarly inspired, was a bad pupil. Hans Castorp becomes a very good one. His soul bursts forth rhapsodically, while his mind patiently learns all about the oxidization of cellular albumen. I wish I were that excellent reader of whom Friedrich Schlegel said that only his voice could do justice to the subtle irony with which the whole work is irradiated.[8] If that voice were mine, you might even allow me to read to you the whole chapter entitled 'Humaniora'.

Q: Friedrich Schlegel taught you how to read *The Magic Mountain*? Haven't you got your dates wrong?

A: Of course. Yes, I have. Friedrich Schlegel meant Goethe's *Wilhelm Meister.* But as a reader of *The Magic Mountain* you should know what tricks Time is apt to play on us when we happen not to be in the mood for playing on it our trick of objective measurement. It is one of the pervasive themes of *The Magic Mountain* that clocks and calendars are both imprecise and dull ways of registering the movements of the elusive river—as imprecise and dull as everything that disregards the human soul. And to the human soul time does not flow evenly, either in retrospect—three weeks of travel seem longer than three months of routine life—or in anticipation—that lecture I have promised to give eight months hence appears to be as distant as the Future Life, and de-

ceptively leaves me with as immeasurable an amount of
time in which to prepare myself. And while time actually
passes (and we pass the time—so that Heaven only knows
who or what it actually is that passes what or whom) there
are time's all but stagnant pools when it appears not to
flow at all, and there are its Niagaras; and there is a state of
the soul when it has no time.

Q: A *state* of the soul?   Well, I agree that nowadays nobody
ever has any time.

A: Because we have nothing but time.

Q: Are you being paradoxical?

A: With your permission. There are two reasons for not
having time. You meant the first: having too much to do.
Why have we too much to do? Because nothing counts
except what we do in our time and with our time, because
we have nothing but time. What I meant was the other
reason for not having time: because the soul enjoys the
timeless state, and has, as it were, God's good time. An
age which has so little of this must find its dealings with time
exceedingly problematical. *The Magic Mountain* is a great
novel of the epoch in nothing so much as in its preoccupation
with Time.   Thomas Mann was a contemporary of Einstein's.

Q: I am very doubtful of such facile offerings of the *Zeitgeist*.

A: I deeply respect your scepticism and shall not mention Time
and Bergson, Time and Proust, Time and Heidegger.   But
it so happens that both Einstein's Relativity and *The Magic
Mountain* are concerned with a concept of time rendered
problematical by the absence of a valid standard of measurement, the absence of an Absolute; and if the *Zeitgeist* can
be defined by what it lacks: this is it.   Perhaps the jam jars
in the larder of Hans Castorp's childhood home have got it.

Q: The jam jars? Have got what?

A: Have got the Absolute. I mean the air-tight glasses full
of jam, fruit, or meat, which Hans Castorp suddenly remembers as Naphta, his gravest educator on the Magic
Mountain, instructs him in the Hermetic Philosophy.
'Hermetic—what a lovely word, Herr Naphta!' Hans Castorp

M

exclaims, 'I have always liked the word hermetic'; and then interrupts his mentor's learned discourse with the homely memory of the conserves: 'What struck me always as magical', he says, 'was their being withdrawn from time, they were hermetically sealed off from it, time passed them by, and there, shut away from time, they stood on their shelves.' [9] This is a typical example of the occasional *Alice in Wonderland* touch of *The Magic Mountain*.   But it is, as I said, the chapter 'Humaniora' which I should like to read to you in the voice prescribed by Friedrich Schlegel.

Q: What is it about?

A: About the rhapsodic and the scientific, and how both are facets of one passion; about Hans Castorp's discovering the high comedy and the high seriousness of the 'Humanities'. Hofrat Behrens, an amateur painter, has painted a portrait of his patient Clavdia Chauchat.   Hans Castorp, already secretly in love with Clavdia, persuades Behrens to show him and cousin Joachim his works.   Joachim is a passive victim of the occasion, cunningly used by Hans as a kind of chaperon to lend the appearance of innocence to the adventurous enterprise.   The episode begins in the garden of the sanatorium—'it was yet another of those incomparable alpine October days: bright without being heavy, hot and yet with a tang in the air'—and ends in the living quarters of the Hofrat.   The epithets given to the October day describe the mood of the whole chapter.   Hans Castorp grows ever more exuberant, almost inebriated as he is by the portrait of Clavdia—a very bad likeness 'which he ought not even to have recognized' but distinguished by an exceedingly faithful, scientifically minute, and unusually 'concrete' rendering of the *décolleté* ('*anschaulich*' is the Goethean adjective Thomas Mann parodistically uses in a situation teeming with parodistic Goethean associations).   For the first time Castorp uninhibitedly displays, to the amazement of the doctor and the embarrassment of the cousin, the interests he has developed, and the extraordinary knowledge he has acquired during his febrile stay on the mountain.   His exchanges with Behrens bring into ironical, and often very comic, play the variety of angles under which man can see himself and his works. 'If a man knows a little about what goes on under the epidermis,' says Behrens, acknowledging the praise he receives from Hans for the masterly execution of Clavdia's skin, 'if he can paint a little below the surface, . . . and stands in yet another relation to nature than just the lyrical, . . . it all comes in handy. . . .' [10]

Q: It sounds like an apologia for the literary method employed in *The Magic Mountain.*

A: An ironical reflection on it, not an apologia. For it is the unashamed intention of *The Magic Mountain* to bring together the lyrical and the prosaic modes. Read once again the chapter 'Research', not because it is the best, but because it carries out the intention most resolutely. You will then soon notice very much subtler ways of handling the theme throughout the book.

Q: Is it about Hans Castorp's studying biology and physiology?

A: Yes, Hans Castorp's reading about life and the mystery of its origin, and reading about it by the light of the dead moon and the red-shaded glow of the table-lamp. And as he lies in his deckchair on the nocturnal balcony above the glittering valley, the image of life, left rather vague and abstract by the scientific books, assumes an imaginatively concrete shape which resembles Madame Chauchat. I have often heard literary critics say in praise of what they take to be particularly happy specimens of literary creation, that in them language 'does' what it describes. I am never quite sure what they mean; I only know that they are after something less simple than the onomatopoetic use of words. But whatever they mean, Thomas Mann's language 'does' it in the chapter 'Research'. It positively 'does' science, and it 'does' poetry. [11]

Q: I remember that spirited flirtation between the rhapsodic and the scientific vocables, the lyrical and the prosaic modes.

A: Flirtation? A consummation—the consummation of German romanticism.

Q: Of German romanticism? I always believed German romanticism was the organized *avoidance* of the prosaic mode —something like the cultivation of raptures and ecstasies, the contemplation of splendid agonies and exemplary Middle Ages, or, in its homelier form, the elegiac intimacy with babbling brooks, moonlit woods, and wild roses. I shouldn't have thought cellular albumen and the epidermis came into it very much.

A: Wild roses *and* cellular albumen, rhapsody *and* physiology— perhaps this is one way of hinting at one of the many varieties of romantic irony. Nocturnal solitudes and the pining spirit and the quest for the blue flower—yes, it is all there; but the bluest of flowers searched for by the first German romantics, that amazing group of people around Friedrich Schlegel, is a 'synthetic' one: the flourishing syn- thesis—how Friedrich Schlegel loved the prefix 'syn'!—of the poetic and the scientific. It is not for nothing that the Romantic Movement can be said to begin with the publication in 1794 of a book called *The Scientific Doctrine*: Fichte's *Wissenschaftslehre*.

Q: Well, scientific . . .

A: You need not think of Newton. But what you are asked to think of seems 'unromantic' enough: systematic ration- ality. What a strange mind was Friedrich Schlegel's! Pro- found, superficial, brilliant, awkward, crazy, reasonable— all in one: self-appointed commander-in-chief to manœuvre the poetic spirit over that zero-point of rationalistic depres- sion which, a little later, Hegel declared to be the end of all art. Schlegel tried to believe that it also marked a climax of intellectual freedom at which man was able freely to choose, and knowingly to create for himself, the good life of poetry which until then had been a dark compulsion of the imagination. 'A wholly free and educated person', he wrote, 'must have the power to attune himself at will to philosophy or philology, to criticism or poetry, to history or rhetoric, to the ancient or the modern—just as one tunes an instrument.' [12] It is a method which Thomas Mann has raised to the level of genius. Remarkable, isn't it, how much both Joseph and Felix Krull have of this infinite adaptability? And in the night of the *mardi gras* even the linguistic ignoramus Hans Castorp speaks fluent French.

Q: 'Just as one tunes an instrument?' It sounds to me like an apotheosis of charlatanism.

A: It is. Of the serious charlatanism of absolute self-awareness. This is the more surprising as our 'romantic' idea of the artist is of a man who, like Luther, 'cannot do otherwise'. He is at the mercy of a demon, an instinct, an inspiration, and knows not what he does. This, we are somehow accustomed to believe, is his 'integrity'. In contrast to this, Schlegel's romantic artist does *know*. He is supremely conscious—so much so that, while he does what he does, he can at the same time do something else: for instance, 'from the height of the mind smile down upon his masterpiece', as Schlegel believed Goethe did in *Wilhelm Meister*.[13]

Q: Did Goethe smile down upon *Wilhelm Meister*?

A: Perhaps not quite as broadly as Thomas Mann upon *The Magic Mountain*. Even if Friedrich Schlegel had been a still more voracious reader than he was, he would hardly have found in the literature available to him more classical examples than Thomas Mann has since produced of this particular brand of romantic irony. For instance: 'Like everyone else we claim the right to our own private thoughts about the story we are telling.' [14] This is how he introduces a reflective passage, ironically apologizing for it—to readers who, I presume, have somewhat naïve ideas about the proper relations between 'creation' and 'reflection'. Or again: 'At this point the author feels it would be advisable for him to express his surprise at what is coming next, or else the reader might try to do it for himself and overdo it.' [15] Or, when he says of the word 'relationship' he uses in describing the feelings, as yet silent, undeclared, and distant, which Hans Castorp has for Clavdia Chauchat, that 'it is Castorp's term, not our own; we disclaim responsibility for it'.[16] This, by

the way, is one of the many passages which floor the translator. The German '*Verhältnis*' means not only 'relationship' but also 'love affair'.

Q: If you go on like this, you will soon reduce me to the status
of those comfortable Platonic dummies who keep on saying
'That would be but natural', or 'True. I had forgotten.'—
Still, I see your point; and even if, measuring 'the height
of the mind', we may not arrive at precisely the same figures,
I too can see the smiling down. It is broad enough. No
doubt in German it is still broader.

A: You sound cross.

Q: Perhaps because the 'somewhat naïve ideas' are mine. For
I do believe that creation and reflection are different activities
of the mind, and that it is one of the weaknesses of Thomas
Mann's that he cannot keep them apart.

A: Who, at this time of day, can? A few talented simpletons—
and they succeed because they have precious little reflection
to keep apart from precious little creation. For the rest any
attempt to cultivate nowadays 'pure creation' in literature
leads to affectation or obscurity or alcoholism.

Q: Why nowadays?

A: I wish I knew the answer. From Hegel to Spengler many
answers have been suggested. They are all uncertain.
Only the symptoms are certain. Friedrich Schlegel already
took these symptoms for granted and tried hard to convince
himself that they meant the approach of 'masterpieces of
romanticism' in which creation was suffused with reflection,
and reflection was released with the spontaneity of the
creative imagination. What he obviously 'divined' was the
emergence of the European novel, which you, insisting so
much upon the 'two activities of the mind', seem still to
judge by the standards of the epic. Schlegel was much more
up to our date. Hence it is not surprising that he gave what
almost amounts to an anticipatory definition of the literary
art of *The Magic Mountain* when he described romantic
poetry as 'progressively universal'—'*progressive Universalpoesie*'. Its task is, he said, 'to re-unite the separate genres

of literature and to bring together poetry and philosophy',
to mix and mingle 'the poetic with the prosaic, creative
spontaneity with critique', to 'satiate the medium of art with
solid learning of every kind and to animate it with the
vibration of humour'.   Such a writer, he continues, 'may so
lose himself in what he portrays that he appears to be concerned with nothing else but the characterization of imaginary
figures, and may yet at the same time, and as if unwittingly,
completely portray himself'.   Only then will his work have
a chance 'of becoming the image of the age', while he himself
remains contemplatively aloof, 'multiplying reflection as if
in an infinite series of mirrors' and 'infusing every single
part of his creation with the identity of the whole'.[17]   It is
amazing how well this fits *The Magic Mountain*—in fact,
much better than the work on which Friedrich Schlegel was
in the habit of calling as the main witness to his conception
of *'progressive Universalpoesie'*.

Q: Goethe's *Wilhelm Meister*?   I seem to remember that
Schlegel's friend Novalis—and he was what Schlegel was
not: a poet—spoke rather unkindly of it.   Did he not call
it 'The Pilgrim's Progress towards a Knighthood'?

A: He did, and said even worse things of it: that it was a
satire against poetry, a 'Candide aimed at poetry', that
from it 'the economic nature of man emerged as his only
true nature', that it was 'a divine image made of straw and
wood shavings', and a 'piece of poetic machinery to deal
with recalcitrant material'.[18]   You can see that it is all much
to the point.

Q: To which point?

A: To my point.   For elsewhere he calls Goethe 'the true
vicar on earth of the poetic spirit', and *Wilhelm Meister*
'the novel *per se*', a work which comes close to the greatest
literary achievements of antiquity.

Q: A moody fellow.

A: As moody as the poetic spirit in a prosaic age.   For he
too regards the history of literature from the ancients to the
moderns as a dialectical quarrel between poetry and prose,

with Goethe as 'the nucleus of a synthesis'. Therefore he feels his way into *Wilhelm Meister* dialectically: now he allows it to affect him as 'prose against poetry' and now again as 'prose resolved in poetry'.[19]   May we now look once more upon our passage from *The Magic Mountain* in the light of Friedrich Schlegel's *Universalpoesie*?

Q: I am not so sure if 'light' is not a euphemism.   I am still in the dark.

A: Like Hans Castorp.   I wish I could be Settembrini for a moment, the man of the Enlightenment.   You recall his first visit at Hans Castorp's bedside?   The young man, until then a mere visitor in the sanatorium, the guest of his sick cousin Joachim Ziemssen, had contracted a cold and was sent to bed by Hofrat Behrens.   There he spends three weeks, if 'spending' is the right word for his passive dealings with time and the time-devouring monotony of the daily routine.   He eats at midday, always the same midday, his 'soup everlasting', and thinks of Clavdia Chauchat at nightfall, always the same nightfall.   But one evening there is a knock on the door, and in comes Settembrini, 'and instantly the room was flooded with light.   For the visitor's first motion, while still on the threshold, had been to turn on the electric light.'[20]

Q: Rather obvious.

A: Because I have made it so.   Besides, everything he does is obvious.   He is without mystery.

Q: Who?

A: Well asked!   I meant Settembrini.   But in a sense it could also be said of Thomas Mann.   Yet if it was well asked it was also asking too much.   True, there are writers—or had we better say: there *were* writers?—whose works have the ineffable quality of a primitive mystery, like the sea, or a landscape, or a truly loved person.   Yes, such works do exist—although much of modern literary criticism seems systematically to exploit the assumption that they don't.   But they do.   We may read them time and again, and at each reading they will be different, mysteriously different,

revealing something new and veiling something new. With
Thomas Mann's works we feel that their secret, which is not
a mystery, is, at least in theory, discoverable.

Q: Well answered! So they are not art. Except, perhaps,
Buddenbrooks.

A: If you are not careful, you will soon understand Friedrich
Schlegel. From *The Magic Mountain* onwards, Thomas
Mann's novels move towards that farthest point of art, its
ne plus ultra, where it yet defiantly asserts itself in the face
of its ultimate deprivation. Art tragically laments the loss
of its own mystery in *Doctor Faustus*, and gaily reports it to
the cosmic police in *Felix Krull*. Friedrich Schlegel, like a
complex simpleton and profoundly prophetic fool, believed
that precisely this would be art's supreme triumph, and read
Wilhelm Meister as if it were *The Magic Mountain*. It is a
book, he said, which 'saves the critic the trouble of judgment'. And why? Because it holds no mystery: 'it judges
itself. And not only does it judge itself, it also represents
itself'—together with the story it purports to represent.[21]
For 'everything that can be done so long as philosophy
[which for Schlegel is only another name for systematic
rationality, self-awareness, and critique] exists apart from
poetry [by which he means all the literary genres] has already
been done. Therefore it is time that they should come
together.'[22] He thought they had done so in *Wilhelm
Meister*. By a mere whim of history Thomas Mann had
lost his most enthusiastic critic. May we now look at *The
Magic Mountain* in the light——

Q: Yes, I think I am beginning to catch a glimpse of Schlegel's
meaning. He thought, did he not, that *Wilhelm Meister*
was the first great literary work produced by a mind in the
state of perfect critical awareness concerning the nature of
literature, and who produced it not despite such awareness,
but, on the contrary, entirely by virtue of it?

A: That is more than a glimpse of Schlegel's meaning.

Q: How unromantic!

A: I have been trying all the time to disillusion you concerning the 'romanticism' of the first German romantics. However, I ought to remind you that Shakespeare and Cervantes belong to Schlegel's history of romanticism as the first great writers who were also conscious *actors* of the spirit of poetry and literature—and therefore great *ironical* writers. Do you know Schlegel's *Lucinde*?

Q: Almost. I know it superficially, and wonder whether this is not the proper way of knowing it. I found it constrained, affected, and intolerably self-conscious.

A: Exactly. He certainly wasn't the writer to practise his theory. But you can see what he was aiming at. His theory was that 'construction', if only it was carried to its utmost limits, would finally re-enter, on a higher level, the sphere of organic growth, while self-consciousness, mounting higher and higher, would ultimately transcend itself in a reasoned ecstasy of spontaneous creation.

Q: And all this happens in *The Magic Mountain*? Small wonder it is so long.

A: Of course it does not happen in *The Magic Mountain*, and is not likely to happen anywhere; for it is the great romantic dream of irony enthroned as the first principle of all literature. But it is only because the great romantic dreams are unrealizable that *The Magic Mountain* is not its fulfilment. It achieves as much of it as can be achieved, and renders the rest undreamable. Maybe this is the nature of all great achievements. Let us at last look at *The Magic Mountain* in the light of Schlegel's theory.

Q: I am sorry. I seem to have succeeded in holding up your exegesis of Hans Castorp's lesson in physiology. Now it is no longer necessary. Our romantic ramble has not wasted *my* time. I can see now: the rhapsodic *and* the prosaic, the poetic *and* the scientific . . . 'to mix and mingle creative spontaneity with critique', and 'to satiate the medium of art with solid learning of every kind'. Yes, there are, in *The Magic Mountain*, pages and pages of critique, science, philosophy, without, I should say, much noticeable admixture of 'creative spontaneity'. There are, believe me, whole chapters where I feel that not only 'the medium of art' is 'satiated with solid learning'. I am too.

A: I doubt the solidity of the learning.

Q: You doubt it?

A: Of course I do. Can any one person have a solid knowledge of all the sciences that come into *The Magic Mountain*? Anatomy, physiology, pathology, pharmacology, radiology, psychology, engineering, philosophy, theology, meteorology, political theory . . .

Q: You are right. Nobody can have a solid knowledge of political theory. But you are confusing me: surely, *I* ought to have said all this?

A: Forgive me. I was only prompting. I know the list of grievances against *The Magic Mountain*. But *had* you said that you doubted the solidity of Thomas Mann's learning, I should have agreed. It is *startling* enough; it is even said that doctors marvelled at *The Magic Mountain*, just as egyptologists marvelled at *Joseph in Egypt*, and musicologists at *Doctor Faustus*. And although Thomas Mann could certainly not afford to be blatantly misinformed concerning their subjects, it cannot be the point of a work of literature to amaze the experts.

Q: I couldn't agree more. But what *is* the point of all that learning in *The Magic Mountain*?

A: Must I repeat myself and Friedrich Schlegel? I must not. May I therefore ask why you think it should *not* be there?

Q: Because a novel is neither a dissertation nor a scientific textbook.

A: Please make it more difficult for me. You know yourself that *The Magic Mountain* is neither.

Q: But long passages in it read like passages from a scientific textbook. They are dead matter in an artistic organization of which we are entitled to expect an aesthetic rendering of human experience.

A: I know *that* textbook all right. Human experience . . . I suppose you mean love and hatred, war and peace, adventure and death, gain and loss. There is plenty of all that in *The Magic Mountain*. But is not learning a human experience?

Q: Not the kind of human experience which can be rendered aesthetically.

A: 'Yet for he was a scholar, once admired
    For wondrous knowledge in our German schools. . . .'
What about Faustus?

Q: That's different. Both Marlowe and Goethe, in so far as 'learning' plays any real part in their works, give us the poetry of the *passion* for learning. Thomas Mann gives us the stuff itself.

A: The 'real stuff'. Just as Clavdia Chauchat is more 'real' than Helen of Troy. For we are dealing with a 'realist'. But Clavdia is not only 'real'; she is also, like Helen of Troy, the object of passion. And what is true of Madame Chauchat is true of the learning. Hans Castorp is in love with both. And as it is the convention of realism to show us the objects of passion not only in their passionate and poetic aspects but 'as they really are', there is no reason— unless we reject the realistic convention—why Thomas Mann should not show us the learning, pursued with passion by Hans Castorp, as realistically as he shows us the woman. But this apologia, addressed as it is to a blind spot in your comprehension, also misses the point of *The Magic Mountain*, which is to present the experience in both its passionate and sober aspects, as 'poetry' and as 'prose', as 'lyrical' and as 'scientific', and to reflect upon it from a multiplicity of angles. Yet of all the demands made by Friedrich Schlegel upon 'universal poetry' none seems to have been as conscientiously and successfully fulfilled by *The Magic Mountain* as the one asking that every single part of a literary creation should be 'infused with the identity of the whole'.

Q: Do you mean to say that Thomas Mann consciously constructed his novel to fit Friedrich Schlegel's design?

A: Certainly not. I even doubt that Thomas Mann was at any point of his work conscious of the prophetic definition. Schlegel was simply a great diviner of the historical probabilities of literature, and Thomas Mann was possessed of a sensibility which functioned as the *Zeitgeist's* most reliable seismograph.

Q: I am not sure whether I understand what is meant by 'every single part of a literary creation being infused with the identity of the whole'. Does it imply more than a certain unity of style?

A: We cannot be quite sure what Schlegel meant. Had he thought of *The Magic Mountain*, he would have meant a great deal more than you suggest, unless the term 'unity of style' covers such radical attempts at perfect integration as whole chapters once again telling in their own terms the whole story of the novel.

Q: A rather boring device. Or, to be just, it would have bored me had I noticed it.

A: I said, 'in its own terms'. The chapter 'Snow', for instance —

Q: In which it happens that Hans Castorp defies the rules of the sanatorium and goes on his lonely skiing expedition into the mountains?

A: Just as he once defied the rules of burgher life in Hamburg and climbed the Magic Mountain. He soon reached regions 'which filled his heart with sensations of wildness, strangeness, and extreme danger'.

Q: In the sanatorium?

A: In the snow. He 'struggled up ever paler heights and knew not whither. It seemed to him they led nowhere. Their upper reaches blended with a sky which was as misty-white as they, and it was hard to tell where it began. No summit, no ridge was visible—Hans Castorp strove towards haze and nothingness. The world behind him, the inhabited valley, fell swiftly away from view. No sound was to be heard. In no time at all, it seemed, he had become as solitary and as lost as heart could wish. His loneliness was deep enough to call forth that terror which is the condition of courage.' [23] Metaphorically, this is a description of the first steps of Hans Castorp's education on the Magic Mountain. Literally, it is only about this particular adventure in the snow. You may even go further, leave this particular Hans aside, and read both book and chapter as a parable of Man, man lost and saved—or perhaps not quite as much saved as he is lost.—Or do you remember 'the ethics of sin and self-abandonment' on which Clavdia enlightens Hans? This is its version in the snow: 'He rejoiced in his inspired freedom and abandon. Before him stretched no path, none lay behind him to take him back whence he had come. At first there had been posts, set up as guides through the snow—but he had soon cut free from their tutelage . . . because they seemed incongruously to intrude into his relations with the great wintry wild.' [24]

Q: I believe you. Yes, the chapter 'Snow' is a synopsis of the whole book. Yes, the whole book aspires to, and perhaps, achieves, a formal unity unparalleled by any other novel. It weaves and inter-weaves its motifs and arabesques into a pattern which, despite its endless variations, seems yet complete on every single page. And if I can find a few more phrases of praise for the formal excellence of Thomas Mann's art, you shall have them all. But you yourself said that analysable formal excellence does not necessarily establish the quality of a work of art.

A: I did say it. Yes, form may be dumb. It may have nothing to say. But *The Magic Mountain* says as much through its form as it says through its content. The two are really one.

Q: I know, I know, they are one and therefore must not get mixed up. And what does it say through its form? That 'form is so finicky'?

A: The whole book is about form and dissolution, the disciplined effort of living and the relaxing lure of death, the honours of achievement and the advantages of dissoluteness. It is about the civilized shape of Europe on the verge of its disintegration. Thomas Mann's insistence on literary form is a parodistic response to his own theme in so far as he treats of the temptation, delight, and danger of disorganization in the most elaborately organized prose. But it is also a militant measure in defence of form.

Q: Whichever it is, it is overdone.

A: As overdone as the white blood corpuscles around the centre of an infection.

Q: Except that it cures nothing. On the contrary, form over-done may itself be a symptom of death.

A: Abstract form. This too Thomas Mann knows. You remember Hans Castorp's learned speculations in the snow—on snow crystals? It is a very good piece—despite its learning, as you no doubt wish me to add. The last sentences of the piece say of those crystals: 'They were far too regular for any substance meant to live. Indeed, the blood of life seemed to run cold at the mere suggestion of anything so precise. The secret of their precision was the secret of death, and Hans felt he understood the reason why the builders of antiquity were in the habit of purposely and fur-tively breaking, with minute deviations from symmetry, the rigid rule of their structures of columns.' [25]

Q: Oh, he is so maddeningly circumspect and has the cowardice of a scholar who enjoys nothing more than frustrating by clever anticipation Professor X's attempt to catch him out! All right, form is death, and form is life, and *The Magic Mountain* is about life and death, and therefore doubly formed.

A: You are unjust. It is not Professor Q's criticism against which he guards. He is considerably subtler than that. He guards against the voice within, the Janus voice, the voice of absolute irony.

Q: The exasperating voice which makes it so difficult for me either to admit or to deny even to myself what I know to be a high probability: that *The Magic Mountain* is, by any available standard, one of the greatest novels ever written.

A: I understand why you cannot deny it. What prevents you from admitting it?

Q: The sun and the moon and the curse of modern literature. I remember a passage from *The Magic Mountain*, the first book of Thomas Mann's I ever read. Even in translation I was struck by the lyrical beauty of the piece: Hans Castorp's remembrance of a lonely boat-ride one evening on a lake in Holstein. I could feel the coolness of the late summer air, and hear the splashing of the water against the boat, and smell the meadows stretching from the bank where the grass was cut for the second time. I don't know whether all this is actually in the passage, but I am sure it was all around me when I read it. But the sun and the moon are certainly there, the almost full moon rising above the bushes that border the lake, and where the moon is, there is night, while the sun still dominates the west with the broad, sober, glassy light of day. I can still see Hans Castorp, sitting in his boat and turning his eyes in amazement from east to west and back again, from night to day and back to the moon. I liked it.[26]

A: I can see the sun and moon. I cannot see the curse.

Q: The curse is that it is a sort of allegory. Hans Castorp remembers the lake, the boat, the sun and moon, while, stirred by Settembrini's account of his family history, he contemplates the difference between his own grandfather in the medieval garments, and Settembrini's ancestor fighting the battles of Reason against the darkness of the past. Perhaps I feel less strongly about it now. But at the time I felt that it was the desecration of a summer evening through unholy literature. The summer evening is too true, too good, and too real, to serve as a mere visual accompaniment to the imaginary family squabbles taking place in Hans Castorp's mind.

A: It is strange that the summer evening, which you find so true, good, and real, is the work of the same writer who so tactlessly relates it to what you call the family squabbles.

Q: It is the terrible compulsion to relate everything to everything, this relentless obsession with the cross-references of the universe, which is the curse of our godless but oh! so 'religious' literature. If you believe in God as the creator of the world, then go and try to decipher His often illegible hand in the scrolls of His creation! But what, I ask you, is gained by relating one sadly meaningless thing to another, sun and moon to two grandfathers, or the superstitious number seven to

almost any arrangement on the Magic Mountain?   Oh, for
those healthy times when metaphors were ornaments of
language, not revelations of spurious meaning!   There is,
believe me, method in those Symbolists' unaccountably
electing the American Edgar Poe their master.   Their whole
school is one of the first manifestations of Americanism in
Europe: more and bigger and better correspondences, all
quivering with vitally appealing intimations of sense and
senses, instead of one clear and sensible truth.   Summer
evenings and grandfathers and criss-cross-references galore—
and when all the relating, referring, and corresponding is
done, we are left with a number of types which are given a
violent sort of 'significance' within a contrived aesthetic
pattern, but are divested of the independent and individual
existence they once had in the eyes of God.   Did I call them
allegorical?   No, they are not even that, for allegories live
entirely by the faith of writer and reader in an ultimate meaning.   Yet everybody and everything in the novel 'represents'
something: Hans Castorp represents Germany, Settembrini
the West, Clavdia the East, the song of the linden-tree death,
but what is represented is certainly not more significant,
and is only bigger, than its representatives, who in their turn
have acquired 'typicalness' at the expense of their uniqueness.

A: Your arguments are formidable and would be devastating if
they were themselves less 'typical'; and by this I mean that
they bring into question not only the work of Thomas Mann
but practically every major effort and achievement of the arts
and of literature in the past hundred years or more.   Besides,
the author of *The Magic Mountain* is well aware of the
difficulty, so much so that the book is in parts an essay in the
relation of the typical to the unique in a world of, as it were,
circular meaninglessness, a world seen in the image of
Nietzsche's 'Eternal Recurrence'.   Listen to Hans Castorp
when, lost in the snow storm, he discovers to his dismay that
after wandering about for a long time, with 'the idea of progress in his heart', he has merely returned to his hopeless
point of departure: 'That was the very devil.   Hans Castorp

N

uttered heartfelt curses although his lips were too stiff to pronounce the labials.   He stumped on his skis around the hut
in order to get his bearings, and came to the conclusion that
he had returned to it from the back, having indulged for the
last hour—as he reckoned it—in the sheerest and silliest waste
of time.   But there it was, precisely as the books reported
it.   You went in a circle, gave yourself endless trouble under
the delusion that you were getting somewhere, and all the
time you were simply describing some big nonsensical arc that
would turn back to its beginning, like the vexatious course of
the seasons.   This was certainly not the way of getting home.
Hans Castorp recognized the traditional phenomenon with a
certain grim satisfaction; he even slapped his thigh in anger
and astonishment at the general law fulfilling itself so punc-
tiliously in his individual, present, and particular case.' [27]
And again we read, as he all but succumbs to the temptation
to lie down in the snow and to rest: 'This temptation was as
great as the books reported, designating it the "typical
danger", which yet did nothing to diminish for him the living
present and the power of it.   It asserted its individual
rights, refused to be simply classified under some general
heading, and protested, as it were, that it was unique and
incomparable in its singular urgency.' [28]   How to equip the
typical with individuality, how to win freedom for that which
is fated, and how to give meaning and direction to a life
running its course in cyclic repetitiveness—this was the persistent problem of Thomas Mann, the writer and thinker,
ever since he realized that the *leit-motif*, which he had used
from the beginning, was more than a literary technique; that
it was in fact the literary symptom of a metaphysical belief
towards which he inclined.

Q: Towards which he inclined, or which he held?

A: Beliefs are not held in the ironical sphere; and in the sphere
of religion it is the beliefs which do the holding.

Q: If it resembles Nietzsche's belief in the Eternal Recurrence,
the love of the *leit-motif* sounds like gloom everlasting.

A: Or a serene faith.   Extremely gloomy, perhaps, when it expresses itself in the parodistic return of Adrian Leverkühn's utterly sophisticated music to archaic primitivity, or in his own defeated return to childhood. But it can also be the happiest faith. Think of those mystical re-embodiments of, say, the servant Eliezer in *Joseph and his Brothers;* every Eliezer who happens to be 'in the flesh' at any given time gains life everlasting through the indestructible type his own mortal self represents and he confidently says 'I' even if he narrates what happened to a servant Eliezer of hundreds of years ago.

Q: I am not Eliezer, and I am going to do something desperate now. I shall ask you, why? Yes, why? Ah, you already look as most critics and philosophers do when asked why—like the Emperor just about not to have his clothes on.   Yet I insist. Why all these changes from the cheerful Eternal Recurrence to the depressing Eternal Recurrence? Why all this romantic fuss about the aspects, and about mixing them, and about the ironical experiments, and about the duplicity of angles? Why?

A: Because of the great calamity.

Q: The great calamity?

A: You yourself used the word *à propos* Thomas Mann's 'indecision', and implied it in your attack on the arbitrary 'cross-references of the universe'. The indecision is, of course, about what is true, and in this respect it is an old calamity.   But the *great* calamity—and some would say that it is also the *new* calamity—is not to be sure even where and how to look for truth, and not to be sure whether it exists.

Q: Why? I mean, why should an artist be concerned with truth?

A: Did you not just complain about those who weren't—the 'aesthetic cross-referees'?   But let us assume, wrongly perhaps, that neither of us knows why they *should* be concerned with truth.   Then it will be easy for us to agree that some artists *are* concerned: Leonardo, for instance, or Rembrandt, or Dante, or Goethe.   Some even call themselves realists, which, if anything, means that they wish to be true to what really is.   And when the great calamity is upon them, such artists are compelled more than ever to experiment—yes, to experiment with aspects and angles and mixing and mingling and 'all this romantic fuss'. For one can never be sure—not even about the face to make in the face of this or that. For there seem to be no faces, only masks. Death, surely, is a solemn occasion, and Hans Castorp's capacity for not remaining as mediocre as he seemed at the outset, all his latent ability seriously to learn and to grow, stems, his story suggests, from the serious and solemn lesson he has, as a child, learned from death: 'One takes one's hat off to him, and goes on tiptoe in his presence. He wears the stately ruff of the past, and we do him honour in austere black.' [29] But Settembrini, on the other hand, calls the power of death 'strong but vicious and lascivious', so that to sympathize with it is 'without the slightest doubt the most ghastly aberration of the human spirit'. [30] And to be sure, death is first mentioned, on an early page of the novel, in a grotesque context. On the way from the station Joachim tells Hans Castorp, who has just arrived, of the bob-sleigh on which, during the winter months, a sanatorium still further up in the mountains transports its corpses into the valley. And when Joachim mentions yet another oddity of the place, namely Dr. Krokowski, the assistant doctor in their own establishment, who practises soul-analysis (the dissolving attack on 'form' is the link between the themes of death and analysis), Hans, already laughing at the macabre winter sport, is seized by an uncontrollable fit of merriment. [31] This is how, as soon as he arrives on the Magic Mountain, he begins to learn of the uncertain meaning of all things. And a little later he is already able to grasp what his soldierly cousin, the old inhabitant of the mountain, means when he says: 'Sometimes I think being ill and dying aren't serious at all, just a sort of loafing about and wasting time up here; life is only serious down below.' [32] *Placet experiri*, says Settembrini, in the humanistic hope that his disciple will discover, by way of experiment with uncertain meanings, the road to liberal certainty. Yet he himself suggests the dubiousness of all

accustomed concepts when he first meets Hans Castorp, the
new arrival and 'mere guest'. 'What,' the Italian exclaims,
'you are but a guest here, like Ulysses in the kingdom of
shades? You are bold indeed thus to descend into these
depths . . .' 'Descend?' asks Castorp, 'I have climbed up
some five thousand feet.' 'Upon my honour,' replies Settembrini, 'it was an illusion. We are deeply fallen creatures.' [33]
It is a parody of Mephistopheles's '*Versinke denn! Ich könnt'
auch sagen: steige: / s'ist einerlei*' . . . from Goethe's *Faust II*,
'Well, then, descend! Which is the same as: Rise!'—a motif
which, in the form of 'the revolving sphere', will dominate
the *Joseph*-tetralogy, and is by no means absent from *The
Magic Mountain*. In Hans Castorp's musings and dreams
there is a constant merging of the ice-covered heights and the
sea down below—the sea of his childhood. And soon Hans
Castorp, in his deceptively mild and gentle way, begins to
experiment with the uncertain levels of being—much to the
embarrassment of Settembrini and his humanely experimental philosophy. And why should he? Because he feels
he must find out all for himself what life is about. Did I hear
you complain about the absence of 'one clear and sensible
truth'? Well, you remember the passage in which Thomas
Mann ironically 'smiles down' upon his novel and 'claims the
right to his own thoughts about the story he is telling'. The
story, at that point, is about Hans Castorp's deepening infatuation with Clavdia, his desire which in all its sensuality
is yet something 'exceedingly elusive and tenuous', a mere
thought or even dream, 'the terrifying and yet infinitely
alluring dream of a young man' whose world had hitherto
offered him 'nothing but a hollow silence as its answer to certain
questions he unconsciously asked'. It is here that the narrator
breaks in with his own observations. Why has Hans Castorp
been taken ill, why has he prolonged his stay on the mountain? It might not have happened, says Thomas Mann,
'hazarding a surmise', if Hans Castorp's 'simple soul had
received from the age in which he lived some even faintly
satisfactory suggestion concerning the point and purpose of

the business of living'.[34]   This is one of the many examples of novel and novelist quoting each other, with the quotation deriving additional meaning from its new context.   For the 'hollow silence' was sounded before, near the beginning, when the reader was given the history of the simple young man, the 'rather mediocre' hero.   But his laziness was bound up with an insight, vague yet profound, which again brought his mediocrity into question.   For a really mediocre young man might well be lazy, but he would hardly notice what Hans Castorp noticed: the absence of any truly compelling reason to exert himself, or, if I may quote you, the absence of 'one clear and sensible truth'.

Q: I remember.   The passage in question has become weary with much use.   It has been quoted so often as 'marking a turning-point' in Thomas Mann's hitherto individualistic 'ethos', and as a first sign of his 'social awareness'.   But I think it merely states explicitly what was implied in *Buddenbrooks, Tonio Kröger,* and *Death in Venice.*   Thomas Mann always knew that 'the age' did not offer to anyone 'a compelling reason to exert himself'; on the contrary, the 'heroism of the age' he always represented, as you have reminded me, through 'the fanatics of accomplishment' prevailing over the sense of senselessness, and making themselves heard above the din of the 'hollow silence'.   I remember that at the presumed turning-point this is put not very differently.   Here: 'In an age that affords no satisfying answer to the question of "Why?" and "To what end?" a man, if he is to achieve something beyond and above the measure of the strictly necessary, must either be possessed of so rare a sense of moral independence and spontaneity that it borders on the heroic, or else of an exceptionally robust vitality.   Neither the one nor the other was Hans Castorp's case, and thus he must be considered mediocre after all, although in an entirely respectable sense.' [35] Now, is it the 'hollow silence' which is the great calamity?

A: An age which, bustling with activity, is yet immediately beneath its energetic surface 'palpably hopeless, clueless and helpless' [36] is calamitous enough.   But this is not what I meant.

Q: Is it not? I am surprised. You always mean the age; so much so that I have come to think of you as sighing under the burden of a wicked epoch—Atlas with a global chip on his shoulder.

A: Do you believe in the immortality of the soul?

Q: No catechism, please!

A: If you don't, you have nothing to lose except your epoch; and if you do believe in it, it is still within your epoch that you win bliss or damnation.

Q: You. And I. And he. Persons. The age is an abstraction.

A: Far from it. It is what you and I and he and she have to say to one another. And how we say it. And what we have to be silent about. And what we do and cannot do. And what we teach and do not teach our children. *The Magic Mountain—*

Q: You meant to say something which you have not yet said.

A: Perhaps because you yourself said it a little while ago in your own inspired manner. I think you made the mistake then of blaming *The Magic Mountain*, or its author, for the age that is the theme of the book.

Q: So it is the age after all.

A: Undeniably so. For what I meant to say was that *The Magic Mountain* is about an age dispossessed of the very sense of definable meaning. Therefore all things are free to acquire whatever meaning they choose. Nothing is what it seems.

Q: Put like that, it sounds like a very old predicament: Plato throughout the Ages. Appearance and Reality.

A: Your own denunciation of European literature from the Symbolists to Thomas Mann suggests that it is more like Plato at the end of his tether: Appearances and no Reality. Hence any appearance may at any moment behave as if it had the sole claim to reality, saying, as it were: 'If anything were real, I should be the *only* real thing.' It is a mescalin world: the red of this tulip would be the essence of reality if reality had any essence, and essence any reality. As it is, we are merely the occasional victims of intoxication, whether it is spirit, mescalin, or art.

Q: What on earth has this to do with Thomas Mann? It fits perhaps Rimbaud's deranging his senses in order to sense Reality, or van Gogh's taking all the meaning which might conceivably be in the universe, and putting it into the face of a sunflower. But Thomas Mann?

A: The magic of *The Magic Mountain* springs from the same procedure, carried out with the latecomer's irony and the moralist's caution. The author says so himself—to the delight, no doubt, of Friedrich Schlegel, who expects a romantic masterpiece not only to do certain things but also to explain what it does: 'We describe the commonplace; but the commonplace becomes very strange if it grows from strange soil.' [37] The thermometer, for instance, or Hans Castorp's cigar, or the deck chair, or the glass door—they are all utensils of disquieting significance, potential messengers of important communications, and trivial usurpers of Reality.

Q: What next?!

A: Do you know that you have just named the ultimate principle of our art and learning? Where the sense of truth is as restlessly keen and as profoundly unbelieving as it is with us, 'What next?' becomes the master question. Every day our eyes are opened to the possible significance of something new, until they are sightless with being kept open too long. You see that we agree.

Q: You see too much in *The Magic Mountain.*

A: For instance this: 'And the step to the atom proved to be without exaggeration absolutely fatal.' [38] Hans Castorp's scientific musings are full of such flashes of anticipation. This, I admit, does not take us away from the epoch and its apocalyptic banalities. Let us avoid them by doing a little literary criticism. I should like you to notice how the motif of the 'hollow silence' brings together three seemingly disparate things: Hans Castorp's laziness, his disease, and his love. These are the three causes which keep him on his mountain and, because they are 'intertwined', keep you in a bad temper.

Q: Talking of intertwining, you forget his learning. For the lazy fellow, feverishly in love, reads with the zeal of a Ph.D. candidate. And still more is intertwined: music and death. Have you noticed that whenever Hans Castorp thinks of death or comes into contact with it, he looks 'as if listening to music': 'slightly dull, sleepy and pious, his mouth half open, his head inclined towards his shoulder'? [39] You see, I am ready for a little literary criticism. Yes, many things are intertwined. I make it seven, the magic number of *The Magic Mountain*.

A: Laziness, learning, disease, love, music, death. Six.

Q: Hollow silence. Seven. 'Only connect', as E. M. Forster says. But what, I ask again, happens when everything has been connected and intertwined? You still owe me an answer to this question.

A: Then we are—let us agree for the time being—on the Magic Mountain, in the midst of that 'lucidly handled chaos' where hardly anything remains quite itself, and in that 'artistically ordered confusion' of which you are so classically suspicious, whereas Friedrich Schlegel saw in it the great merit of romantic literature. This literature, with its 'enchanting symmetry of contradictions, its wonderful and ceaseless oscillations between enthusiasm and irony' seemed to him 'in itself an indirect mythology'.[40]

Q: What does 'indirect mythology' mean?

A: I suppose it means the kind of mythology that might emerge if Oedipus, endowed with Freudian knowledge about himself, still saw fit to enact his myth; or if Moses, having read Thomas Mann's *The Tables of the Law*, were still to climb Mount Sinai and wait for the voice of God to speak. They would do it 'indirectly', by way of knowledge, and perhaps in spite of it—would do it ironically or ambiguously.

Q: Would the voice speak?

A: Friedrich Schlegel seems to think that it would speak more clearly even than before. I doubt it. But we are not on Sinai of the Ten Commandments. We are on the Magic Mountain of the Seven Ambiguities, which, as you can

easily see, have their own improper dealings with the Seven
Deadly Sins.   Let us listen to Hans Castorp and what he has
to say to Clavdia Chauchat.   By this time he has learned a
great deal—not only French but also Novalis.   This is what
he says: '*Le corps, l'amour, la mort, ces trois ne font qu'un.
Car le corps, c'est la maladie et la volupté, et c'est lui qui fait la
mort, oui, ils sont charnels, tous deux, l'amour et la mort, et
voilà leur terreur et leur grande magie.*' [41]   Werther, Novalis,
Platen, Wagner, *Death in Venice*—obviously, *l'amour et la mort*
is the most German of all romantic refrains.   Thomas Mann,
the perfect Romantic of Schlegel's expectation, has made *The
Magic Mountain* both the consummation *and the critique* of
the old theme.   It is the critique which you mistakenly ignore.
And what is true of *l'amour et la mort*, also applies to that
other romantic fascination, *la maladie et l'esprit*.

Q: This, surely, is a less respectable theme—the phthisical myth
of *La Bohème*, tuberculosis and art dwelling together in the
untidy attic?

A: In German it is of immaculate intellectual respectability.
Thomas Mann could hardly have chosen a more suitable
scene and background for his 'critique of the European mind'
than a sanatorium; not only because the European mind is
the patient, but because mind and sickness go together within the romantic tradition of German thought.   Disease is a
mark of spiritual distinction, and Hans Castorp merely
voices a Germanic platitude when, innocently provoking
Settembrini to his first great aria in praise of the classical
mens sana in corpore sano, he speaks, romantically, of the
emotional dilemma that some patients in the sanatorium
cause him by their being so ill and at the same time so stupid.
Stupidity and sickness is a combination but little dreamt of
in the romantic philosophy.   'What I mean is, it's not right,
it doesn't fit; I can't get used to the idea.   One always thinks
of a stupid person as perfectly healthy and ordinary, and of
illness making him refined and clever and unusual.' [42]   This
is what Hans Castorp says, and, as he is German, might indeed
feel even without having read *Buddenbrooks* or *Death in*

Venice. Do you know that Novalis becomes positively a Darwin of natural pathology when he meditates on disease and evolution? Listen to this: 'Vegetable diseases are animalizations, animal diseases are rationalizations. Vegetation is an illness of the rocks.'

Q: From which it would indeed follow that human sickness is an approach to divinity. The transfiguration of German measles.

A: A joke worthy of Settembrini at his humanistic worst. Europe had, in actual fact, no need of German romanticism in order to think that through some denial of his animal health man might draw nearer to the divine. Novalis's romantically Darwinist fragment also says: 'All diseases have this in common with sin that they are symptoms of transcendence: heightened sensibilities which strive to become higher powers. Man sinned when he desired to become God.' [43] In other words: he fell ill.

Q: Goethe seems to have had better reasons than he knew when he identified romanticism with sickness.

A: On the other hand, he admired Schopenhauer—at least before the philosopher expressed himself pessimistically about *The Theory of Colours.* And as we can see from *Buddenbrooks,* nothing is easier than to give to disease a very definite and very positive function in the philosophy of the Will: it weakens the Will and therefore strengthens Mind. And Nietzsche believed—at least sometimes—that an artist thrives on conditions which 'are akin to, and organically connected with, the pathological, so that it seems impossible to be an artist without being sick'.[44] Above all, we must not forget that Hans Castorp's education is unthinkable without his becoming ill—in a sense it is even true to say that his education and his illness are identical. Little does Joachim Ziemssen know how much he brings into question when he says to his cousin: 'Oh, you with your learning! Getting wiser all the time, with your biology, and your botany . . . ! But we didn't come up here to get wiser. We came to get healthier. . . .' [45] Professor Weigand is, of course, right in saying of Hans

Castorp's surrender to disease that 'it has the same symbolic significance as Faust's pact with the Devil' [46]—and is almost prophetically right, or even suggestively right: Thomas Mann, much later, literally made his own Faustus sell his soul to the Devil by contracting syphilis and with it a spell of immense artistic creativity. Yet *The Magic Mountain* is also the *critique* of the romantic equation *la maladie c'est l'esprit*, as of *all* those romantic equations the luxuriant growth of which arouses your classical anger.

Q: Because critique is often merely the morally insured way of indulging the criticized fascination.

A: In *The Magic Mountain* disease is no longer the sure ally of mind and unfailing promoter of 'spirit' which it was in *Buddenbrooks*. Frau Stöhr, the apogee of vulgarity and stupidity, is very ill, and with this *coincidentia oppositorum* confuses Hans Castorp's native philosophy of life. And true enough, before *The Magic Mountain* Thomas Mann could not possibly have allowed a sufferer from tuberculosis to say 'cosmic' when she means 'cosmetic'. 'Stupid, healthy life' is what Frau Stöhr would have been. The aesthetic proof that Thomas Mann is ironically in earnest with his critique of the old obsession is the vehement success with which the tubercular Frau Stöhr, abandoned to imbecile giggles behind her handkerchief, comes to life in the novel—indeed, crashes into life—while the man who appears to be born for the highly diseased and highly intellectual career of the hitherto typical Thomas Mann hero, Naphta, is a rather pale literary creation, and a little too obvious as the poor sacrificial tiger, that unmistakable co-author of *Meditations of a Non-Political Man*, who has to be killed on the altar of a spiritual conversion.

Q: True, what a romantic novel! *L'amour et la mort, la maladie et l'esprit* (or let's say 'learning'; we are among Germans)— these are four of our seven themes ambiguously intertwined in the novel. It is easy enough to fit the remaining three into the romantic household: the 'hollow silence'—or shall we say 'the desperate search for meaning'? Then there is laziness— called 'dreaminess' in the politer romantic idiom——

A: —or the Philosophy of the Good-for-Nothing in Eichendorff's *Aus dem Leben eines Taugenichts*, a book hailed as 'purest romanticism' in Thomas Mann's *Meditations*.[47]

Q: And, lastly, music. There is the celebrated chapter about Hans Castorp's favourite gramophone records. Are they not all, although only one piece is German, about our great romantic fascinations, above all about death?

A: Yes, romantically played, as if by arrangement with Friedrich Schlegel, on a most advanced electro-technical contraption. The chapter is yet another instance of the extraordinary organization of the novel. Again, it seems to re-tell the whole story, this time in the guise of meditations on pieces by Verdi, Bizet, Debussy, Gounod, and Schubert.

Q: A strange assortment. The selection not of a musician—

A: —but of a novelist who calls Hans Castorp's great love by the abiding name of Hippe.

Q: Abiding? The love story Thomas Mann tells is about Hans and Clavdia. Hippe is merely a memory. But what's in the name?

A: Death. Pribislav Hippe. Pribislav is a Polish name—like Tadzio in *Death in Venice;* and Hippe is the German for scythe, an instrument which belongs to the medieval image of Death. Clavdia Chauchat, to whom Hans Castorp finally 'returns the pencil', which in a first boyish feat of passionate daring he borrowed from the admired schoolmate, is Pribislav Hippe's feminine incarnation. She has his 'Kirghiz' eyes and husky voice, and her profound identity with him is sealed by Hans Castorp's blood.

Q: Blood? I can remember no such drama.

A: Can't you? Hans Castorp has been a visitor in the sanatorium for only a few days. One morning he ventures on a first lonely walk into the mountains. As he is lying on a bench by a stream, trying to stop an ominous bleeding at the nose (soon he will be a patient himself), his mind is suddenly invaded by the school-yard scene with Hippe. The memory of it has the articulate presence of a vision. And only after this experience does Hans Castorp know that he is in love with Clavdia Chauchat.[48]   But what is more: it *remains* the same love. The sex does not matter.   Think of Hans Castorp's sleepy thoughts when, in extreme danger of falling asleep in the snow, he meditates, without any apparent motivation, upon pencils and genders in French: '*Son crayon!* That means her pencil, not his pencil, in this case; you only say *son* because *crayon* is masculine.   The rest is just a silly play on words.' [49]

Q: Do you mean to suggest that Hippe is to Clavdia as Proust's Albert is to Marcel's Albertine?

A: There is no need for suggestion.   I merely mean what Thomas Mann not only meant but made abundantly clear: that Clavdia is to the young man Hans Castorp what Hippe was to the boy Hans Castorp.   In neither case is it a passion from which marriages are made.   On the contrary, it is the 'unreasonable love' which Hans himself, in a conversation with Clavdia, equates with death and calls by the names of *res bina* and *lapis philosophorum,* names he has learned from Naphta, who, however, added to them 'the double-sexed *prima materia*'.[50]   And of Hans's passion for Clavdia Thomas Mann says that it was 'a risky and homeless variety of the lovesick folly, mingled frost and fire, like a dangerous fever, or the October air in these altitudes.   What it lacked was those emotions which could have bridged the two extremes.' [51]

Q: Which two extremes?

A: The two extremes between which romantic love enacts its comedies and tragedies: a definable desire and an indefinably tenuous hope.

Q: That she will yield?

A: That life will yield.

Q: Oh, I remember: yield a meaning rather than a hollow silence.   The kind of thing the Flying Dutchman expects of Senta when he sings of the 'sinister glow' of which he is not sure whether it is love.   No, no, he sings, 'it is the longing for salvation'.   If only he could have it 'through such an angel'.   I daresay you are right, and the sex of the angel makes little difference if it is salvation one wants by it, not children.

A: That is why I said the name of Hans Castorp's abiding love
was Hippe.   Death.   Life is always in danger of obliteration
when those two extremes touch each other and the yearning
for salvation becomes fused with the desire of the senses.
Listen: 'The term he had set for his holiday had long since
passed.   He no longer cared.   The thought of returning
home did not even occur to him.'   Why can't he ask her to
return with him?   Because of external obstacles?   These are
merely the feeble external symptoms of the inward state of
affairs: Hans Castorp does not want a wife; he wants the
adventure in permanence, he wants ecstasy as the daily level
of living, he wants the bliss which transcends life and lasts
for ever.   It is the romantic variation on death and salvation.
Hence he does not even wish to know Clavdia—except bibli-
cally.   He seeks to preserve that yearning of which Thomas
Mann says that it is 'the product of defective knowledge', the
exciting tension which exists 'between two beings who know
each other only with their eyes', and 'the hysteria of suppressed
communications and undeliverable messages'.   You remember these passages?
Q: I do.
A: You are quite wrong.   Forgive the didactic trick.   They do
not come from *The Magic Mountain*.   Of course, they might;
but they come from *Death in Venice*.[52]   Tadzio or Clavdia—
the nature of the passion is the same.   You remember how
it ends: after Hans Castorp's long and patient waiting—for
on the morning following the night of the *mardi gras* Clavdia
departed—she comes back to the mountain in the company
of Mynheer Peeperkorn.
Q: Senta with the Flying Dutchman.
A: I doubt it.   He needs no angel of salvation.   She is his
mistress, woman to a man.   And Hans Castorp's passion all
but dissolves.   Only now has he outgrown the Hippe love the
other name of which is Death.   To the slight annoyance of
Clavdia he makes friends with Peeperkorn, the big, inarticulate, tottering mystery.
Q: Yet another representative.   He represents Life.

A: Without the slightest detriment to his own. Representative
or not, admit that as a literary creation he is a surpassing
success. Admit—grudgingly, if you like, but admit—that
your outburst of a while ago did grave injustice to Thomas
Mann on at least one point: you implied that he divests his
creatures of their individual existence for the sake of their
typicality. It is untrue. Thomas Mann time and again succeeds in achieving the apparently impossible—namely, in
squaring Schlegel's literary circle and giving life to seemingly
preconceived ideas as if they were naturally conceived children of the imagination; which is only another way of saying
that you are wrong in thinking of his ideas as literally 'preconceived'. They belong to an imaginative order, not an
excogitated scheme. Think of Thomas Buddenbrook, or
Tony, or Christian! Think of Mynheer Peeperkorn!

Q: Who is a representative of Life.

A: If so, then not without irony. True, he is Dionysus, almost
as painted by Rubens, and a colonial Dutch coffee-planter,
as unforgettably described by Thomas Mann. But his model
is not Life but Art: a poet—Gerhart Hauptmann. Also, he
kills himself.

Q: Yes, he kills himself. I remember an extraordinary weapon.

A: Specially constructed for suicide. It is a mechanical imitation of the fangs of a poisonous tropical snake, the engineered semblance of a demon from such a jungle as Gustav
Aschenbach saw in his Dionysian nightmare.

Q: An engineered demon—your Friedrich Schlegel would have
loved it. But before you draw your representative conclusions from the fact that Life kills itself with a most in-
telligently and scientifically constructed monster, don't
forget that Naphta, unmistakably representative of Mind, also
commits suicide—in an act of sheer supererogation. He had
never been alive.

A: And is, like Settembrini, dwarfed by the advent of Peeperkorn. They cease to exist in his presence.

Q: Mind dwarfed by Life.

A: Whereas Peeperkorn, in his Dionysian inarticulateness, cuts an excellent figure in the company of his true peers, the mighty mountain cataract and the eagle in the sky.   He acknowledges, almost applauds, their great performances like someone who intimately knows what an achievement it is to be a good mountain cataract or a good eagle—a force of nature. Not to be one is to him the deepest humiliation.   This is why he must kill himself at the approach of impotence.   He fears that the tropical fever from which he suffers will destroy, or has already destroyed, his power of answering, as he calls it, the demands of feeling.

Q: Life without Mind.

A: Your prompting is better than your intention.   Life without Mind.   Then you also know why Naphta never comes to life: Mind without Life.   Peeperkorn's and Naphta's suicides may be Thomas Mann's way of killing his oldest pair of irreconcilable opposites.   Neither Life nor Mind can exist the one without the other.   'It is impossible to separate Nature from Mind without destroying both Life and Art.' [53]   Goethe knew that.   Thomas Mann comes to know it again after much '*Weltentzweiung*', much 'sowing of categorical discord', as Hans Castorp calls the intellectual activities of Naphta and Settembrini—or perhaps of the author of *Meditations of a Non-Political Man,*

Q: So it is for the sake of overcoming a 'categorical discord' that Dionysus has to be made sick and Priapus impotent? Irony with a vengeance.   *Placet experiri.*   Yes, it pleases Thomas Mann to experiment.   With what?   With all the aspects of—did you say, truth?   Or did you say that all the aspects together constitute the 'hollow silence' of the age? You did speak of 'that lucidly handled chaos' of *The Magic Mountain*, where 'hardly anything remains itself', and spoke of it with a puzzling undertone of romantic hope.

A: Which reminds me of Novalis's saying that 'true anarchy will beget religion, and religion will rise from the chaos of destruction as the glorious founder of a new world'.[54]   You are wrong in suspecting that I find it easy to share such cataclysmic hopes.

o

Q: But you do seem to see something positive in that chaos where everything is not itself but something else. Laziness is learning. Living is dying. Love is disease. Music is death. Clavdia is Pribislav. No amount of debate will clarify matters so hopelessly tangled.

A: No amount of debate. As Hans Castorp watches Settembrini's and Naphta's dialectical battles, this is how Thomas Mann describes his feelings: 'The principles and points of view constantly trespassed upon one another's domains, there was no end of inner contradictions; and as it became more and more difficult for Hans Castorp's civilian sense of responsibility to make a choice between opposed positions, or even to keep them neatly apart in his mind, so the temptation grew to plunge headforemost into Naphta's "morally untidy universe".'—Even in your most biased mood you must at least concede that Thomas Mann is far from being an uncritical supporter of this state of affairs. The passage continues: 'It was the universal topsy-turvydom, the world at cross-purposes with itself, the great confusion, which, more than the "wrongheadedness" of the partner, oppressed the soul of each disputant. And Hans Castorp sensed that this was the true cause of their exasperation.' [55] These are not the words of a champion of chaos.

Q: The true cause of my exasperation is the virtuoso literary manner with which Thomas Mann self-consciously creates a 'significant' work of art out of the apparently desperate uncertainty concerning the significance of anything. I understand that it is the vaguely sensed meaninglessness of his life which, in the novel, sends Hans Castorp to the Magic Mountain and keeps him there for seven years. This meaninglessness colours every one of his experiences, even his love. But where everything is coloured by meaninglessness, of what can anything be truly significant? If I let you go on, you will say in a minute what every single interpreter of *The Magic Mountain* has said: that, among other things, it is a 'symbolic novel'. And as the book—how did Friedrich Schlegel put it? —'judges itself', *The Magic Mountain* probably says so itself.

A: It does.   You may be thinking of Naphta's description of the initiation rites to which a novice is subjected if he wishes fully to enter the community of Freemasons. 'Magic pedagogy', 'alchemist levitation', 'transsubstantiation', 'hermetics', and finally the tomb, 'the place of corruption' which is also 'the receptacle wherein the material is prepared for its final transformation and purification'—these are the terms Naphta uses when he tells Hans Castorp of the mysteries of the mystery religion.   It is clear, I think, that they stand at the same time for the education young Castorp receives as the hero of the *Bildungsroman.*   And then again: 'The way of the mysteries and of the purification . . . leads through the fear of death and the sphere of corruption; and the apprentice, the neophyte, is the spirit of youth in person, guided by shrouded figures who are nothing but the shadows of the mystery.' [56]   All this, I am sure, is meant to reflect upon the novel itself.

Q: And the most shadowy of the shadows is no doubt Herr Naphta himself, the Nietzschean Jesuit and full-time mouthpiece.   Yet I expect that what is meant is the whole shrouded party of Hans Castorp's educators: Settembrini, Behrens, Madame Chauchat, Mynheer Peeperkorn.   If these are the shadows of the mystery, pray you, what precisely is the mystery?

A: You don't mean 'precisely', do you?   Anything may be precise except a mystery.   May I remind you of Thomas Mann's very Goethean definition of 'symbolic significance'?   The occasion is Hans Castorp's growing enchantment with Schubert's song of the linden-tree, and his ever clearer realization of its 'meaning'.   The song acquires great significance for him, and Thomas Mann asks: 'In what does the significance of a significant subject lie?   In the fact that it points beyond itself, that it is the expression and representation of something general, something universal, of a whole world of thought and feeling. . . .' [57]   There is only one 'precise' way of describing a mystery, or suggesting a 'whole world of thought and feeling': to find their concrete symbols.

The passages I have just read out to you are, I think, disguised declarations by the novelist concerning the intention of his novel. Yes, he meant to write a symbolic novel.

Q: You see! I am asking you how anybody can arrive at anything significant in a meaningless world, and you answer: by writing a symbolic novel. Symbolic of what?

A: And what if I said: symbolic of the difficulty of writing a novel, significant of the vital irony of an artist who produces works of art against, and almost from, the ubiquitous suggestion that it is meaningless to produce works of art?

Q: It would not be an answer. It would be a joke.

A: You were polite enough not to laugh when a little while ago I spoke of the *ne plus ultra* of irony in Thomas Mann's literary art from *The Magic Mountain* onward. I really meant the same thing. However, it would be a joke if I meant anything less than a work of art. As I mean a work of art, it is serious. For a work of art is the vindication of meaning.

Q: Even if it is symbolic of meaninglessness?

A: If it is a work of art, it will be in some sense symbolic. If it is symbolic, it can only be symbolic of meaning—although it may say: 'The world is meaningless'.

Q: We are ourselves approaching the grand confusion, the *quazzabuglio* of Messrs. Naphta and Settembrini. I shall soon be as speechless as young Castorp is on those occasions.

A: And you will *tell* me that you are. 'I am speechless', your speech will say. And it will not be unlike a work of art saying: 'Everything is meaningless.' If it were quite true, it could not be said—not by a work of art. The worst is not, so long as we can say, 'This is the worst.' There is reason for rejoicing as long as tragedies can be written. The preserved form of a piece of literature gives the marginal lie to the expressed conviction that everything is in a state of dissolution. It is an exceedingly ironical situation—a situation which has found in *The Magic Mountain* its appropriately ironical literary shape. Never before has the falling apart of all things been treated with so intensely conscious an artistic determination to hold them together.

Q: By the arrangement of words on a page?

A: Yes.   And therefore as facts of the mind.   And therefore as a human reality.   If this were not the case, literature would not be worth the paper it is written on.   The story of *The Magic Mountain* is, as it were, told twice: once as a series of incidents and experiences, and then again as a series of intimations conveyed through the very shape of the work.   The arrangement between the two is not smoothly harmonious, but ironical and contrapuntal, like the two parts, the one Apolline, the other Dionysian, of the dream Hans Castorp has in the snow, the 'dream poem of humanity' he composes on the verge of death, which teaches him the true state and status of *Homo Dei*, the lord of all contradictions, 'between mystic community and windy individualism'.[58]   It would be a bad and unconvincing dream had it to rely for its authenticity only on the story told.   Its proof is in the telling.

Q: You mean in the form, not in the content?   I understand. The form, you mean, tells a story of its own, a story which stands in a contrapuntal relationship to the series of incidents?

A: Yes; and as a *Bildungsroman* it stands in the same ironical relationship to the rules of the genre.   Wilhelm Meister, the model hero of such a novel, begins as an *Originalgenie* and ends as a useful member of society.   Hans Castorp begins as a useful member of society and ends approaching the state of being an *Originalgenie*.

Q: Yet he eventually leaves the Magic Mountain to do his duty by his country.

A: Which happens to be about to destroy itself in war; and most probably will destroy its citizen Castorp.   We catch a last glimpse of him amid the shrapnel of a battlefield in Flanders.

Q: And if he survives?

A: If you insist on playing this literary parlour game, my guess is that he would write a novel.

Q: I agree.   With all that hermetic education in him, he cannot possibly go back to being a shipbuilding engineer in Hamburg.

So he will be a writer and write a novel—most probably *The Magic Mountain*. The Eternal Recurrence—

A: —will not take place. For here we end our conversation.

Q: It is an unsatisfactory ending—a little *too* ironical. You appear to be saying two things. Firstly, that it is the aim of an education for life to produce writers of fiction; and secondly, that to acquire true identity means to lose one's identity. For you have previously told us that, according to Thomas Mann, the loss of identity is the professional hazard of literary men.

A: 'Literature' and 'non-identity' are, in this case, the aesthetic incognito which a man, incapable of accepting a meaningless existence, chooses in a world which insists upon living as if life were meaningless. Kierkegaard meant something similar when he defined irony as the incognito of the moralist.

Q: Why has Kierkegaard's moralist got to use an incognito?

A: 'Because he knows that his manner of existing inwardly cannot be expressed in terms of the world.' [59] Such is our world that sense and meaning have to be disguised—as irony, or as literature, or as both come together: for instance in *The Magic Mountain*.

VI

The Theology of Irony

1

FOR good reasons (too good perhaps to be quite true to the life of literature, which does not always suffer reasons gladly) the questioning partner in the preceding conversation persisted in asking what the mystery was of which 'the shrouded figures' on the Magic Mountain were the symbolic communicants, or, in other words, what the symbols symbolized. No doubt the answer he received did not satisfy his curiosity. How could it? His question cannot be so easily disposed of. It has been asked by art and literature ever since they became a riddle to themselves and thus the occasion of much aesthetic philosophizing. If he wanted a definition, he had his answer: it is the definition of a mystery that it is undefinable. But it is not necessarily indescribable. On the contrary: art and literature are its description, describing it in an endless series of more or less precise intimations. Although these have, in the course of their recent history, acquired a more and more abstract, and therefore less and less realizable, precision, it has yet remained the *raison d'être* of the artistic impulse to name the mystery, sound it, and give it shape. It is this which even the most individualistic artist has in common with the collective mythological imagination. For a myth is the mystery in the kind of conspicuous disguise which makes it publicly recognizable. Time was when poets and artists merely improved upon the common mythology, giving it the subtlety and depth of their exact imaginative minds; yet in more recent times it has fallen to the lot of art and literature to engage in the

215

paradoxical business of creating publicly unrecognizable myths. Neither the occasional restoration nor the subtle adaptation of past mythologies could affect this state of affairs. Oedipus, Antigone, Electra, and Orestes are no longer universally acknowledged symbols of the human destiny and the common psyche, but the private patients of men sworn to professional secrecy. Nobody can hope fully to be taken into the poetic confidence. The public has to make do with uncertain hints. Indeed, there exist good reasons for asking questions.

'You above all must know what I mean,' exclaims Friedrich Schlegel through one of the imaginary participants in his 'Conversation on Poetry' as he addresses the poets with his 'Oration about Mythology', 'you have all made poetry and must often have felt that your activity lacked a firm centre, soil in which to grow and invigorating air in which to breathe. The modern poet must create his works entirely from within his own self, and many have done it magnificently, but each in isolation, and every work was a new beginning, and came as if out of nothing. . . . What is absent is that centre which the ancients possessed in their mythology. That modern poetry is at a disadvantage compared with theirs is due to one fact: we have no mythology.' [1] Schlegel's orator thinks that we shall soon have one, and that, like all mythologies, it will be 'a hieroglyphic expression of the world around us, transfigured by imagination and love'. [2] Yet it will also differ from all previous mythologies. How it will differ is not easy to glean from the oracular vagueness which follows upon the promise, except that it will emerge, not like the ancient mythologies as 'the first flower of a youthful imagination', but, on the contrary, as the late incarnation of the most sophisticated, abstract, and abstruse ideas, namely those produced by 'the great phenomenon of the age': philosophical idealism. The new mythology will, in fact, be its 'realization'. Thus it will be realistic, enjoying the kind of reality which only the concrete poetic spirit can bestow upon ideas. [3]

The meaning, if not the actual content, of Schlegel's 'new mythology' becomes much clearer if we read the 'Oration' in

conjunction with his celebrated essay 'On the Study of Greek
Poetry' which is even more on modern literature than it is on
the poets of Greece. Modern literature, Schlegel predicts
there, will either regain the *objectivity* of the ancients or else
destroy itself in its frantic pursuit of the eccentric and the over-
individualized; for it is the complete lack of the conviction
that anything can be 'universally valid', or mythically true,
which has driven 'the whole aesthetic education of the moderns'
in the direction of 'the Interesting'.[4]   The Interesting, throughout the essay, is Schlegel's term not, as in our introductory
chapter, for 'that which matters', but for that which is disturbing and has an innate tendency towards the morbid.   It is
surprising how accurately Schlegel, the appreciative witness of
the great classical achievements of German literature, foresaw
that modern readers would more and more demand, and
modern writers more and more supply, 'that which is piquant'
to stimulate the tired fancy, and, 'in a last convulsion of the
dying sensibility, that which is shocking' as the final stage of
'the Interesting'.[5] Schlegel's forecasts of the approaching
condition of European literature do indeed read like Nietzsche's
much later essays on literary decadence, which, however, were
based on symptoms already abounding in the works of his
contemporaries; and Schlegel would probably not even have
disagreed with him on the 'decadent' nature of Richard
Wagner's revival of Teutonic myths.   When Schlegel spoke of
mythology he certainly did not think of Wotan.   Nor did he
necessarily think of biblical figures like Joseph and his brothers.
What he did have in mind was the possibility that the imagination might once again comprehend man and his world in the
image of a noble truth, and not as the doubtful thing that may,
or may not, emerge from the scattered fragments of insight,
instructive, or edifying, or fascinating, or shocking, or paralysing, which literature and science afford in their separate
pursuits.   He contemplated a new 'mythology' such as would
come about, not through some wilfully cultivated obscurantism,
but on the other side, as it were, of the great rational disillusionment of the race; not, that is, a mystery shabby with ignorance,

seedy with vice, shrivelled with cynicism, or wizened with false rationality, but intact, realistic, and unaffected by those outrageous trivialities or scandalous rumours which modern man is wont to tell himself to his face.

There are moments in *Joseph and his Brothers* when it seems possible that Schlegel's utopian literary hopes may be fulfilled. Time and again the intricate play of irony, psychology, archaeology, and anthropology, which Thomas Mann has arranged in honour of the biblical tale, comes close to producing the effect of poetry. Sometimes it even conveys, shyly hiding behind archaic artifice and extreme virtuosity—that is, in the broken accents which the age prescribes as the correct pronunciation—the mystery which Pascal perceived when, long before Thomas Mann, he called the Joseph of Genesis the Old Testament model and mundane anticipation of the Redeemer: for Joseph, like Jesus, was 'the beloved of his father, sent by his father to see his brothers, sold by his brothers for silver, and thereby becoming their lord, their saviour; . . . which would not have been but for their plot to destroy him, their sale and their rejection of him'.[6]

Tolstoy, it is true, seems to have had some anxious premonition of the literary destiny that was in store for Joseph when, in *What is Art?*, he called the biblical record of Joseph's life a truly exemplary piece of literature, placed it above all acknowledged masterpieces (including his own) and praised it because of its simple profundity and brevity. These indeed are virtues which Thomas Mann (encouraged by Goethe's wish to have the story told more fully) made no attempt to emulate, and emulating which would mean, as Tolstoy well knew, ceasing to be an artist of this age. Yet in the end the mythic truth emerges from Thomas Mann's vast elaboration, just as, over thousands of years, the meaning of a text emerges from an inspired commentary.

In his ironical and humorous manner, which sometimes merely seems to conceal an extreme of artistic seriousness and experimental daring, Thomas Mann tries to resolve in *Joseph and his Brothers* a problem which from *Buddenbrooks* onwards has held the centre of his literary imagination and aesthetic philosophy: the tension, diagnosed by Friedrich Schlegel as the inescapable lot of modern literature, between the unique and the typical, the singular and the universal, the 'psychologically interesting' and the 'mythological'. In subject-matter as well as idiom, all the major writings of Thomas Mann show this divided fascination. Its paradigm is, of course, *Death in Venice*, the 'interesting' story told in the 'mythical' manner. But the current flowing from one pole to the other can be felt everywhere. It is in the antithetical pairing of adjectives which always hyphenate their descriptive forces in order to ensure the most perfect particularity for their employer nouns, and yet achieve in the long run, by persistence and repetition, the effect of the typical: so that, for instance, Peeperkorn, 'robust yet scant', inarticulately communicative, and master of the most informal ceremonies, finally resides on the Magic Mountain, safely established, despite his shattering eccentricity, as the archetype of Being. Then there are Thomas Mann's 'things'— dresses, cigars, chairs, blankets—which are all individualized almost to the point of becoming caricatures of the very idea of 'the particular', and yet gradually seem to acquire the roughly hewn simplicity of objects which from time immemorial have furnished the mythological imagination of man.

It is essentially the same tension which Thomas Mann's youthfully radical antitheses already express: the conflict between Art and Life, between the 'artistic' and the 'burgher-like'. Persuaded by his upbringing, by Nietzsche, and by the intellectual temper of the age, the young artist came to identify art with the 'extraordinary' and the 'interesting', and was unable morally to come to terms with it as long as, at the same time, he had to see everything that to him was morally desirable at the opposite pole of the tension: in the life of the burgher which, solidly rooted and solemnly monotonous as it appeared, followed its traditional and classical pattern. This is why, when in *Meditations* he searched for the origin of his own being, its prototype in history, he saw the face of a burgher from medieval Nuremberg, and not an artist.[7] For the burgher is 'typical', and only as he ceases to be a burgher does he become 'interesting'.   Thomas and Hanno Buddenbrook are, in Schlegel's sense, incomparably more interesting than old Johann Buddenbrook, and the education on the Magic Mountain raises a simple young man to a precariously high level of complexity and interest—by cutting him off for good from his 'typical' life. Yet the 'interesting' life is a short life: compared to grandfather Castorp, whose lasting image, eternalized by death, is the model for an endless succession of grandfathers and medievally attired councillors of the old city, Hans becomes, so to speak, far more 'mortal', indeed as decidedly transient as Thomas and Hanno are if seen side by side with the first Buddenbrook. This, of course, has nothing to do with actual longevity, but everything with the idea of the solidly established and individually renewable type.   Ever since Adam and Eve more and more mortality, it would appear, has been exacted as the price of more and more interesting conditions.   For the ways of death are more devastating with the unique than with the typical. The singular is also the singularly perishable.   All 'interesting' stories end with death, but mythologies are about resurrections.

There is hardly a chapter in *Joseph and his Brothers* which does not sound this *leit-motif* of Thomas Mann's mind; and as the work proceeds, it occurs with ever subtler thematic echoes and in ever more complex orchestrations.   The musical simile is entirely relevant.   Writing in 1937 of Richard Wagner's *Ring*, Thomas Mann said of 'that incomparable work, as one may call it without exaggeration or disloyalty to creations from other and perhaps purer spheres', that 'it seems to side-step all contemporary preoccupations and yet could hardly be more modern in the subtlety, sophistication and all but decadent complexity of the artistic resources' with which it presents 'the primitively elemental drama of existence, . . . a conversation between archetypes of the human race'.   It is impossible not to read this as autobiography, as an indirect self-appraisal. For it is, for instance, true of either the *Ring* or *Joseph* that one cannot think of it entirely as an 'inspired' work, produced in 'transports of the imagination', because it is so rich in 'wit and thought, allusion, construction and minute elaboration'; it is true of both works that their 'fascination results from an unexampled grafting of the most advanced, most modern intellectuality upon the perennially appealing primitive myth'; and, finally, it is true of both Richard Wagner and Thomas Mann that they were not to carry out their works—the one the *Ring*, the other *Joseph*—'at home. . . . From one day to the next he became a political refugee and was, as our language has it, "*im Elend*", which means "in misery" and originally meant "*im Ausland*", that is, abroad. But it was not his new country . . . it was Germany herself which was his misery and his heartbreak.'[8] And in the Foreword to the one-volume edition of *Joseph* Thomas Mann himself confesses that his work was 'secretly determined by the recollection of Wagner's grandiose composition'.[9]

However, the central theme of *Joseph*, which is the relationship between the 'uniquely interesting' and the 'mythically bound and rooted', receives its most daringly humorous and most 'baroque' treatment in the scene of Joseph's second resurrection from the pit and final translation to power and glory—in the chapter 'The Cretan Loggia' where Joseph reveals to Pharaoh the meaning of his dream. With historical wit, ingenuity, and learning, Thomas Mann has placed Joseph's Egyptian sojourn in a time of the loosening of the mythic rule, the time of the Eighteenth Dynasty, when foreigners would, as never before, meet with liberal curiosity and cosmopolitan generosity in the hitherto rigidly conservative country, when the sun god Atôn-Rê gained the theological upper hand over such darker and severer deities as Amun and Osiris, and when even art entered upon its unclassical, exploratory, and 'modern' phase. And it is Amenhotep IV whom Thomas Mann has appointed the dreamer of the celebrated dream, making him, with some freely exaggerated prompting from history, into a very late latecomer, much enlightened despot, romantic art critic, and student of comparative religion. This Pharaoh is greatly relieved to learn that his chosen soothsayer

Joseph, although he is a 'genuine prophetic lamb', is yet a prophet who will not 'ham' his part, not 'foam at the mouth' and not collapse at the end, for the sake of tradition, in prophetic epilepsy; that he is not merely 'true to type', but also 'true to himself', just as he, Amenhotep, plays the mythical part of Pharaoh, but plays it in personal style—too personal, as the Queen Mother thinks, the Great Mama, who is wisely shocked at her ruling son's informality, his love of foreigners and foreign words, his artistic extravagance and his unorthodox religiousness. She is alarmed at his losing himself in abstruse speculations as soon as the foreign prophet has prophesied the seven fat and the seven lean years. Ought he not to think immediately of the practical measures to be taken? Yet his thoughts, forming a kind of abstract monument to Thomas Mann's principal concern, run as follows:

> Now it is brought to light by this genuine but peculiar lamb. Yes, *I* had to be, so that the King might dream, just as *he* had to be, so that the lamb might prophesy. Where we are, there is the meeting place between that which has never been and that which always is; in our own time we are the vessels of eternity. And yet not only that. Ah, there is the problem which I should like to put before the thinkers of my Realm! Which bestows the greater gift: the Eternal upon the Here and Now, the Unique and Particular, or the Here and Now upon the Eternal? It is a beautiful question, one of those to which there is no answer. Hence they can be contemplated without end from nightfall to the dawn of day.[10]

As early as *The Magic Mountain*, Hans Castorp's dream in the snow, which for one brief moment of clear-sightedness raised him above the interesting oppositions of his educators, had already been a mythological dream—mythological not because Dionysus and Apollo were its obvious patrons, but because it revealed to the dreamer the state and status of *Homo Dei*, a mythic truth about man, and thus robbed death, in the only italicized words in the novel, of the dominion it had held for so long over the hero's increasingly 'interesting' thoughts.[11] This dream, no sooner dreamt than forgotten, prefigures the

lasting mythological realities of *Joseph and his Brothers*, and
one scene in particular. It is the scene which shows Joseph,
the Egyptian dignitary, whose true identity is as yet unknown
to his brothers, dining with them in his house and teasingly
proving to Benjamin, the favourite brother, his power of
clairvoyance by telling him old family stories he pretends to
read in his magic silver cup. In this cup he feigns to see a
grave, which is in fact the grave of their mother, and sees a
youth kneeling by its side and wearing a coat of many colours.
'He is a foolish boy,' Joseph remarks, 'he thinks he has just
embarked on a pleasant trip and knows not that he is riding
towards his own grave.' And Benjamin, while his eyes fill with
tears, mutters: 'That is my brother Joseph.' Whereupon he
hears his great host say:

> 'Oh, forgive me . . . I would not have spoken so lightly of him
> if I had known it was your lost brother. And what I said of
> the grave, his grave, you must not take too seriously. . . . True,
> the grave is a solemn thing, a pit deep and dark. Yet surprisingly
> weak is its power to hold what it receives. You may be sure
> that its natural state is emptiness: empty is the tomb when it
> awaits its prey, and if you come after it has taken it in, lo, it is
> empty again—the stone is rolled away. I do not say it deserves
> no tears. Indeed, it calls for them, and even calls for wailing,
> loud and shrill, to do it honour. For alas, the pit is there, a
> solemn dispensation of the world, the sad season of the feast.
> I even go so far as to say that it would be sheer complacency and
> an insult to the venerable institution if we displayed too confi-
> dently our knowledge that by its very nature the grave is empty
> and impotent. No, no, let us pay it the homage of our weeping
> and wailing. But in the secrecy of our hearts we may be sure
> that there is no descent without the resurrection which belongs to
> it. For I ask you, what a poor and fragmentary thing would be
> the tale about the feast of life if it stopped short at the pit and knew
> not how to go on? No, the world is not half; whole is the world
> and holy the feast, and in its wholeness lies the trust which shall
> not be betrayed. So do not let yourself be troubled by what
> I said about your brother's grave, but be of good cheer.' [12]

It was with Hans Castorp's elusive vision of *Homo Dei* that
Thomas Mann had reached the edge of that 'bottomless well

of the past' in which the merely capricious and singular is lost for ever, but from which rise the loyal resurrections and faithful renewals of the soul and its eternal memories. Yet how, without violence and destruction, can the spirit of exploration, the curiosity of the pilgrimage, and the adventure of individuality be reconciled to this order of things? Can there be a mythic truth which does not ask for the sacrifice of creative freedom? As the well is reached, the very logic of his imagination, which had already travelled from the interestingly declining provincial merchants in Lübeck to the vaster European panorama afforded by the Magic Mountain, demands that he should descend; and preparing himself for the work to be done, he discovers 'a very ancient tradition of human thought, based upon man's truest intuition of himself and going back to exceedingly early days, whence it has been inherited by the religions, prophecies and successive doctrines of the East, by Avesta, Islam, Manicheism, Gnosticism and Hellenism'.[13] The discovery must have come to Thomas Mann with a shock of recognition. For the story of Creation as it is told within the Manichean and Gnostic tradition is the exact theological version of Schopenhauer's metaphysics; and being theology, albeit of a heretical brand, it offers a chance of transcending pessimism. Thomas Mann seizes the opportunity and re-writes, as it were, the ironically pessimistic story of *Buddenbrooks* in terms of the ironically hopeful 'Romance of the Soul', the central part of the 'Prelude' to *Joseph and his Brothers*. The warring opposites of his past, having come to irremediable grief at the hands of the non-political man and in the *quazzabuglio* arranged by Settembrini and Naphta, are at last on speaking terms again, and that in a language which has a word for peace.

2

The various Gnostic and Manichean sources, differing in many details but agreeing on all the essential points, say that, long before Creation began, there was Evil. Whence it came, nobody can be sure, as little as anybody knows what the origin is of that formless matter from which the Creator created the world. Certain is only, according to all the sources, that matter was there, and that Evil was there, and that somehow the two had got together or perhaps had always co-existed. God's problem was how to destroy Evil, although the amorphous, world-less and life-less state of affairs suggests that Evil would not have been able to do much harm. There is even a lingering suspicion that action was urged upon God by those extremely puritanical Angels who formed His Realm of Severity and represented the legal aspect of His existence. Still, He acted, and this action had far-reaching consequences of a kind which make it highly improbable that the Realm of Severity foresaw them. God, we are told, appointed a spirit whom the Hebrew texts call *adam quadmon* as His warrior against Evil, a spirit made of pure light and equipped with soul but no knowledge—a pure soul, in fact. He sent it into the Realm of Matter, knowing, but perhaps not quite wanting to know, what would happen to it. What did happen was this: Soul, pure, innocent, and unaware of the dangers which the mission involved, was, as the books report, 'laid in chains by the demons of Evil' and gradually alienated from its divine origin and task. In other words, it fell in love with the Realm of Matter, desired to set up its home there and create forms and shapes for its self-forgetful play and pleasure. Yet all the labour of its love seemed to be in vain; for matter, lazily and obstinately, preferred to stay in its amorphous state, would hear nothing of assuming form just to please the Soul, and was as difficult about it as one can possibly be.

At this point, however, God intervened, took pity on His poor defeated warrior, the ignorantly and unhappily loving Soul, and created, to the Soul's enormous delight, the world of forms and shapes, of growing and dying, in which the Soul instantly and rapturously set to work to produce human beings. Thus, according to those persistent heretical rumours, Creation itself was the Fall. Why did God do it? Had He blundered before by sending the innocent Soul, without giving it knowledge,

P

into the demonic sphere? Was He in His omniscience incapable of imagining the embarrassments of ignorance? Or had precisely this been His master plan for creating Man, and was the whole dramatic complication nothing but a ruse, a pretext He needed, in order to explain the creation of Man, inexplicable before a court of absolute morality, to His severe Angels? God only knows. One thing, however, is certain: He would not have been the God of Love, had He simply made use of His omnipotence, torn the net of enchantment in which the Soul was caught, and brought it forcibly back to His throne. To safeguard the moral law, He did something else. He gathered from His mysterious substance yet another Soul (and this is literally what the ancient sources say), bestowed knowledge upon it, transformed it into Spirit, so as to avoid a repetition of the first disaster—if disaster it was, and not one stage only in a well-considered divine drama—and made him His emissary in the now truly created realm. His mission was to teach the Soul that it was a grave mistake to indulge its passion and thus to call forth the world, to rouse it from its voluptuous dream of bliss and woe, and make it yearn for the peace it once enjoyed—until one day it would tear itself away from the world of desire, anguish, and death, and return to God. This would be the end of the world, Evil would be vanquished through the Soul's renunciation, death done away, and matter restored to its ancient freedom.[14]

So far, so good—or so sad, so much like Schopenhauer who thinks that

> Death is the result and résumé of living, its sum total, which shows us all at once what life teaches us piecemeal: that the will and desire which have assumed the form of life are futile, vain and contradictory. To be taken out of it is no loss; it is pure deliverance. . . . What gives to life its strange and paradoxical character is the fact that in it two diametrically opposed intentions perpetually work against each other: on the one hand, the aim of the individual will seeking the chimera of happiness in an ephemeral, dream-like and deceptive existence which, as soon as it passes—and every moment transforms a present into a past— makes happiness or unhappiness into matters of absolute indiffer-

ence; and on the other hand, the working of the universal will which only too clearly aims at destroying our happiness, mortifying our individual will, and freeing us from that delusion which keeps us in bondage to this world.[15]

To enlighten the Soul about its fatal blunder is, according to Schopenhauer as well as the Manichean sources, the task of the Spirit. But at this point the 'Romance of the Soul' merges into Thomas Mann's own 'Romance of the Spirit' through a series of speculations not unworthy of the 'divine acumen' of the ancient sages, or indeed of Joseph himself. There is, observes Thomas Mann, the puzzling insistence of the texts on the identity of Soul and Spirit: for the Spirit, they say, is 'the Soul once more'. If they are of the same nature, Thomas Mann asks, is it not more than likely that they would share the same fate? *Have* they not shared the same fate? For clearly the world has not yet come to its end: the Spirit too, in all his knowingness, lingers and takes his time, and is slow in effectively delivering to the Soul his message of deliverance. Why? It often happens that an ambassador, staying too long, is won over to the morals and habits and points of view of the country in which he serves; and in the case of the Spirit and his message the situation could hardly be more confusing. For what is pure light in the country of his origin is a dark menace to the world in which he now dwells, and the messenger of salvation is only too easily felt to be a curse to the unrepentant will which by its very nature wills its own continuance. But why, one may ask, should the Spirit have waited long enough to let this fatal change of perspective distract him from his purpose? Might he not have become the Soul's advocate simply from an illicit sympathy with the Soul's impassioned state?

There is further the strained relationship between God and the Realm of Severity. The texts and sources unmistakably suggest a certain tension between the two, as indeed there always is between the divine and the moralistic, between love and the law, between the imaginative and the literal, between grace and the close reading of the text. It is possible that the drafting of that severe mission with which Spirit went into the created world to save it from love and death through Love and Death, was a mere concession to the puritanical Angels, and even a trick to hoodwink the impatient critics. *Was* the Spirit the same as the Soul? *Is* he the same? It is not easy to attach the right tense to the operations of the mystery. We are moving in a sphere where history is indistinguishable from prophecy, and 'once upon a time' may point into the past *or* into the future.

> The saying that Soul and Spirit *were* the same means perhaps that once upon a time they shall be one. This seems the more tenable as the Spirit is of his nature and essentially the principle of the future, of the 'It is to be' and 'It shall be', while the soul, devoutly loyal to everything that has received its form and shape over the ages, has its eyes on the past, on the sacred 'It was'.
> . . . But it may well be that the secret hope of God is for their union, for their inseparable intertwining, for the sacrament of their marriage, and for their bringing forth a race of men blessed with blessing from the heavens above and from the depths that lie beneath.[16]

The last words are the same as those which, according to Genesis (xlix. 25), Jacob spoke on his deathbed when he blessed Joseph. In them Thomas Mann finds the definition of the Hebrew word *tâm*; and *tâm* denotes the very being of Joseph. *Tâm* is a fascinating word; it has an iridescent charm and gracefully bridges the gulf between light and darkness, between the upper and the nether regions, and he who is *tâm* is the natural mediator between above and below, between the angelic heights and the chthonic depths. Yet he is only a mediator and counsellor, not the bearer of the prophetic blessing, not the chosen son. The *whole* story which, after all, is *not* a romance, neither of the Soul nor of the Spirit, but the story of God's dealings with His world, seems to come to rest for a blessed while in *tâm*, but *tâm* is not its conclusion. Therefore the 'Prelude' in the end retracts the words of the Joseph blessing by adding a sceptical recantation which is strangely reminiscent of the final question Thomas Mann asked in

Meditations of a Non-Political Man about the *inner* truth of his Germanically conservative beliefs. ' Could it be ', he asked then, 'that what I am does not correspond exactly to what I think and believe, and that I am destined to further precisely that which in these pages I have called "Progress" through the very act of conservatively opposing it—opposing it by means of literature?' [17]

On the mythological plane of the 'Romance of the Soul' this very same doubt concerns the Spirit's apparently treacherous conduct, his amorous betrayal of his mission, and his siding with the formed, created, sensuous, and mortal world against the luminous designs of his employment. Does the Spirit truly *mean* to behave like that, the question runs, *can* he truly mean it? And if so, can his compromising conduct do him any good? For even behaving as he does, and indeed *by* thus behaving, he can in the end not help serving the purpose for which he was sent, namely to bring to an end the material world by taking the Soul away from it. It is even likely that the Spirit knows all this, and permits himself such dubious behaviour only because he is sure he can afford it. [18] And so the Gnostic tale of the Soul ends with words which unmistakably convey the non-political man's guilty conscience transferred to the exaggerating and distorting perspective of the cosmogonic heights:

> Let the Spirit lend all his wit to the dumb passion of the Soul, let him celebrate the tombs, call the past the only source of life, and declare his wicked zeal and will to have the world enslaved by death! It is an ineffectual pose. He cannot but remain what in truth he is: the voice of conscience, the principle of critique and opposition, the messenger of the pilgrimage whose call, in a world benumbed with pleasure and conformity, brings disquiet and sublime unrest to the single heart, urges the wanderer on his journey, drives the herdsman from the familiar pastures into the adventures of the distance, and makes him like unto a stone which, by detaching itself from its mountain, is destined to set up an ever-increasing motion of which nobody can say where it will end. [19]

The reader who cannot help being reminded by this of

Meditations and *The Magic Mountain* may also ask whether this disavowal of the Soul's advocates, of the non-political man and of Naphta, does not bring the *Zivilisationsliterat* and Settembrini into an unwarranted relationship with Abraham. For in this description of the ineluctable embassy of the Spirit, memories of *Meditations* are ironically mixed with anticipations of the divinely troubled Abraham, the 'Wanderer of Ur' who, dissatisfied with all the blindly worshipped idols of the Soul, the tribal gods embodied in the forms and shapes of the created world, sets out to oppose and criticize them, and to seek the Highest, whom finally he discovers residing above them all in pure transcendence. The answer is that neither of the old opposites is any longer what it was: both the 'non-political' conception of the Soul and the Settembrini championship of the Spirit are transcended in the theology of irony contained in the 'Prelude' to *Joseph and his Brothers*. Thomas Mann has called it 'Descent into Hell' because with it the narrator, the 'murmuring conjuror of the past and imperfect', sets out to seek the true image of man deep down among the dead in the underworld, as Ishtar once sought Tammuz, and Isis sought Osiris.[20] It has, however, its counterpart in the 'Prelude in the Higher Circles', which introduces the fourth volume of the tetralogy, *Joseph the Provider*; and if the 'Romance of the Soul' is the basis of the ironical theology, its ironical climax is reached in the 'Higher Circles'. It is parodistically modelled on the 'Prologue in Heaven' of Goethe's *Faust*, and has the same characters: the Lord, the angelic Realm of Severity, and the Prince of Darkness, named here Shemmael. The occasion is the need that has arisen to punish, an event which, as always, is greeted by the Angels with hardly concealed malicious satisfaction at seeing confirmed their jealous mistrust of Man, the Lord's apparently incorrigible problem child. This time, it is true, the Wrath is less abundant than it was at times in the watery or fiery past. It is not the whole troublesome race which is sent to the pit, as happened in the Great Flood, not even a whole city like Sodom, but only 'one single specimen of the breed, albeit an uncommonly hand-

some and supercilious one, and one exceptionally equipped with
the advantages of divine predeliction and firmly made designs
in his favour'.[21]   It is Joseph, who goes to prison in Egypt.
For the second time it has proved necessary to teach that young
man a lesson.   Hence the Realm's suspicion, and its doubt
whether the punishment is meant seriously at all: it may soon
become evident that it was a mere detour on the way to greater
and greatly undeserved glory.

What was man that God should be so mindful of him?
Time and again the psalmodizing Angels had asked the question
without receiving a definite answer.   Small wonder that they
lent their ears to rumours on this point, rumours of an exceedingly plausible kind.   According to this gossip the Lord was
in the habit of furtively seeing Shemmael, whom officially He
had banned from His sight.   As He sees everything, this was
difficult to avoid; but He did not only see him: He held disputations with him.   Creation itself, some believed, was the
result of such an interview; and scandal had it that Shemmael's
ideas would almost always find a benevolent hearing whenever
they appeared to be concerned with an increase in divine
liveliness.   They said that man was created in the image, to
some extent, of the Lord because He, in His transcendent
spirituality and incomparable uniqueness, was curious about
Himself; and to know oneself means to compare oneself:
'man was a means to His own self-knowledge'.[22]

But why this particular interest in Joseph?   Because, they
argued persuasively, he was an exceptionally gifted descendant
of that man Abraham who more than anyone else before him
had contributed to this self-knowledge.   It was, in fact, through
Abraham and his proud determination to serve and acknowledge no lesser god that the Lord became aware of Himself
as the Highest.   When Abraham, after much searching in his
soul, and anxiety, and unrest, discovered Him and instantly
knew that there could be no god above Him, God was over-
joyed and cried, to the secret annoyance of the Angels: 'It is
unbelievable what knowledge of Me is possessed by this son
of earth!   Have I not begun to make Myself known through

him?   Verily, I will anoint him!' and did anoint him with the oil of gladness more than all his fellows.[23]   Transcendence in itself is not enough; it must be acknowledged.   And through Abraham God was confirmed in His infinite superiority over all the tribal gods.*

But were the tribal gods not livelier?   More vital?   They were fed and feasted and embodied.   Shemmael knew only too well what had happened to the first warrior sent against Evil: how the Soul was seduced by Life and how God in the end assisted its desire and provided for its passion.   The appeal of liveliness seemed irresistible.   Why should He not be persuaded to choose the body of a tribe for His embodiment and thus become as lively as all the Gods whom He surpassed in every other respect?   Shemmael whispered and hinted—and succeeded.   God chose His tribe.   For a while at least Shemmael triumphed.   He caused God to fall, just as he had done in a

* Thomas Mann's story of how Abraham discovered God is remarkably close to the mysticism of the German seventeenth century.   Abraham and God, Thomas Mann writes, 'were two, an I and a Thou, although it is true to say that Abraham could never have discerned the properties of God except by virtue of his own greatness of soul; without it they would have remained in darkness.   But God, none the less, was a Being who said "I am" in an infinitely more powerful way than Abraham ever could . . . Yet He was also in Abraham who, through his own strength of mind and soul, had discovered Him . . .   It was on this foundation that God made His covenant with Abraham.'   Through this covenant, however, 'something was come into the world which had never been there before: the accursed possibility of man's breaking the bond and betraying God' (*Joseph and his Brothers*, pp. 287–8).   It would be possible to quote for almost every sentence of Thomas Mann's chapter a couplet from *Der Cherubinische Wandersmann*, the mystical work of the seventeenth-century poet Angelus Silesius, who knew that 'without me God could not live for one moment; if ever I came to nothing, He too would have to perish', and yet also knew that 'the whole difference between myself and God lies in one word, and that is Otherness'.   And again: 'God cares as much for me as I for Him: I help as much to guard His Being as He guards mine' (*Der Cherubinische Wandersmann*, I, 8; II, 201; I, 100).   It is characteristic of the elaborate organization of *Joseph* that Abraham's discovery of God is given its close correspondence in the theological searches of the Egyptian Pharaoh, the 'dreamer' Amenhotep IV, who recognizes that his true Father resides 'in Heaven' and not, like the sun god of his predecessors, 'in the sky' (*Joseph and his Brothers*, p. 969).

very similar manner in the case of the Soul. But his triumph could not last. For the chosen tribe was such that its particular theological disposition and intelligence would know better, as it were, than God Himself, and soon realize that 'The world moves in His space, but He is not confined to the space of the world' (and, quoting *The Magic Mountain*, Thomas Mann adds: '. . . just as the narrator's mind provides the space of the story, but is not confined to it, a fact which gives him the chance to comment upon it'). Of course, God must have known from the outset that this was bound to happen, that He would be released again from the liveliness and the burden of the flesh, and restored in even greater glory to absolute spirituality and magisterial transcendence; but Shemmael exploited even that tremendous occasion and spread the malicious tale that God could never have returned from His 'Fall' to the position of surpassing sublimity without the intellectual exertions of the patriarchs. All this was muttered in the Higher Circles, so the 'Prelude' ends, while the scion of the Chosen Seed travelled to his Egyptian prison.[24] *

3

We have recapitulated the theology of irony at such length, and tried to render its tone as faithfully as is possible in another

---

* A perusal of the sources on which Thomas Mann drew for the two 'Preludes', not to mention the voluminous material he used for the tetralogy, reveals his quite extraordinary skill in fusing scholarship and literature, anthropology and speculation, theology and fancy. In a much more spectacular manner than even *The Magic Mountain*, *Joseph and his Brothers* seems to live up to Friedrich Schlegel's extravagant expectation of a future *Universalpoesie*.—The most easily accessible guide to a study of Thomas Mann's sources are the notes in Käte Hamburger's book *Thomas Manns Roman 'Joseph und seine Brüder'* (Stockholm, 1945), and the correspondence with Thomas Mann which Professor Karl Kerenyi, the well-known student of Greek and oriental mythologies, published under the title of *Romandichtung und Mythologie* (Zürich, 1945).—When in 1950 Thomas Mann described the method adopted in writing *Joseph*, he said: 'I emphasize the scholarly aspect of the work. The archaeological and theological discussions are not extraneous to it; on the contrary, they are extremely important for the literary realization of the subject' (*Die Neue Rundschau*, 1930, p. 763).

language and without the help of still lengthier quotations, because, like an elaborately composed overture, it contains the whole thematic and stylistic structure of the work. The nature of its irony may have emerged with sufficient clarity. It is the apotheosis of all previous ironies. The Spirit's amorous tarrying, against its appointed vocation, in the realm of the Soul, and God's own secret hankering, against His own better omniscience, for more liveliness than He can afford in His transcendence, and even for the bliss of the commonplace tribal deities, provide the cosmological model—posthumously discovered, as it were—for Tonio Kröger's anxieties. Equally clear is the pattern, designed in the Higher Circles, which determines Aschenbach's fall. In fact, all the heroes of Thomas Mann, from Thomas Buddenbrook to Hans Castorp, are men on whom the Spirit has visited a generous measure of the deeply ironical problems he has created in his perplexed and perplexing dealings with the Soul, and who were not *tâm* enough to resolve them within their discordant social existence. Not the least of these problems arises from the archetypal Buddenbrooks situation: the question of the true relationship between the forms which, as if for ever, the Soul has begotten in the world, and the goal which, try as he may, the Spirit is not allowed to forget.

If it were for nothing else, *Joseph and his Brothers* would be an astonishing work for the ease and naturalness with which the biblical story, unharmed in its original structure, takes its apparently predestined place within Thomas Mann's literary career. In retrospect it almost looks as if, had it not existed, he would have had to invent it. For the conservative imagination, wounded by its outcast destiny, could not have comforted itself with a happier tale than that of the son who loses his patriarchal home and the paternal blessing but gains the world and the power to save his brothers. Small wonder that Thomas Mann dwelt upon it so long. What does seem a wonder is his power to resolve in serene irony the besetting dilemmas between faithful acceptance and disloyally creative critique, between the house and the journey, between the eternal recurrence and the adventure of the pilgrimage. Not so far back, after all, in *Meditations of a Non-Political Man*, the two pugnacious souls in his breast appeared to be ready to destroy each other—a little in the manner of the two lions in Schopenhauer's story who one night quarrelled so ferociously that in the morning only their tails were found in the cage.

Irony—the reader will no doubt have noticed that the word has had to cover, in the course of this discussion of Thomas Mann's works, a multitude of moods. Deeply discouraged by even the best writers on the subject (with Hegel and Kierkegaard among them) as well as by Thomas Mann's extremely resourceful employment of the term, I have attempted neither a definition of it nor a catalogue of its varieties (which are such that it is impossible to grasp hold of the thing they vary). For like 'romantic', with which ever since Friedrich Schlegel 'irony' has enjoyed a firm and intriguing alliance, or like 'tragic', with which it has lived for an even longer time, it has maliciously provoked and invariably defeated hosts of definitions; and an earnest discussion of irony is likely to prove as incongruous and as tiresome as a dispassionate debate on love or a prosaic dissertation about poetry. Every attempt to define irony unambiguously is in itself ironical. It is wiser to speak about it ironically, and one good epigram may reveal more of its nature, if nature it has, than even Kierkegaard's profound thesis on the elusive phenomenon, written, as its title announces, 'without ever losing sight of Socrates'.[25] For every assertion ever made about irony (unless what is meant is simply the figure of speech or the conversational pleasantry which goes by that name) is such that anyone might legitimately reply: 'Ah, but that is not irony!' Many things, for instance, are irony to Kierkegaard and it is not easy to say what exactly it is they have in common. When he speaks of the ironical mode of living, he means now absolute aesthetic detachment, and now the 'negative freedom' of absolute scepticism; now a self constantly withdrawing from all serious commitments in order to save itself, and now again, with irony 'controlled', a self enjoying ideal wisdom.

To take another example: Goethe's Mephistopheles, the 'spirit of eternal negation', is, according to his author's own testimony, a creature of irony.   But Goethe calls ironical also the condition of a mind which, having risen 'above happiness or unhappiness, good or evil, death or life, beholds a truly poetic world'.   Elsewhere again he recommends that all scientific theorizing should be done, 'to use a daring word, with irony'.[26]   Irony, then, is in the first instance indistinguishable from nihilism or cynicism, in the second identical with that sublime contemplative bliss which, as Schopenhauer teaches, rewards the conquest of the subjective will, while in the third case it means the sagacity of a mind which will never look upon a scientific theory as if it could reveal an absolute truth.— Who, after even these few instances, will be unkind enough to ask for a satisfying definition of the word irony?   Clearly it would be a forbidding task to try to find the exact common denominator of Socrates and Mephistopheles, cynicism and pure poetic contemplation, the fate of a tragic hero and the flight of a self escaping from itself, nihilism and the wisdom of a sage.

In an index to Thomas Mann's essays the entries under 'irony' would fill columns and be no less varied and ironically contradictory than the examples produced by his predecessors in the field.   He once called irony 'the most alluring problem in the world';[27] and indeed, allured he was!   There were times when he treated it with a passion of thought which was in curious contrast to the sense of detachment the word usually conveys. In *Meditations of a Non-Political Man* it became literally a *nom de guerre*.   From every district of literature and thought ironical warriors were mustered to defeat the invasion of radical intellectualism with which the *Zivilisationsliterat* threatened Germany.   In a manœuvre which might have led to the self-annihilation of irony, Thomas Mann brought it into *radical* opposition to radicalism and exclaimed, unknowingly echoing Kierkegaard at his most anti-ironical: 'Irony and radicalism— this is an alternative and an Either-Or.   An intelligent man has the choice (*if* he has it) to be either ironical or radical.

There is, in all decency, no third possibility. Which he is depends on the argument he accepts as *ultimately* and *absolutely* [my italics] valid: life or spirit . . . For the radical man life is no argument. *Fiat spiritus, pereat vita!* But the words of irony are: "Can truth be an argument if it is a matter of life?" ' [28] After this great radical gesture, however, irony mellowed again: 'Irony always aims at both sides, at life as well as at the spirit, and this makes it incapable of great gestures, and gives it its tone of melancholy and humility.' [29] But at about the same time we met in his Frederick II a type of irony which, also aiming 'at both sides', was yet the idiom of a 'nihilistic fanaticism of accomplishment' and of a 'sovereignty as vicious as it was melancholy'. [30] A few years later, in the republican oration of 1932, irony ran into still greater difficulties: for there is now a profound kinship between the ironical spirit of romanticism and Walt Whitman's democratic republicanism, between Novalis and the Weimar Republic. [31] And if in Frederick the Great irony was the expression of immense energies, it could also be a mere ruse of the inferior to acquire the semblance of superiority—'and that is what it almost always is', Thomas Mann added in a Nietzschean mood. [32]

On the other hand, it may be, as it was in *Tonio Kröger*, 'erotic irony', the life-enchanted self-negation of the spirit which at that time, however, did not yet realize that its desire was reciprocated: 'life too yearned—and yearned for the spirit'. [33] And even while, considerably later, he assigned the roles of this 'romance' to the theological entities of the Gnosis, with God desiring to embody Himself in a people, and the people desirous of His pure transcendence, he provided yet another stage for its performance: the 'Indian Legend' *The Transposed Heads*.* With love and irony now mediating between the once irreconcilable

* The problem of Thomas Mann's irony is discussed with lucidity and learning in two works already mentioned: in Hermann J. Weigand's *Thomas Mann's Novel 'Der Zauberberg'*, and in Bernhard Blume's *Thomas Mann und Goethe.*—Its most comprehensive and philosophically thorough discussion I have found in Reinhard Baumgart's Inaugural Dissertation *Das Ironische und die Ironie in den Werken Thomas Manns* (Freiburg i. Br., 1953).

opposites, Goethe gradually moved into the centre of
Thomas Mann's interest, and opened a vista beyond Schopenhauer and Nietzsche, the old '*Weltentzweier*' and champions of
the metaphysical division. Goethe's friendship with Schiller,
the not always easy alliance between the 'vital' and the 'spiritual',
or—in Schiller's terms—the '*naïve*' and the '*sentimentalische*',
became the symbol, found in the highest literary ranks, of the
new *rapprochement*. And in *Lotte in Weimar*, the work Thomas
Mann produced between the third and the fourth volumes of
the tetralogy, he emphasized again and again, by direct quotation from *Joseph* and by many an allusion, that he saw a deep
kinship, and at times even a kind of 'mythic identity', between
his biblical dreamer and statesman, and the Weimar poet, sage
and minister of state.[34] It is Goethe now who, ironical and
great, bears the double blessing from the spirit above and the
dark ground below, and lives, '*geprägte Form, die lebend sich
entwickelt*', a life formed from the beginning in the mysterious
mould and energetically growing into the clarity of knowing
selfhood. Whatever irony, in its apparently numberless guises,
shades, and nuances, means or has meant to Thomas Mann,
it is the irony of the double blessing which pervades *Joseph
and his Brothers*. Indeed, it may be more than irony and
come close to humour; and although we know how futile it is
to expect reliable definitions of such intangible qualities, it
cannot do any harm to remember that Kierkegaard, for one,
distinguished irony from humour. Humour was his name for
the state of a soul existing at the approaches to faith.

At the end of the banquet scene from which we have quoted
Joseph's show of clairvoyance, Benjamin almost, but only
almost, recognizes his brother in Pharaoh's great minister, and
his heart is in a tumult of doubt and belief. Throughout the
whole meal he had been feverish with vague and 'indescribable'
premonitions, but now, as Joseph takes his hand by the wrist
and waves it in the air like a fan, just as he used to do when
as boys they played together in the olive grove, his emotional
condition 'reaches a pitch of indescribability; right then it was
quite certain that nobody would ever describe it'. Whereupon

Thomas Mann, with exquisite craftsmanship, draws a picture, not of his feelings, but of their expression on his face, and concludes: 'Ah, yes, let anyone come and try to describe the state of a soul which is on the point of believing.'[35] This is a telling example of Thomas Mann's method of ironical narration. Perhaps it tells of more than a method.

4

In *The Magic Mountain* Time was all but the protagonist, silent, yet voiced in the speculative discourses of narrator and hero. What is it, we read there, that brings forth Time? Change, was the answer. But, so the reflection went on, as the changing motion by which we measure time is circular, 'it is a motion which we might just as well describe as rest; for the There constantly recurs in the Here, the Then in the Now'.[36] And it seemed to Hans Castorp, lying in bed and killing time, that in the changeless routine of his sickroom every moment of his day was the same as every moment of any other day, and therefore all the days literally the same—*one* and the same day. Yet Time was, in *The Magic Mountain*, not only a subject of reflection. Its circular motion determined the very form of the work: the omnipresence of the *leit-motif* as a means of realizing the idea of the ever-present.

This realization was one aspect of the magic which gave the novel its name, and in alluding to it Thomas Mann displayed inexhaustible resources of stylistic subtlety and telling invention. There was even a scene in which both past and future were conjured up together in *one* person: the spiritualist seance, arranged by the sinister Dr. Krokowski, in which Hans Castorp's dead cousin, the good and soldierly Joachim, appears, wearing the as yet unknown battledress of the approaching war. Yet what precisely, as our Q asked, was the nature of that which is everpresent? A 'soup everlasting'—as the very chapter is named in which circular motion is equated with rest? Or a beautiful mystery worthy of man's affirming faith? In the air of *The Magic Mountain*, only climatically pure, it was by no means easy for Hans Castorp, except perhaps in one moment of extreme exposure to ice and death, to give so much as a timidly tentative answer. But the answer given by *Joseph and his Brothers* is in all its irony (and irony always answers tentatively) far from being timid. On the contrary, the work reads as if the imagination had at last, under very great pressure, struggled free from the besetting negations of soul and mind, and courageously decided, during the most difficult and harassed years of the author's own life, to indulge the heart's desire and have a Good Time.

Therefore, it is only in *Joseph and his Brothers* that the literary method of the *leit-motif*, which ever since *Buddenbrooks* had steadily gained in meaning and in eloquence, together with the idea which it seeks to realize, comes clearly into its own. For only here is complete unity achieved between the structure of the work and the structure of the world it not only portrays but humorously affirms: a world conceived in the mythic image and 'beautiful mystery' of the revolving sphere. As young Joseph receives his first lessons in astronomy from his teacher Eliezer, who is himself, as we shall see, a creature of the 'Eternal Recurrence', and is taught the configurations of the stars and their courses, and how they are mirrored in the seas, the mountains and men's destinies on earth, 'he distinguishes not between the earthly and the heavenly'.[37] And if the descent into the past, which the narrator undertook in the first 'Prelude', proved to be a journey into a 'bottomless well', this was due, as we learn a little later in the book, to his unwittingly travelling not in a straight line—a movement which would have held no mysteries—but along the mysterious curves of the sphere. Consisting of an earthly and a heavenly half, this sphere is in a state of constant revolution: 'Bottom is top, and top is bottom, if in such circumstances it makes sense thus to distinguish. Not only do things in Heaven and things on earth recognize themselves in each other but, thanks to the rotation of the sphere, that which is in Heaven soon comes down to earth, and that which is on earth goes up to Heaven.'[38] This establishes the revolving sphere as the tectonic principle of

Joseph and his Brothers. Together with the ideas of incarnation
and metempsychosis, which almost inseparably belong to it, it
determines the shape of the whole work by way of seemingly
numberless variations of incident, thought and stylistic device.
Thus the tetralogy is the happiest consummation and *ne plus
ultra* of the *leit-motif.*

Thomas Mann was, of course, well prepared for 'the mystery
of the revolving sphere' by Schopenhauer's philosophy of the
eternal *nunc stans* which resides at the centre of the illusory
motion of Time, and by Nietzsche's Eternal Recurrence (and
Thomas Mann's favourite plaything, the *imitatio mystica*, is a
reflection of metempsychosis, even if it is somewhat bleached
by the light of 'realistic psychology'). But it is certainly a stroke
of exceptionally good luck, or the doing of a secret guide of his
imagination, that with *Joseph and his Brothers* he found a world
in which Schopenhauer's and Nietzsche's philosophical speculations meet, as it were, their historical reality.* Yet the homecoming of these inherited ideas, which Thomas Mann himself
had taken on a long and varied excursion throughout his works,
takes place in an amazingly changed mood. We shall see how

* He might even have learned from his early reading of Schopenhauer
that 'the Egyptians, as Herodotus tells us, believed in the revolving sphere
and metempsychosis. Even the Jews partly accepted the belief, as
Tertullian and Justin (in his *Dialogue*) report. The Talmud teaches that
Cain's soul became re-embodied first in Seth and then in Moses. Also
in the New Testament, the passage Matt. xvi. 13–15 makes sense only
if read with the idea of metempsychosis in mind' (op. cit.—see Appendix
—pp. 1293–5). Thomas Mann himself speaks in the first 'Prelude' of
metempsychosis as a popularization of the doctrine of *nunc stans*: 'Let
the common people be taught that the soul wanders. But the initiates
know that this teaching is only the garment of the mystery of the Soul's
omnipresence' (*Joseph and his Brothers*, pp. 32–3). As far as the New
Testament is concerned, St. John iii, 12–13, may have suggested to
Thomas Mann the very words with which he describes the sphere in
rotation : 'If I have told you earthly things, and ye believe not, how shall
ye believe, if I tell you of heavenly things?—and no man hath ascended
up to Heaven but he that came down from Heaven. . . .' Alfred Jeremias's
Handbuch der Alt-Orientalischen Geisteskultur, which, as Käte Hamburger
tells us, was one of Thomas Mann's sources, shows the predominance
the revolving sphere has also in the Sumerian-Babylonian mythology.

Q

easy it is to apply Schopenhauer's very own words to some of
the 'immortal' characters of the novel, but the transference will,
as it were, trick the words out of their native metaphysical mood.
For the soothing warmth of Schopenhauer's many reflections
on the unreality of death and the indestructible nature of man's
innermost being is deceptive: the comfort he gives is metaphysically cold. Let him exclaim in his consoling voice:
'Where *is* that all-consuming void which terrifies you? You
have only to recognize your own nature, and indeed precisely
that in you which so much thirsts for life, to find it again in the
pulsating force which, from the mysterious deep, sends the tree
into the light and remains unchangingly one and the same
throughout the changing generations of budding and withering
leaves!' Let him seemingly celebrate the *nunc stans* at the
heart of all the coming and going, and assure the creature
intimidated by death that 'at every moment we may be serenely
sure that, despite time, death and putrefaction, we shall all be
here, always!' Yet the eternity he so lyrically invokes is and
remains with him an offence to the spirit, and his true hero is
the man who defies the 'always' and breaks the never-ending
round: 'He alone must be exempted who says from the depth
of his heart: It delights me not. I do not will it any more.' [39]

The beautiful calm of Schopenhauer's prose, however, reflects the large measure of spiritual security which still enabled
him stoically to contemplate the undesirable 'Eternal Recurrence'; but in his disciple Nietzsche (and he carried his disciple-
ship even into his radical denials of the pessimist) stoicism
turned to despair. For it is despair that gives to Zarathustra's
dithyrambic prophecies of the Eternal Recurrence their shrill
hysterical notes, the despair to which time and again Nietzsche
confessed even while his Zarathustra uttered his loudest Yea-
sayings. Nietzsche called the Eternal Recurrence his 'great
test': 'Who can bear the thought?' And again, behind
Zarathustra's back: 'Let us think that thought in its most
terrifying form: existence, as it is, senseless, aimless, yet inescapably returning, without a finale in non-being.' Like a
Darwin of the spirit, he himself took Nature's selecting initia-

tive and decreed that the idea of the Eternal Recurrence should be the great catastrophe which was to destroy the spiritual weaklings and mark out for survival the spiritually fittest.[40] It was certainly no very reassuring faith which the revolving sphere inspired in Thomas Mann's intellectual ancestors. Only an heir, creative in his irony and rebellious in his humour, could choose it as the cosmic home for 'God's beautiful invention', the story of *Joseph and his Brothers*; and the revolving sphere which is, at the same time, the most conservative model of the world, must have pleased his conservative imagination. Yet his conservatism is ironical too; and so there was yet another task for the humorous inventiveness: to accommodate within the revolving sphere God's progressive designs as made known in the Higher Circles.

Zarathustra too had recklessly wanted two irreconcilable things: the Eternal Recurrence and the unique, unheard-of creation of the Superman. The manner in which Thomas Mann, in better humour than Zarathustra, sets about it is, of course, closely related to the mission Spirit was given in the 'Prelude'. Certainly, the sphere revolves, and the sphere is the world, and the world has been created by God. But God, as we know already, is not confined to the space of the world, although the world moves in His space. It is His will, as His covenant with Abraham made clear, to realize Himself *in* His world through man. Indeed, it is demanded of man that he should assist in the process, and it is even true to say that his assistance is essential. Through the covenant a truly tremendous responsibility has descended upon man: the freedom to fail God's hope. It is this freedom which dramatically changes man's mythically determined repetitiveness: now he has to 'repeat' in the right spirit, in a spirit which, as precisely as can be, is appropriate to the particular moment within God's movement towards His chosen creature. In Thomas Mann's work it is Jacob, not Joseph, who is the hero of this 'story above the story'. He is 'the caretaker of the right spirit, anxiously contemplating God's uncertain stations'.[41] It is he who has taught Joseph that nothing ought

to be done too naïvely 'according to pattern', that the sphere
revolves through the seasons of God, and that everything which
comes back to us by way of the spherical revolution must be
carefully inspected for a message of His approach: for what
did its duty yesterday may have to be discarded now because
it obscures our vision of the exact place where the Lord chooses
to be today in relation to us. 'The outworn is repulsive to
Him, for He wishes us to be beyond it, and He rejects and
curses it.' [42]   Jacob's 'divine anxiety', his loyalty to the created
order of things, and his untiring watch over the Creator's
exercise of freedom, are so much at the centre of Thomas
Mann's work that he sometimes thought he would have to
call it *Jacob and his Sons*.[43]

The established pattern and the freedom of the Creator,
typical living and new departures, are the subject of one of the
disputations between Jacob and young Joseph in a scene rich
in humour and profundity, and providing perfect examples of
both Jacob's and Joseph's spiritual characters.   Of Jacob it
was said that he had two passions: God and Rachel (and in
the telling of the love-story of Jacob and Rachel Thomas Mann
shows a tenderness which, in its disciplined purity and poetic
firmness, would in itself prove that his irony is not what it so
often can be: a mere defence against sentimentality).   Jacob
has lost Rachel, and could never quite help feeling that with
her death a jealous God had rebuked his extravagant heart.
This is why his love for Joseph, who has taken her place in his
affection, is not free of secret misgivings.   And now, while
conversing with Joseph, he is overcome by a vision that terrifies
him: God has demanded from him what He once demanded
from Abraham, the sacrifice of his son; and Jacob, in his day-
dream, enacts the drama of Abraham and Isaac to the very
point where the knife is lifted up over the child.   But here his
strength leaves him and he cries: '*You* kill him, you, my Lord
and Slayer, for he is my one and all, and I am not Abraham,
and my soul fails before you.'   'At the last moment', Joseph
asks, 'your soul failed?' and, in his resourceful intimacy with
'the pattern', he continues: 'But why, at the next moment,

the very next moment, the voice would have sounded and called to you: Lay not your hand upon the lad and do him no harm!—and you would have seen the ram in the thicket.'

In the ensuing dialogue, conducted with all the intellectual alacrity of the Talmud and the humour of Joseph, the light of two minds, one profound, the other profoundly witty, is turned upon every facet of the problem created by the individual sphere within the revolving sphere, and on the question of how the singular is related to the exemplary, the being cast in a traditional role to the being cast into the unexampled predicament of the unique decision—into that fear and trembling which ever since Kierkegaard has been the 'traditional' mood of 'existential' speculation. For Jacob now firmly replies: 'I did not know. I was as Abraham and the story had not yet been told.' And Joseph: 'You did not know? Ah, but did you not say that you cried out: I am not Abraham? And if you were not Abraham, then you were Jacob my father, and the story was old and you knew its ending. This is the advantage of not being first but coming late: we already know the course on which the world is set, and know the tales which tell its story . . . You might have trusted in the voice and the ram.' But Jacob dismisses the 'advantage of coming late'. For had he done as Abraham did *because* he knew the issue, what could his show of strength have meant to the Lord? It would not have been that which alone pleases the Lord, not the great obedience of faith. And finally, it was a dream and did not really happen: it was not the Lord who tried him as He once tried Abraham; he, Jacob, tried himself with the trial of Abraham, and found himself wanting: his love was stronger than his faith. And Jacob seems inconsolably distressed. But Joseph persists in consolation. In Jacob's very failure, he now says, was the wisdom of the Lord. For what was the meaning of Abraham's trial? It was twofold: to test his obedience *and* to teach him a lesson; and Joseph tells the story of the Isaac sacrifice in his best interpreter's manner:

The Lord said to Abraham: 'I am Melech, the bull god of Baalim. Bring me your firstborn!' But when Abraham made haste to do so, the Lord spoke: 'How dare you! Am I Melech, the bull king? Far from it! I am the God of Abraham. . . . What I commanded, I did not command so that you should do it, but that you should learn that it must not be done. For it is an abomination in My sight. And besides, here is a ram.' And so my father has diverted himself with the trying question of whether he could do that which the Lord forbade Abraham to do; and now he grieves because he found that he could not.

And Jacob ends this part of the disputation with the words: 'You spoke like an angel near to the throne of God. . . . But only half the truth is in your words, the other half remains in mine.' [44] For man must not be too familiar with the progress of the drama; his part is made up of both familiarity and the suspense of waiting.

5

The following passage occurs in the first 'Prelude' to *Joseph and his Brothers*:

Through the kings of Babel and the two Egypts . . . the sun god manifested himself in the flesh—in them the myth became the *mysterium*, leaving no room to distinguish between what they *were* and what they *meant*. Not until three thousand years later did people begin to debate such questions as whether the Eucharist 'was' or only 'signified' the body of the Sacrifice. But even those slightly superfluous disputations could not at all affect the true nature of the mystery, which is and will remain the timeless present . . . This is the meaning of the observance and the feast. And when Joseph, in mid-summer, at the feast of the Weeping Women, the feast of the Burning Lamps, the feast of Tammuz, amid much sobbing of flutes and joyful shoutings, witnessed in elaborate presentation, that is to say, in the present, the murder and the resurrection of the lamented Son, of Osiris-Adonis, then it came to pass that time was dissolved in the mystery. This is important for our story because it shows a manner of thinking which, without being in the least logically objectionable, recognized in every visitation by water the Great Flood.[45]

It is a manner of thinking, or rather a mode of experience, which for long held a kind of negative fascination for Thomas

Mann: that is, not as the *mysterium* of the oneness of 'being' and 'meaning', but on the contrary, as the agony of their falling apart. This was the only subject of one of his first literary exercises (and the earliest he allowed to be included in the volume of collected stories). Written in 1896, the little sketch *Disillusionment* is the sad monologue of a man who, so to speak, lost himself in the gulf which one day opened before him and for ever separated language from reality, 'meaning' from 'being', so that nothing he experienced, neither success nor failure, not love, art, or disaster, ever 'was' to him what words had promised it would 'mean'. [46]* And the story of Thomas Buddenbrook, the meticulous burgher who had ceased 'being' what he 'signified', was only one of many in which the uprooted individual lamented, or searched for, his lost tradition as the only sanction of an authentic and 'exemplary' existence. Yet in recalling Thomas Buddenbrook we also remember that one night he experienced the 'timeless presence' and, in a feverish vision, saw his essential being live on 'in all those who for ever and ever will say "I" '.[47] But only in *Joseph and his Brothers* do we encounter men who wholly live in the mythic tense of the perfect present. Thomas Mann once said—and it was the saying of a writer who intimately knew the pain of being excessively 'separate'—that what above all matters to man is to recognize himself in the past, catch its echo in himself, and find in everything he is and does the familiar form and feel of humanity.[48] It is this which distinguishes— that is to say, 'distinguishes' not too much—all the characters of *Joseph*. Of some of them it is even true to say that they are, without much detriment to their liveliness, no selves at all, but entirely 'manifestations in the flesh' of a timeless principle.

Eliezer, who is Jacob's oldest servant and young Joseph's teacher, is such a man. He is, in his mythic mode of existence,

---

* This sketch shows that Thomas Mann began at the very point where Hofmannsthal, already much advanced in his literary career, suffered the crisis of the 'Chandos Letter' (1902). The theme of the 'Letter' is almost the same as that of *Disillusionment*.

unaffected by the *principium individuationis*: an 'open identity', as Thomas Mann himself has called him.[49]   And as Thomas Buddenbrook's fleeting vision of immortality was induced by his reading of Schopenhauer, so was Thomas Mann's imagination thoroughly prepared by the pessimistic philosopher for the conception of the gloomless and deathless Eliezer. A comparison, however, between Eliezer's imperturbable calm and the turbulence of mind which released Thomas's metaphysical delirium shows once more how startlingly easy it is to lure Schopenhauer's ideas from their pessimistic setting. The share which *The World as Will and Idea* has in the creation of the 'open identity', Thomas Mann indirectly acknowledges by almost word for word quotations. He says, for instance, of the Eliezer type of man that to him 'the life of the individual is only superficially distinct from that of the race, and birth and death seem mere vibrations of that which always is'.[50] This could all but be replaced by Schopenhauer's observation that 'if we think of the changes brought about by death and birth as infinitely rapid vibrations, we shall behold the lasting Idea of the individual creature, motionless as a rainbow above the rush of the waterfall'.[51] Or: 'If I protested in all seriousness that the same Eliezer who taught Joseph was still the same old man who served Abraham, I would be considered mad.   Yet I know that it is still madder to believe that the Eliezer here and now is in any true and profound sense an entirely other man. . . .   This is why Eliezer stood before Joseph as if this very day were his first, and none could be his last, and his eyes were alight with the radiance of an indestructible principle.'   Adjusted to Eliezer's un-self-awareness, this is the same passage out of *The World as Will and Idea* from which we quoted before in speaking of the 'indestructible principle' Tony Buddenbrook felt she represented, and of which, in fact, she was a comic version.[52]

Eliezer, however, is not comic, perhaps because the imagination that has created him is no longer pessimistically suspicious of the 'principle' by which he lives. He has the dignity and intelligence of the myth. It would make no sense to say of him that he does not know who he is. On the contrary, he knows it better than more individualized selves. Eliezer he is, and this means being a mythic institution. He occupies a place on earth which, from time immemorial and for all eternity, has been allotted to 'the Eliezer'; and if by mischance he stumbles and comes to be elsewhere, then the earth 'leaps towards him', as it is said to have done when Abraham's Eliezer went out to woo Rebecca on behalf of his master's son, so that Eliezer stands again where he ought. Not even young Joseph, endowed with much precocious irony, takes any critical exception to his expansive and majestic manner of saying 'I', as he sits with him by the well, under the tree of wisdom, and listens to the Eliezer stories which are as inexhaustible in meaning and number as the past itself. True, he 'sees through him' as his eyes are fixed on the great storyteller, and gazes 'into an infinite perspective of Eliezer-figures who all said "I" through the mouth of the one who was present in the flesh; but as they sat in the twilight shade of the great tree and the sun-drenched air quivered behind his teacher, the long succession of identities lost itself not in darkness but in light'.[53] This does indeed sound like a farewell to the pessimism of Schopenhauer.

Although Joseph does not mind Eliezer's mythic manners, he nevertheless 'knows'; and as he grows up he comes to distinguish ever more clearly between the mythic truth and the actual present. For in him and through him, according to Thomas Mann's conscious design, the 'ego emerges from within the mythic collective'.[54] And so, even within the novel itself, it is not quite true to say what the 'Prelude' says, namely, that 'only three thousand years later did people begin to ask themselves whether "being" and "meaning" were quite inseparably merged into each other'. We have seen Joseph's manner of assuaging Jacob's anguish at not being able to do as Abraham did; but on a later occasion young Joseph proves himself, in his abundant *tâm*, the wittiest charmer not only of his father and his father's difficult Lord, but of the *mysterium* itself. This time the patriarch's theological anxieties are about a feast and observation of long standing which, dear to the people, is linked with certain primitive tribal memories, and is therefore distrusted by Jacob. It is, in Thomas Mann's interpretation, a kind of pre-Mosaic model of the Passover; he even makes Jacob call it 'Pessach' in a calculated *Golden Bough* anachronism. Is it not likely to displease God, Jacob asks himself, and had it not better be abolished? But young Joseph offers the following advice—as if indeed he had learned from *The Golden Bough* that 'the history of religion is a long attempt to reconcile old custom with new reason, to find a sound theory for an absurd practice':[55]

> If your child may presume that he has been asked, he would advise that the feast be spared and not too jealously handled on account of its stories. Might these not be replaced by another which perchance you will be pleased to tell when the roast meat is served at the meal of the celebration? Would not, for instance, the saving of Isaac be very suitable? Or let us wait and see whether God will not one day honour Himself in us by some great intervention and deliverance. The feast would then be there, ready to receive the story and ready for us to sing songs of rejoicing.[56]

There is, clearly, in Joseph's mind ample room to distinguish between that which *is* and that which is *meant*, between the observance and that which is observed; and once there is room to distinguish, there is also irony—the irony of the conscious need to interpret, to *make* sense rather than to find it as a given attribute of the world. It is the very irony with which, as Goethe thought, even all scientific interpreting should be done. Thus defined, irony seems indeed the natural condition of the human mind at a certain stage of its growth: at the emergence of the multiple vision which was bound ironically to undermine the throne of those unironical royalties of Babel and the two Egypts by revealing that they were embodiments of the sun god only 'from one point of view'. Once 'points of view' have come into the world, the suspicion spreads that all 'meanings' are only so many texts read into life; and who can be sure then that what he reads is the text of the authorized version? This is the inescapable predicament of irony and the source of many virtues and many sins of the human mind, of frivolity, arbitrariness and despair as well as of humility, humour, and faith. Somewhere between humour and faith Joseph, the first-born of irony, lives his life, a life that enchanted Thomas Mann's imagination for longer than any other life he ever contemplated.

Within the mythic world of the Eliezers and the patriarchs the first-born of irony is, of course, a late heir, 'witty, problematical and interesting', as Thomas Mann calls him,[57] well-equipped from the outset to become 'a success' in that Egypt which in Thomas Mann's rendering shows many signs of a *fin de siècle* civilization. We need only think of all the other late heirs of Thomas Mann's imaginative world, of Thomas and Hanno, Tonio and Adrian, in order to appreciate his lasting enchantment with this one: for the first time, if we disregard the brief comedy interlude of *Royal Highness*, the 'outcast', the man set apart from his tradition by self-awareness and exceptional sensibility, is not the sufferer of a curse but the bearer of a double blessing, a *déraciné* with roots in the divine intelligence. Joseph knows only too well how to 'compare himself' (to use once more the motto to *Meditations*, the advice Antonio, in Goethe's *Tasso*, gives to the despairing poet). If he also is incomparably 'unique', his uniqueness lies in the surpassing art and virtuosity with which he plays the part written for him by the author of the world, and in the singular intuition with which he improvises in the many gaps in the text of that notoriously difficult playwright.

To be left without a text and to stand on the stage in utter embarrassment, oblivious of the words to be said and the things to be done—this nightmare of the actor is a theme which, in numberless variations, has risen to dominance in modern literature. Among Thomas Mann's works little Hanno is its most affecting victim. '*Wer aber* sind *sie*—?' ('Who in truth *are* they?')—the opening question of the fifth of Rilke's *Duino Elegies* echoes and re-echoes, unanswered and unanswerable, through our literary spheres and manages to encircle their problematical inhabitants with swarming question-marks. Rilke's own Malte Laurids Brigge is only one of the heroes thus surrounded and enclosed. And in the ever narrowing space that is left, K. of Kafka's *The Castle*, who does not know whence he came, why he arrived, or whither he is to go, tries in vain to assert himself, with desolate heroism, against his cursed uniqueness and his ignorance of the role. What he lacks above all is the faith that there is a story, and in it a part for him to play, and therefore, in case of need, the humour of confident improvisation. 'What have you to complain about?' he once asks his two assistants, who appear to have denounced him in the Castle. Their answer is: 'That you have no sense of humour.' [58]

Joseph possesses it in abundance because he knows the story and knows his part, and knows that both the story and the part are good. Ironical heir that he is, he also knows, unlike Eliezer, that it is entirely his own part, which none but he could play. Yet the supreme confidence with which he acts it—and in his younger years to the point of hubris, for which he had to be punished twice—constantly alludes to the higher authorship which manifests itself in him, and startles everyone he meets with this divine allusiveness. His very beauty is the beauty of a young god; and whether it be Adonis, Tammuz, Osiris, the god who is slain, descends into the underworld, and rises again, or Thoth, the Egyptian Hermes, who, with wit and charm, mediates between the heights and the 'deep that lieth under', Joseph acts both parts with inspired skill, so that he is Tammuz as Jacob's child, and Thoth as the Egyptian courtier. When his brothers bury him in the dry well, his terror is his own, and yet not quite his own, for it is enchanted with the terror of the buried god and the story of his rising again; and although his mythic faith is less solemnly in earnest than that of Jacob, mixed as it is with not a little ironical sophistication and more than a touch of shrewd roguery, it is yet as unshakable in the conviction that a story 'would not even know how to happen and would, as it were, not occur to itself', if it were not exemplary, not modelled upon its plot in Heaven, and not a phase of the 'revolving sphere' which, in its incessant exchanges between the divine and the human, again and again brings down to earth what had been high above. Whatever Joseph lacks of Jacob's theological seriousness (and he lacks so much that he must ultimately be denied the paternal blessing), he is nevertheless his father's true son in being unable to think of life as deserving its name if it is 'not founded upon the sacredly established, not a mirror of the divine, and not recognized by God'. This, says Thomas Mann, 'was as it should be'; but what was slightly dubious was 'Joseph's inclination to use to his advantage this general manner of thinking, and to dazzle people by means of quite a little self-dramatization' [59] (a habit which he shared with his author, who dazzled not a few of his critics by his Goethe *imitatio*, of which he himself once said that 'it can, from the sub-conscious, mythically determine a writer's life . . . although what is unconscious in an artist may at any moment turn to smiling awareness').[60]

With unobtrusive care and subtle art Thomas Mann divests Joseph's 'ego', as he rises to power in Egypt, of bond after bond of the 'mythic collective'. The more he becomes a god in the eyes of the world, the more human he becomes to himself and the more humorously he 'acts'. Language follows suit and the vocabulary of the theatre abounds: 'rehearsals' are held, 'supers' are engaged, 'spectators' are invited, 'prompters' are at hand, the stage is set and the curtain rises. Yet not for one moment does Joseph lose his serene faith that he is in a 'real' story, however much he himself must see to it that it takes its proper course; and as the story nears its climax, he even feels a little stage-fright. The brothers are expected, their reception has to be prepared, and Joseph discusses the arrangements with his steward. 'What a story this is in which we are', he exclaims, 'one of the best! And now it is up to us to give it the finest shape and extract the great delight that God has put into it. Indeed, now He needs all our wits. How shall we set about doing justice to it? That is what excites me so much.' And as he rehearses this and that possibility, and how to behave and what to say, and when exactly to reveal himself as their brother, his friend and helper wonders why he should be so unsure.   At this point, if only for one moment, the last trace of 'mythic certainty' seems to leave him in his all-too-human agitation: 'I don't know what sort of man I am', he says.   'Can anyone know beforehand how he will behave in his story?   He cannot.   As soon as it happens it will be clear.   Oh, I am so curious to get to know myself, and to hear what I shall say to them, for now I have no idea. . . .' [61]

6

The innate character of a work, the literary species towards which it tends, is often revealed to its author, Thomas Mann once said, through the reading he instinctively chooses while he is writing it.   During the years in which he produced *Joseph and his Brothers*, Thomas Mann found such 'invigorating reading' in *Tristram Shandy* and Goethe's *Faust*, particularly Part II; and he soon discovered that it was the ambition of his work to become 'a humorous symbol of humanity'.[62] Yet no less relevant to the intention of the work in hand are, in his case, the literary interpretations he wrote at the time. An example of this is his essay on Kleist's *Amphitryon*.   What captivated him most in that drama was Jupiter's play with his own identity when, for instance, in the shape of Alcmene's husband, Amphitryon, he answers her anxious question whether it was he, Amphitryon, who was her consort during the night: 'I was he,' says the god.   And Thomas Mann comments: 'This "I was he" is a strangely ambiguous reply.   Who says it?   Amphitryon, but also the god, the one speaking for the other; and this fascinating ambiguity is characteristic of everything he says.' [63]   This, of course, is also Joseph's manner of saying 'I', and is perhaps, as even language seems to suggest, the only right way of saying it.   'I am', or 'I am that I am'— thus speaks God (or perhaps the fallen angel).   A man is always 'it', is something, is related, and is in danger of losing his humanity and his soul if he approaches the state of being an 'I' in the gloomy absoluteness of the *principium individua-*

tionis. Thomas Mann's Joseph is an ego whose self-aware-ness is inseparable from his awareness of 'the story' in which he is 'he': a little too much he himself to be the chosen bearer of the blessing that points towards the eternally 'other', and yet not heavy enough with selfhood ever to lose the lightness and the Hermes humour of which he says that 'they are God's best gifts and our dearest wisdom; for on it alone can we depend when He asks us His difficult questions. He gave those gifts to us so that we might bring a smile even to life's most serious face.' [64]

'I am he' is one of the *leit-motifs* of *Joseph the Provider*, and with each recurrence it comes closer to the full meaning it assumes in Joseph's self-revelation to his brothers.[65] It is then that he is finally and entirely 'himself', steps out of the mythic play and announces its mythic consummation. At this moment he attains the unambiguous identity of the most successful hero a *Bildungsroman* ever had. Yet it is also at this point that he renounces Jacob's blessing and shows himself prepared for the denial to come. 'Your brother', so he speaks to his brothers who are overcome with wonderment, awe, and not a little fear, and are about to genuflect before him,

is no hero of God and no harbinger of spiritual salvation. He is just a farmer of corn and a provider of bread; and if in my dream your sheaves bowed down to mine, as once I prattled and boasted, and if the stars made curtsies—well, you can see now that it did not mean anything out of this world. It only meant that father and brothers would thank me for feeding their hunger. And when a man is given bread he says, not 'Hosanna in the highest', but simply 'Thank you very much'. Still, bread there has to be and it comes before the hosanna. . . .[66]

And so he is well prepared for the great hour of his reunion with Jacob and for 'the love that denies the blessing'.

There are readers who, not a little encouraged by some of Thomas Mann's later utterances, wish to see the meaning and message of the novel in the bread that comes before the hosanna (and it undeniably does so, as undeniably as the air and many other things created before the soul of man). But even if such a reading had been the intention of Thomas Mann's political self (which was, in fact, as divided then as it was at all times from *Meditations* to the essay on Chekhov, and found its cosmic justification in the compromise between the conservatively revolving sphere and the progressive spirit), his work knew better—a little in the manner of Abraham, who, as the Higher Circles whispered, 'knew better' than his Creator. For this work never loses sight of the 'still greater story' of which, as Pascal perceived, the story of Joseph is a secular anticipation, and within which it is, as the novel itself says, 'only an interlude'.[67] These words, prepared and echoed by many more throughout the four books, and indeed prefigured in the programmatic 'Prelude' with the Spirit's ineluctable mission, occur at the end of yet another interlude within the Interlude: the story of Tamar, the alien woman who won Jacob's friendship, sat at his feet intently listening to his tales and, upon divining their meaning and ultimate prophecy, resolved to be included in them. With persistence, cunning, and even subterfuge, she finally succeeded in becoming the mother of two of Judah's children and so had 'made her way into the line of descent with amazing determination'.[68] This woman, who would not be defeated in her purpose of playing a part in the drama of the blessing and the Spirit, is one of Thomas Mann's most successful creations and, together with Rachel and Mut-em-enet, Potiphar's wife, the most important female figure of the tetralogy. Yet any doubt that might still remain about Thomas Mann's serious purpose in conceiving four volumes of a novel as 'only an interlude', would be removed by Jacob's arrival in Egypt. It is then that he is finally confirmed as the hero of the 'story above the story'—and confirmed not merely by the plot but by the verdict of Thomas Mann's literary art, which is nowhere more at ease than in the denial of the blessing: 'God has raised you and rejected you, both in one, I say it in your ear, beloved child, and you are wise enough to understand. He has raised you above your brothers as once you dreamt. . . . But He has raised you in a worldly way, not in the sense of the blessing. . . .'[69] And so the blessing will go to Judah, the great sinner and the un-happy son. He needs it, just as the story, within which the story of Joseph is only an interlude, needs his sin and un-happiness for its ultimate wholeness and fulfilment.

In more than one sense *Joseph and his Brothers* is the work of an emigrant, of a mind whom his age and country left with the alternatives of either despairing or finding the profounder reasons of love, and of an imagination seeking refuge from the terror of the time. The first volume of the novel appeared in the year of Hitler's coming to power, and when Thomas Mann in California wrote the last words of the 'divine in-vention', announcing—ironically enough, in hardly translat-able German—that '*so endigt die schöne Geschichte und Gotteser-findung von Joseph und seinen Brüdern*', the Second World War was at its height. In the course of writing the four volumes Thomas Mann lost his home, his German readers, and his country, to rulers who, as their prelude to violent action, invaded the minds of their followers with stupefying myths and myth-ologies of their own. From the backwoods of misguided literacy there emerged the axe-grinding explorers of the past, researchers into ancestry, racial theorists, who assembled around the god risen from the depths of the beer cellars. Reason began to dream, and nightmares talked science in their sleep. With the 'sure touch of a dream-walker' they settled the rational concerns of society but laid down, with tables of measurement, pedigrees and hereditary calculations, their absurd laws for the practice of love. And while they destroyed all trust between men, they extolled the phantom of a community founded on the purity of blood and other mystico-natural ingredients.

It was against this background of domestic perversity that Thomas Mann went in search of the true relationship between myth and reason, poetry and rational knowledge, community and the individual, and created from present tears and horrors his most serene book, a *gaya scienza* of man and the world, and of that good government of human affairs which Hans Castorp, sincerely and ineffectively, used to meditate (and 'governing' was what he called his meditations) as he sat among

R

the alpine flowers, the irreconcilable opposites, and the sick
disputants of the Magic Mountain. Irony? *Joseph and his
Brothers* is, if nothing else, one of the greatest and friendliest
conquests the imagination has ever made of irony.

VII

Parody, Tragic and Comic

1

IT is not the least irony of Thomas Mann's literary career, and the most obvious proof of his artistic integrity, that the longer he lived abroad, and the more he had to depend on being read in English, the more difficult he made his translator's business. Of *Doctor Faustus* even the full title is untranslatable; for this 'Life of the German Composer Adrian Leverkühn, as told by a Friend' is in the original the life of a '*Tonsetzer*', a word which, although 'composer' is its only possible English equivalent, is a deliberately chosen archaism and as such points to an important aspect of the story. Equally lost in the foreign idiom is the allusiveness of the hero's name, as of all other names in the book: for Leverkühn suggests 'to live audaciously', as Zarathustra preached that man should live, and thus hints at the close kinship between the imaginary composer and Friedrich Nietzsche. And what is true of the title is also true of the first sentence which Serenus Zeitblom, Ph.D., friend and fictitious biographer, commits to paper, a grievously laborious and interminably wavering construction—intentional self-parody of the real author—for which any other language lacks the native training in sustained breathlessness. And Zeitblom himself instantly remarks: 'I read over the above lines and cannot help observing that they reflect a certain discomfort, an almost physical oppression only too indicative of the state of mind in which I sit down today ... on the 27th May 1943, three years after Leverkühn's death. ...' That first untranslatable sentence does in fact collapse in the middle, and the embarrassed author makes a fresh start with 'I beg to begin again.' [1]

I am quoting this not only because it instantly sets the tone of parody (and perhaps it was rash to use the words 'tragic parody' in speaking of *Death in Venice*, which is a classical epic by comparison with the parodistic intricacies of *Doctor Faustus*), but also because the position held by the novel among the works of Thomas Mann suggests that 'I beg to begin again' might also be my cue. If so, I shall not take it, but try instead to be brief. For on the preceding pages much has already been said, both explicitly and implicitly, about *Doctor Faustus*, a work which thematically would seem to follow more closely upon *Buddenbrooks*, *Tonio Kröger*, *Death in Venice*, and *Meditations*, than upon *Joseph and his Brothers*, although it could not have been written without either the relief Thomas Mann's mind had found in a friendlier sphere, or without the immense store of intellectual and technical resources he had assembled in the meantime. Indeed, to discuss *Doctor Faustus* means, in more than one respect, to return to the past; but it is above all Thomas Mann's own past which is recalled by this life of a composer in whom genius and the passion to create are yet threatened with sterility, possessed as he is of the knowledge that the tradition of his medium is so utterly exhausted that to work within it would condemn the artist to banality, and to 'break through' require sacrifices and ingenuities not thought of in Heaven.

There was, to review briefly Thomas Mann's earlier work, Thomas Buddenbrook's losing himself by losing his sense of a valid convention of living, and Hanno's lethal musical inspiration; there was Tonio Kröger's denouncing as 'infamous' the fate of the artist who has to pay with his life for as much as one leaf from the laurel tree, and Aschenbach's surrender to the chaos which lurks at the very heart of the aesthetic sensibility; and there were, finally, the non-political man's Germany intent upon music and military 'break-throughs', and Hans Castorp's discovery of the ethics of sin and the 'heightening' effect of disease. All themes come together once more in *Doctor Faustus* and, greatly intertwined and infernally illuminated as they now are, make the work a *summa demonologica* of Thomas Mann's imagination. For this novel has something in common even with *Joseph and his Brothers*: the reconciliation, prepared on the Magic Mountain, of the old irreconcilable opposites. Yet this time they do not meet with the double blessing from above and below. All *tâm* is gone; and it is not only the desperate spirit of Adrian Leverkühn that enters into a pact with Satan. Life too, German life, is nothing if not bedevilled. Both Life and Spirit meet in 'the deep that lieth under'.

Although Adrian Leverkühn is in a sense a magnified Tonio Kröger, his 'detachment' has acquired demonic properties. Not a trace is left in him of that idyllic irony with which Tonio yearned for the simplicity and triviality of life, and which he held so dear as the saving grace of his art and existence. The 'life' which is the setting of *Doctor Faustus*, the world into which the composer Leverkühn grows up, has frustrated the humiliating love which had wooed and courted it only because it was so handsomely stupid. It would not endure any longer the boredom of its own banality and found means to 'spiritualize' itself. By the time Adrian's life reached its tragic climax, in 1930, the Hans Hansens of Germany were no longer quite innocent of the demonic; and so the artist had to seek his inspiration in other quarters. The Devil himself took over from the healthy simpletons and brainless young athletes; and as Leverkühn composed his masterpieces, 'instilled with the poison of the angel from the deep',[2] and Zeitblom wrote the master's biography with a hand unsteadied by the fall of high explosives, the discord between the robustness of Life and the infirmity of the Spirit was resolved in the unison of Hell. This is at least one conclusion, and not the most unfitting one, to Schopenhauer's metaphysical story where only the flesh is willing but the spirit weak, and the artist's place is in the vacuum of 'nothingness'. For it is the Devil who has the strongest *horror vacui*. This is why, to repeat what has been said earlier, the transition is so imperceptibly smooth from 'art as salvation to art as damnation'. Already with Hanno Buddenbrook we had arrived in the age of Adrian Leverkühn, a time when 'in pious sober wise, naught of work is to be wrought and art is grown impossible without the Devil's help and fires of Hell under the cauldron'.[3]

Doctor Faustus, however, returns also to a far remoter past than the space of the author's own life could yield. It links a voluminous amount of present to the mainspring of that literary inspiration which, through four centuries, has proved irresistible, with both splendid and calamitous results, to many a poet and writer: the first German Faustbook of 1587, published by one Johann Spiess in Frankfurt-am-Main. This told for the first time the story of the learned Dr. Faustus who was 'fain to love forbidden things, after which he hankered night and day' until he 'decided to try out and put into action certain magic words, figures, characters and conjurations, in order to summon up the Devil before him', and whose 'apostasy was nothing more nor less than his pride and arrogance, despair, audacity and insolence, like unto those giants of whom the poets sing that they ... made war on God, yea, like unto that evil angel who opposed God, and was cast off by God on account of his arrogance and presumption'. And so Faustus sold his soul to the Devil in return for twenty-four years of researcher's bliss during which Hell was to 'profit him greatly', if he but renounced 'all living creatures, and the whole heavenly host and all human beings, for so it must be'.*[4]

It is to this Faustbook that Thomas Mann owes not only, as many writers before him had done, the rough framework of his plot, but also many long quotations which, in their original

* For a learned, thorough, and animated discussion of the successive literary Fausts, see E. M. Butler's *The Fortunes of Faust*, Cambridge, 1952. I have quoted the above Faustbook passages in her excellent translation. In the chapter Professor Butler devotes to Thomas Mann's *Doctor Faustus* she also shows clearly the correspondence which episodes and personages in this latest Faustbook have to those of the first (and, to some extent, to Goethe's, although the parallel she draws between the Wagner of Goethe's *Faust* and the Serenus Zeitblom of Thomas Mann must not be stretched too far. On the whole, I think, Thomas Mann obeyed the inner logic of his central idea by limiting all his essential allusions and 'structural borrowing' to the sixteenth-century model.)

sixteenth-century German, he has most skilfully woven into his own text: above all in those passages which have a direct bearing on the pact, so that, for instance, Adrian, a student of Lutheran theology, uses the archaic idiom in writing the letter about his fatal visit to the brothel, and again in the farewell oration to his friends when, as he is about to play them his last and greatest work, 'The Lamentation of Dr. Faustus', he succumbs to that madness which is the final stage of the disease he contracted from his *hetaera esmeralda.*

To follow the motif of *hetaera esmeralda* throughout the novel would provide yet another example of Thomas Mann's virtuosity in 'connecting', a method which is carried to its extreme limit in *Doctor Faustus*, together with art itself, both as a practice and as a theme. For we meet *hetaera esmeralda* first as the name of an exotic butterfly, uncannily beautiful and poisonous, in Father Leverkühn's collection of some of Nature's ambiguous creations, a collection which the man, so fond of 'speculating the elements' (the first Faustian allusion in the book), likes to display to his children. The name later gets attached in Adrian's mind to the woman whom he met in his student days in the Leipzig brothel. He was conducted there by a porter whom he had asked to show him a restaurant; but he was a pimp in disguise, reminiscent in appearance of the specialist in demonology from the theological school in Halle. This episode Thomas Mann has taken almost verbatim from Deussen's *Recollections of Nietzsche*; it is not the only instance of quotation and sheer reportage, a technique deliberately adopted by Thomas Mann in order to demonstrate one of his main themes, which is the exhaustion of art and the defeat of invention. Like Nietzsche, the embarrassed Adrian made straight for the piano, struck a few chords, and left in confusion. Yet there was time for one of the women to approach him and stroke his face, thereby creating in him a kind of obsession which some time later drove him into her arms and into the disease which, for twenty-four years, the very time Dr. Faustus bought from the Devil, released his latent genius. Henceforward a sequence of notes, derived from the name *hetaera esmeralda,* was to recur in Adrian's music. It is this brothel episode which Thomas Mann has transferred from Deussen's report about Nietzsche to Adrian's letter, parodistically written in sixteenth-century German, in the Lutheran Devil's own language.

Yet this archaic parody is only the external aspect of the inner meaning which the return to the past has throughout the work, a meaning so perplexing and shocking in its associations and ramifications that, quite understandably, it has baffled both the writer and his critics. The theme in question is as dominant and domineering in *Doctor Faustus* as the revolving sphere was in *Joseph and his Brothers,* and through it more than any other Thomas Mann seeks to establish the much-debated, much-criticized, and much-abused connection between the destiny of a German genius and the politics of the German tyranny. If he fails in its full realization, he fails once more in the manner of *Meditations*: he is distracted by Germany. For the theme is not a 'German' theme alone, as little as Germany has any exclusive proprietary claims to modern art or modern tyranny, or even to those 'magic words, figures, characters and conjurations' with which to summon up, in despair, audacity and insolence, forbidden things. The revulsion from the Third Reich can hardly be overstated morally; yet as a product of the intellectual imagination, *Doctor Faustus* is an overstatement of the 'problem of Germany', and is in this respect, and in its own incomparably grander way, as deeply stirring and as flawed as *Meditations* was. But as it is not a treatise, the shocks and blows it deals to the imagination are likely to hurt and quicken it much longer than will last any contradictions which it evokes in the mind. And if Adrian Leverkühn is not a perfect symbol of Germany, he is yet a symbol. He will, alas, be recognizable to many minds as one they know with dangerous intimacy.

It is in Serenus Zeitblom's discussion of Adrian Leverkühn's great oratorio '*Apocalipsis cum figuris*', based on the series of Dürer woodcuts, that the theme in question is most clearly brought out, and its importance must justify my making it, at the expense of almost everything else, the focus of this chapter.

The following quotation also 'unwrites' and 'revokes', as it were, that 'sphere' which in *Joseph and his Brothers* revolved in God's good humour and space, just as Adrian, in his most desperate hour, felt that Beethoven's Ninth Symphony must be unwritten and revoked.   Serenus Zeitblom, in describing Adrian's principles of composition, cannot help recalling certain discussions he had attended with him during the 'twenties in a Munich circle of intellectuals.   Their favourite subject was the critique of the 'bourgeois cultural tradition', which had, so they thought, destroyed much profounder values, namely the true values of the communal life and the true communion of the human spirit, by cultivating a highly individualistic and aesthetic culture with which to replace the 'collective cult'.   In this anti-bourgeois mood they turned, for instance, against the 'aesthetic theatre', which (and here it might be Bertolt Brecht speaking) had become a matter merely of refined pleasure and bourgeois '*Bildung*' and lost its ancient meaning and significance as an expression of man's communal nature.   It is such ideas Zeitblom remembers as he witnesses Adrian's composing, which denies the form of the drama and replaces the dramatic and operatic by the epic form of oratorio and cantata, and this

in a spirit which agreed precisely with those derogatory judgements about the individual and all individualism. . . . It was an attitude of mind which, no longer interested in the psychological, searched for that which was objective, binding, and compelling, and imposed upon itself the dedicated discipline of a pre-classical austerity of form.   How often, while intensely watching Adrian's work, did my mind go back to those early impressions which we boys received from his teacher when he elaborated his antithesis of 'harmonic subjectivity' and 'polyphonic objectivity'! The track round the sphere, of which they used to talk in those agonizingly clever conversations [in the Munich circle], along which regress and progress, the old and the new, past and future, became one—I saw it all realized here [in Adrian's composition] in a regression full of novelty, going back beyond Bach's and Handel's harmonic art to the remoter past of true polyphony.[5]

That antithesis between 'harmonic subjectivity' and 'polyphonic objectivity' was indeed a favourite subject of Adrian's teacher, the volubly stuttering Wendell Kretzschmar (the spelling of whose name, which surely ought to have been preserved in the English translation, is again an allusion to Nietzsche). He prophesied, stutteringly but forcefully, that the time was close at hand when all the world would see that 'harmonic subjectivity' had become a contradiction in terms, that the laws determining it were obsolete and unable to maintain authentic order. And why? The reason is most lucidly stated, as are so many other reasons, in Adrian's hallucinatory conversation with the Devil—again a deliberate 'borrowing': this time from Dostoevsky's *The Brothers Karamazov*—who has come to discuss the pact long since concluded in the embrace of *hetaera esmeralda*. For four hundred years, says 'he', all great music rested on the assumption that there could be harmony and peace between a universally established convention and the subjective concerns of the individual, that 'soul' and 'order' were profoundly—yes, profoundly—at one, and that it was therefore possible for the human passions truly and freely to express themselves within prescribed formulae. But this 'play' is over; the 'law' no longer recognizes itself in the 'mirror' of human inwardness, and the human heart no longer feels that any 'general order of things' can be valid. Its 'genuine' expression would resemble chaos rather than a pattern.[6]

Can the human mind dissociate itself from this predicament? Adrian himself had, on a previous occasion, answered this question too in a not less catastrophic manner (and almost verbatim as, before him, Nietzsche had done). The present state of our consciousness, Adrian said, as of our knowledge and sense of truth, ever more commandingly suggests (and is assisted in this by the utter insecurity and complete lack of harmony in our social existence) that art as 'a beautiful illusion' has simply become a 'fraud and a lie', and the more a fraud and a lie, the more beautiful it is.[7] The observation is later echoed by the Devil, who protests that the only way in which art might still try to maintain itself is to become totally absorbed in its own technical problems and play at being art by solving puzzles. For these have become so difficult that their solutions demand the whole mind. 'Art becomes its own critique.' But does not 'the danger of sterility' lie precisely here? And as if to correct Adrian's earlier remarks which we have just quoted, and to frustrate the Marxist interpreter, the Devil adds: 'Don't blame it on social conditions! I know you tend to do so, and are in the habit of saying that these conditions . . . are incompatible with the self-sufficient harmony of a work. True, but accidental. The prohibitive difficulties of the work lie deep in its own nature. It is the historical development of the musical material itself which has turned against the idea of harmony.' [8] (And let no Marxist interpreters say that this is just a devilish saying. Thomas Mann's Devil says many things with which they would not wish to disagree.)

It is for the sake of an important problem, and not in order to indulge a polemical fancy, that we refer here once again to the book on Thomas Mann by the Marxist critic Georg Lukacs, and to his interpretation of *Doctor Faustus*. For he certainly was not deterred by the Devil's warning. The book in question has all the virtues of intelligence, learning, and perception, which distinguish most pages of his other volumes, and it is unfair, and only justified by our context, to quote a characteristic example of the occasional lapses into crudity which are always caused by his doctrinal addiction. 'It is a strange coincidence', he writes, that he 'finished reading *Doctor Faustus* just at the time when the Central Committee of the Communist Party of Soviet Russia announced its [condemnatory] resolution concerning modern music. Thomas Mann's novel reads like analytical-artistic support for the condemnation.' [9] But he forgets to add that Adrian Leverkühn's music could not be performed in Hitler's Germany either. It is true that in *Doctor Faustus* Thomas Mann, more consciously than he had ever done before, presents the tragedy of his hero within the setting of a social tragedy; and also true that Leverkühn includes in his mad farewell address a confession of his a-social conduct, his unconcern about what is 'needful on earth'.[10] But what precisely the connection is between the state of music and the state of society must elude the doctrinal interpreter. For it emerges from the novel itself as something highly contradictory and paradoxical, and is unambiguous only in one respect, which we shall presently discuss. Besides, why Adrian's 'modern music', glaringly anti-bourgeois in inspiration, should so much displease both the Central Committee and a Hitlerite Ministry of Culture, is yet another paradox not easily solved, and certainly not solved by Georg Lukacs.* The reason here may well be that no modern tyranny can endure the revelation by art of its own spiritual foundations. This, at least, is what *Doctor Faustus* suggests by virtue of the only unequivocal connection it establishes between the nature of Leverkühn's music and the abdication of freedom. At this point, however, we had better return to Serenus Zeitblom's reflections on Adrian's '*Apocalipsis cum figuris*' and its bearing on Wendell Kretzschmar's teaching as well as on the conversations in the Munich circle.

Is there, the question runs, any way out of the radical predicament which we have seen arise from the deeply felt incongruity between the state of the individual soul and the conventions which history has to offer for expression and communication, between that which in all truthfulness must be said and that which can be said in traditional language? One answer—and it is one of Leverkühn's answers—is not even to

---

* To read Lukacs produces, in one reader at least, the unsettling sensation of a wisely conducted tour over firm ground with sudden detours, taken at the beckoning of the *idée fixe*, over large patches of thin ice. The result is a vague distrust of the wisdom even of what is undeniably wise.—I once heard of a strange case of mental affliction. A distinguished writer one morning at breakfast refused to sit down, protesting that the relevant part of his body was made of glass and was bound to break on impact with the chair. He had to be taken to a hospital, where he spent his time walking in the garden, dictating his distinguished books, and lying in bed on his stomach. One day, however, his nurse found him comfortably seated in a chair. 'You are cured!' she cried, 'I knew it would happen! Such an intelligent man . . .' 'Cured?' he replied. 'Of what? Perhaps of a slight misapprehension. Why did nobody ever tell me that it is unbreakable glass?' He was rightly released as being perfectly adjusted to life, but unfortunately among those who knew him there lingered a slight doubt which even affected their reactions to his distinguished books.

attempt any longer to express and communicate that which has become inexpressible and incommunicable: the 'self', but to submit to 'objective order', and to forswear that lawlessness which, having posed much too long as the law of 'harmonic subjectivity', has tricked the individual into the false belief that its relations with truth were 'harmonious'.   For it is freedom itself, and the illusory faith in its preordained oneness with the true nature of human reality, which has settled upon the soul 'like mildew', sent artists, with the question 'What next?' on their lips, on their chaotic chase after still more fascinating curiosities of the inner life, and has finally rendered the 'interesting' so tedious that, as the Devil puts it, 'they begin to persuade themselves and others that the tedious has become interesting'.[11]   'Everything which comes from God is ordered', said the very young Leverkühn on one occasion, significantly misquoting Romans xiii ('It became clear to me then that he was religious', notes his biographer [12]) but sometime later this became: 'Even a stupid order is better than none at all.' [13]

2

It is this theme of the unmanageability, in art and life alike, of the mildew freedom, the enthusiastic readiness to escape from the embarrassments of 'subjectivity' into an ordered 'polyphonic objectivity', from uniqueness into history, and from the drama of being a self into the choral discipline of the collective, through which, above all, the music of Adrian Leverkühn is related to the noise of the popular tyranny.   It is a theme which ought to be of little use to affectionate interpreters of Central Committee resolutions.   For after all, the theory of the 'epic theatre', held by the Marxist Bertolt Brecht, is informed with the same insight as are Adrian Leverkühn's musical ideas. Indeed, Brecht might have had lessons about the obsoleteness of 'harmonic subjectivity' from a Wendell Kretzschmar of the stage. The puzzle, therefore, is once again why 'Central Committees' should wish to suppress Leverkühn's manner of composing.

Perhaps the reason can be found in Serenus Zeitblom's further meditations on the subject. At the time when Adrian was writing his '*Apocalipsis cum figuris*', Zeitblom received a letter from him which he signed 'Perotinus Magnus'. It was, the recipient remarks, 'a suggestive joke and a playful identification full of self-mockery':

> . . . for this Perotinus was in charge of church music at Notre Dame in the twelfth century, a composer whose directions much contributed to the development of the young art of polyphony. The jesting signature vividly reminded me of a letter of Richard Wagner's, which he wrote at the time of *Parsifal*, and in which he added to his name the title 'Member of the High Consistory'. . . . It is an intriguing question: how serious is the artist in what ought and seems to be his most earnestly sincere concern; how seriously does he take himself in relation to his work, or how much masquerading and playfulness is involved—a kind of higher flippancy? . . . This is what I asked myself on seeing Adrian's signature. Indeed, my questions and my anxiety went further, and in my heart I doubted the authenticity of what he did. Had he, a man of our time, any true claim to the sphere in which he immersed himself, and which he struggled to recreate by means of an extremely sophisticated technique? I suspected, in short, the kind of aestheticism which exposed to most aggravating doubts the opinion my friend once uttered: that the antithesis to bourgeois culture is not barbarism but collectivism.[14]

Serenus Zeitblom goes on to explain this suspicion, of which he says that nobody will quite understand it unless he has experienced in his own soul how close to each other aestheticism and barbarism are. Does not a revival of ritual, he asks, initiated by a profane epoch, herald grave danger? For a dedication to the principle of ritualistic order 'as such', a devotion to it which does not spring from a clearly articulate faith but is born from despair and directed by the desire that there should be any collective order rather than the ever less endurable 'freedom of the atom', may suddenly find itself in calculated sympathy with even the crudest and cruellest cult. And finally Zeitblom admits to himself that the '*Apocalipsis cum figuris*' lies open 'not only in part, but as a whole', to two apparently contradictory charges: that of barbarism and that of bloodless intellectualism.[15] It is through the analysis and artistic presentation (deliberately combined by Thomas Mann) of a highly sophisticated primitivism that *Doctor Faustus* becomes, and will no doubt remain, one of the profoundest literary documents of the age. For the phenomenon of ideological primitivism is, in politics as well as in art and thought, the great fascination of our time; and it is this, much more than his 'Teutonism', which makes Adrian Leverkühn a truly representative artist. Indeed in the novel itself, particularly in the brilliant episode with the impresario Fitelberg, he is shown as having every chance of becoming an 'international celebrity'.

One of the basic motifs of the novel is, as Thomas Mann himself said, 'the approach of cultural sterility and that despair which predisposes a man for a pact with the Devil'.[16] And consistently enough, it is the Devil's business in the novel to conquer the threat of sterility which, as we know from Serenus Zeitblom's and Leverkühn's own reflections, comes from the incongruity, paralysingly felt by the artist, between that which 'is' and that which 'can be said', between reality and language; comes from a merely 'aesthetic' and deeply faith-less experimenting with revolutionary 'content' and primitive 'forms'; and comes finally from the all-pervasive suspicion that our very sense of truth has reduced the artistic manipulation of illusion to irrelevance, or even to frivolity, in the face of suffering. For having been deserted by the suffering God and His promise of redemption, agony no longer permits the lie of 'meaning' with which the play of art molests and mocks it: only its 'undisguised and untransfigured expression' may still be permissible.[17]

What, then, is the Devil to provide? The answer reveals the shocking character of the historical hour of which this Faustus stands as a symbol among the Faustus symbols of other ages— a symbol, moreover, which leaves the critic no room to ask the question as to its comparative literary rank: it gives the irrefutable answer itself. For it is, in the novel, only the Devil who can still provide creative enthusiasm, ultimate authenticity, and absolute faith in the relevance of the order revealed through a work of art; and it is Adrian Leverkühn, not his biographer, who has assigned his soul to the Devil. Without the Devil's help the artist is condemned to the sphere of higher parody, the only thing that is still left when the 'real thing' has become impossible, and the 'direct method' of creation, as the Devil has it, 'incompatible with genuineness'.[18]   Might a man not know, Adrian asks, that the traditional forms of art have been deserted by life, and might he not nevertheless find his playground beyond such knowledge, and ingeniously play with these forms as if they were counters in an intelligent game? 'I know, I know,' replies the Devil, 'parody. Yes, it might be a merry game if it were not so melancholy in its aristocratic nihilism. Would you expect much happiness or greatness from such subterfuge?'[19]   For parody, at least in the sense in which Thomas Mann uses the word, is essentially aesthetic critique. The Devil has better gifts to bestow. 'They tell me that the Devil passes for a man of criticism!' he exclaims. 'Calumny, my friend, sheer calumny! . . . What he wants and gives is the triumph over and above criticism, is the uninhibited creative rapture!'[20]

Such is the thoroughness with which Thomas Mann 'unwrites' Goethe's *Faust*. For with Goethe it is Mephistopheles who is all critique, irony and mockery, and Faust himself the enthusiastic creator; and while Faust secures his place in Heaven with his eternal striving, Mephistopheles is engaged in the hopeless business of trying to trick him into the damning contentment. Times have changed—the commonplace acquires sad significance when we compare the two Fausts. Is there, one wonders, a brief way of saying in what the change consists? In the complete reversal, it seems, of the relationship between the soul and the world. The hero of Goethe's drama cannot possibly damn himself by his passion for knowledge, experience and creation. He has out-witted Hell even before Mephistopheles appears on the scene, just as Leverkühn has been his victim long before he comes to discuss the pact. Goethe's Faust needs no saviour because he is safe in the pre-established harmony between the intellectual, moral, and aesthetic aspirations of man and the real nature of things. There is for him only one damnation: not to aspire to that *self*-realization through which he realizes the *world*. For self and world are at one. It is in this sense that Goethe's drama is the poetic climax, late, and therefore not unversed in doubt, of that 'harmonic subjectivity' within which, if our soul 'wills us to wear ourselves and never rest', it does so because its 'faculties can comprehend the wondrous architecture of the world'. Leverkühn's soul enjoys no such Marlowean reassurance. His faculties are deeply at odds with the architecture of the world which, even if comprehended, might be found wanting in wonder. For its discovered truths are certainly of little use to the soul, and it is hard not to sympathize with Serenus Zeitblom's observation: 'I shall never understand the "Hosanna" mood which befalls some people when they contemplate the "works of God" in terms of astrophysics. Can an arrangement be properly called the "work of God" when one may just as reasonably say about it: "Well, what of it?" instead of "Glory be to God"?' [21] Yet this is merely a comfortably philistine reflection of that catastrophe of the human soul, the representative victim of which is Adrian Leverkühn. It is in the contemplation of this disaster that Thomas Mann's *Doctor Faustus* is the 'unwriting' of Goethe's. For now the relationship between soul and world, between self and reality, is not one of fundamental harmony but of total 'absurdity'. Its only legitimate literary expressions are then parody, tragic or comic.*

* I am using the term 'absurdity' in the sense in which, ever since Kierkegaard, it has come to play a dominant role in existentialist thought. Existentialism is, of course, a philosophical expression of the state of affairs described above. The same, however, is also true of the other extreme of contemporary philosophizing, which tends to regard as the only legitimate theme of philosophy the critique of language and the construction of 'language games'. For it too is informed with the suspicion that the ultimate relationship between the cognitive faculties of man and the 'true nature' of the world may be one of 'absurdity'. In this context I may be allowed to mention that the only 'real person' of whom I am reminded by Adrian Leverkühn's genius (though certainly not by his biography) is the philosopher Ludwig Wittgenstein. There was the same almost paralysing 'absoluteness' in the demands he made upon his work, the same withdrawn character, and in his own sphere the same fear that the pursuit of authenticity may have become 'too difficult'. He also shared Leverkühn's mathematical inspiration and not

S

3

Thomas Mann's *Doctor Faustus* is the tragic parody of the first Frankfurt Faustbook of 1587. What is the fundamental point of the parodistic transformation? The ancient Faustus bought licentious freedom of the spirit from the Devil, to use it against the authentic order of his age. Adrian Leverkühn seeks, helped by the 'magic words, figures, characters and conjurations' of the Devil and his music, to recover that which is 'objective, binding and compelling', so that he might be delivered from the frustrations of the 'mildew' freedom and be given the sense of an authentic spiritual order. It seems to be the wheel of Ixion turned full circle. Not so long after the first Faustbook the theologians had to think of ways to accommodate Dr. Faustus's irresistible urge, and decided to give their blessing to his researches. With Thomas Mann's *Doctor Faustus* we have entered a world which, in one form or another, craves again for theological rigour; but alas, the only true *religiosus* to be found in Leverkühn's world is Satan, as already Thomas Mann's model knew, Dostoevsky's Devil, who said to Ivan Karamazov: 'It's reactionary to believe in God in our day, but I am the Devil, so I may be believed in.' [22] Is Adrian surprised that he, the 'Great Adversary', speaks of religion and mystic passion? Who else, the Devil answers, 'is to speak of it today? Surely not the liberal theologian! After all, I am by now the sole custodian of the theological side of existence.' [23] And he has much to offer.

Consciously to submit to the discipline of abstract form and absolute order is one thing; it is quite another to fill it with the life of the soul, to give it that which Serenus in his comments on Adrian's Perotinus Magnus signature suspected it could never possess: genuineness, authenticity, and the sanction of the human heart. Adrian himself once remarked that the man who succeeded in 'breaking through' from intellectual coldness

a little of his grasp of music. The similarity has always struck me as the more significant as it is purely accidental. For Thomas Mann is unlikely to have had any knowledge of either the man or his philosophy.

of construction into new adventures of the passions would be
'the saviour of art'.[24]   It is this break-through which the Devil
offers, and which is accomplished in Leverkühn's later music.
Already his '*Apocalipsis cum figuris*' showed unmistakable signs
of it.   Although Zeitblom accused it of both barbarism and
bloodless intellectualism, there are passages in it of which he
says that they sound 'like a fervid prayer for the granting of a
soul', and which 'could bring tears to the eyes of a man more
callous than I'.   But the power to whom this prayer is directed
and who is ready to answer it is unambiguously announced; for
'the work is dominated by the paradox . . . that in it dissonance
stands for everything sublime, solemn and dedicated, everything
that is of the spirit; while consonance and firm tonality are
reserved for the world of Hell'.[25]   The ultimate triumph, however, is '*D. Fausti Weheklag*', the Lamentation of Doctor
Faustus, which is the first Faustbook set to music.   Only here is
the seemingly impossible achieved.   Of this composition it is
said that it adheres to the very strictest form, indeed that in it
order becomes so absolute and 'totalitarian' that the mere suggestion of a fugue would be absurd: 'there is no longer one free
note'.   Yet every trace of 'parody' has gone.   The Devil has
done his work and granted a soul.   The deepest feeling has
found authentic expression.   For just because the material is so
utterly organized, the composer can afford to surrender to the
utmost 'subjectivity' without the slightest fear lest he should
break the form—a fear that would inhibit him if he worked
within a less unbreakable framework.   Thus it happens that
this technically most rigid work, a work calculated to the last
detail, is at the same time purest self-expression; and what it
expresses is 'the ultimate sorrow', 'the final despair'.

Yet it *is* self-expression, albeit on the margin of silence; and
it is only in the composer's own musical defiance of the Devil's
words spoken to Faustus in his last hour—'Be silent, suffer and
abstain, of thy ill lot to none complayne'—that a faint echo of
the old cynically-parodistic manner can still be perceived.   For
the rest, this music is so pure that it inspires Zeitblom with the
courage to ask whether the great 'artistic parodox'—the paradox

of an extreme of calculation and construction issuing in an extreme of agony expressed—might not have its correspondence in a religious paradox: 'that out of irremediable desperation might rise (though utterable only in the lowest whisper) a vestige of hope.   It would be the hope beyond hopelessness, the transcendence of despair—not its betrayal, but the miracle that passes belief.' [26]

4

Greater still than Zeitblom's courage is Thomas Mann's.   For he has dared invent not only the composer who only just succeeds in defying the command of silence, but also the loquacious man who does not quite succeed in telling his story, even if he could hardly be more successful in telling the music (and is, in fact, so unbelievably successful that the question has been asked what prevented Thomas Mann from composing it himself).   As a work of literature, *Doctor Faustus* is the defeat of the critic, and this in an incomparably more radical sense than Schlegel had in mind when he said the same of *Wilhelm Meister*.   Much has been said about the work by way of commentary and exposition, and not least by Thomas Mann himself, who wrote a book about writing *Doctor Faustus*.   We know by now the model 'in real life' for almost every character in the book (and the time may not be too far off when innocent researchers will set about discovering the true identity of true identities—'I know who Schildknapp is, but who is Bruno Walter?').   We can follow Adrian's movements on a map of Germany, know that his birthplace, Kaisersaschern, is a synthetic town made up of Thomas Mann's Lübeck and Nietzsche's Naumburg, and I am sure I have been to Pfeiffering although its name comes from the first Faustbook. The sources of most borrowings of text and incident are by now familiar, and Schönberg even insisted on being named as the true author of certain musical ideas, jealously claiming his property back from the Devil himself.   But such entertaining interpreters' trifles apart, the novel is a fortress against criticism.

Doctor Faustus is, to quote Friedrich Schlegel once more and for the last time, its own critique, and that in the most thorough-going manner imaginable. There is no critical thought which the book does not think *about itself*. With its theme that 'art has become too difficult', it has made criticism either too easy or impossible, and manœuvred the critic into a position where he is bound to plagiarize the object of his critique. If the book is tragic parody, Thomas Mann has seen to it that the Devil has the last word about the possible happiness or greatness afforded by the genre. If it is a novel, it has ostensibly been written by a man who has no thought of writing one, and time and again complains about the inadequacies of his talent for even writing a biography. And indeed, the literary device of the fictitious narrator has in its long history never had weightier implications. For by letting Serenus, the humanist and pedagogue, tell the demonic tale, Thomas Mann declares that the subject is out of all proportion to the traditional means of literary communication. Serenus Zeitblom is the novelist's offer of abdication, the *nom de plume* of silence. The following is what the *nom de plume* says about one of Adrian Leverkühn's compositions:

> Admiration and sadness mingled strangely as I contemplated this music. 'How beautiful', my heart said, and 'how sad'. For here was an ingenious and melancholy *tour de force*, an intellectual achievement which deserved to be called heroic, something which escaped disaster by the skin of its teeth, and yet conducted itself with parodistic exuberance. I know not how otherwise to characterize it than by calling it a tense, sustained, neck-breaking performance, played on the verge of impossibility.[27]

Somewhere between this and the tragic consolation 'that man has at least been given a voice to speak his anguish' lies, in all probability, the place reserved in the canon of literature for *Doctor Faustus*, Thomas Mann's eloquent compromise with silence, a work which is stupendous if not great.

5

At the time of *Doctor Faustus* Thomas Mann entered in his diary a number of observations which have no obvious connection with the work in hand. They seem related more to his reading than to his writing. He quotes, for instance, what Sainte-Beuve admiringly said about Molière: that he was one of the few great writers who had the good fortune to live and work 'between a Homeric and an Alexandrian epoch', who were 'still "naïve" and yet already sophisticated', and thus surpassed even the greatest among less fortunate artists in abundance of inspiration and grace of spirit. Was Goethe among the exceptionally favoured ones? Thomas Mann asks; and without debating a judgment which is blind to at least two-thirds of Goethe's genius, he simply notes that Sainte-Beuve called him 'the Talleyrand of literature', calculating in his detachment and icy in his impartiality. Such 'critical *raffinements*', Sainte-Beuve added, were as yet unknown to the age of Molière. Immediately after this Thomas Mann puts down what St. John-Perse said about Voltaire's *Charles XII*: 'extraordinary but not great'; and himself comments: 'A remarkable distinction.' This again is followed by a quotation from Jacob Burckhardt, who observed that in Voltaire 'rationalism had become poetic, indeed magic'. And finally there comes Kierkegaard's definition of humour as the attitude of mind that cannot help 'thinking of God always in juxtaposition to something else, something contradictory to the idea of God', a mind which thus becomes the meeting-place for all the paradoxical exchanges between the divine and the profane, and, while perceiving the paradox with wit and profundity, is 'without any religious passion of its own'.[28]

From all we have said about Thomas Mann it will be clear that these apparently arbitrary diary entries are manifestly related to his own literary existence, and above all to his later works, *Joseph and his Brothers* and *Doctor Faustus*. They form in fact an extraordinarily fitting summing-up of his self-questioning as well as of his hopes. The 'critical *raffinements*', however, find at last their completely unproblematical home in the comic novel *Felix Krull*. 'I was not destined to return to it', Thomas Mann wrote in 1936, introducing the English collection of his *Stories of Three Decades*, a volume which contains the short fragment of *Felix Krull* as he left it in 1911; and although he had added a little since then, it was not until after *Doctor Faustus* that he went back to it with the confidence that it was, after all, his destiny to write it. In 1911 he had forsaken it for *Death in Venice* because, he said, he could not 'hold that note for too long without relief', a remark which is echoed in *Doctor Faustus* when Adrian interrupts the composition of his comic opera *Love's Labour's Lost* because 'the parodistic artificiality of the style was hard to keep up'.[29] Ample relief, however, was granted to Thomas Mann: all his major works, with the exception of *Buddenbrooks* and *Tonio Kröger*, came into being while Felix Krull waited for more than forty years, until at last a substantial part of his life saw the light of day. It is difficult to realize that its author was almost eighty when he finished these 'Memoirs Part I'. For what he said of the first fragment is certainly not less true of the whole volume: that he wrote it 'with such zest that I was not surprised to have many excellent judges pronounce it the best and happiest thing I had done'.[30] And when in 1943, after the completion of the *Joseph* tetralogy and before embarking on *Doctor Faustus*—a work he contemplated with deep anxiety—it was suggested to him that he should take up *Felix Krull* again, the idea appealed to him, as a diary note says, 'mainly because it would round off the unity of my life. . . . To continue after thirty-two years where I left off before *Death in Venice*, this had an attraction of its own. Everything I did in between might be seen then as a mere break, claiming a whole life-time, in the enterprise of a man of thirty-six.' [31]

When finally he decided to continue the story of the rogue and adventurer, he began on the very page where the old manuscript broke off, without changing a word of what had been written before. Considering the damage which might have been done to the original fabric by the wear and tear of the years between 1911 and 1954, this is likely to remain one of the most astonishing cases of invisible mending recorded in the history of literature. Stylistic analysis will no doubt one day manage to perceive the imperceptible seam which joins the handiwork of the old hand to the weaving of the younger, but perhaps the matter should be left to the Marquise de Venosta née de Plettenberg in the novel itself, who becomes the victim of an exquisite epistolary fake of Felix Krull's and writes to him in the unsuspecting belief that he is her son: 'Your handwriting, my dear Loulou, always left much to be desired and is now as ever not without its mannerisms, but your style has decidedly gained in elegance and polish. . . .'[32]

Perhaps it is homage to the homeland of the genre to which this novel belongs—or rather, which it parodies, for it parodies everything which it touches, including of course the pen of its author—that its concluding scenes are set in the Iberian peninsula. For one of Felix Krull's literary ancestors is undoubtedly Matéo Aleman's *Guzman de Alfarache*, Picaro, the rogue who gave the genre its name, and still further back in time Juan Ruiz, the author of *Libro de buen amor*, of whom it is said that he launched the career of the outlawed sensibility, of the aesthetic criminal, and who shared with Felix Krull the inspiration provided by the quietude of the prison cell. Neither is it difficult to detect some of the scattered legacy of Don Juan in Krull's possession. It was, however, German literature which, in the seventeenth century, produced a unique fusion of the picaresque with the spiritual, of the *Schelmenroman* with elements which were later to make up the *Bildungsroman*: Grimmelshausen's *Der abenteuerliche Simplizissimus*. As the legitimate literary offspring of the Thirty Years' War this great work reflects the temper of the epoch, that tohu-bohu of coarseness and sophistication, licentiousness and piety, violence and formality, and finally reveals the formative powers of the spirit set free by the very dissoluteness of the soul.

We need only transfer this theme from the battlefields, castles, and hermitages of the seventeenth century to the borderland between bourgeois ethics and decadence, and we have brought it within the magnetic field of Thomas Mann's imagination. Simplex is the name of Grimmelshausen's immortal rogue; and the 'simple' young man who received his education on the Magic Mountain possessed not a little of that 'Hermetic' roguishness (*Schalkhaftigkeit*) of which Joseph is an all but divine, and Felix Krull an exceedingly mundane, incarnation. Indeed, in the end it may have been the secret and, as he would have it, mysteriously guided ambition of Thomas Mann's *imitatio mystica* to include in its examples the literature of the sixteenth and seventeenth centuries, and thus to leave behind a body of work which could truly claim to be the parodistic résumé of German literary history. This would certainly not be surprising and might even be found to lie in the nature of things: in the nature of that age in which, time and again, affinities have been discovered to our own, as well as in the nature of Thomas Mann's style which, as time went on, became increasingly 'baroque' in more than the superficial sense of the word. For there are not only the ever richer and more daring convolutions of verbal architecture (which in *Doctor Faustus* belie the narrator's ostensibly classical education) but also the incessant alternations between pathos and laughter, pity and mockery, the tragic and the grotesque—in fact, enough to justify Pharaoh's exclamation, showing the true appreciation of a literary historian for the story Joseph has told him about his father and how he stole Esau's blessing: 'What a baroque tale! It calls for mirth and pity, both at once!' [33]

We have seen how much of the mystical theology of the *Cherubinischer Wandersmann* has gone, consciously or not, into the story of Abraham's discovering God, and we may add here that the only noticeable precursors Thomas Mann has had as the author of *Joseph and his Brothers* were writers of the seventeenth century. It was in keeping with the preoccupations of the time that the theological, political, and erotic possibilities of the biblical story should have appealed to the literature of the period.* More perhaps to our present point are the

---

* The story was treated in Grimmelshausen's *Historie vom Keuschen*

numerous similarities of incident between Grimmelshausen's *Simplizissimus* and Thomas Mann's *Felix Krull*.   There is, for instance, the serious erotic confusion involving both sexes, one caused by Simplex with his *'glatter Spiegel'* and *'gerader Leib'*, the other by Krull with his *'hübsches Frätzchen'*; or their temporary elevation into the ranks of the aristocracy; or the audiences with kings, much relished by either rogue; or Simplex's playing, in one episode, the part of Hermes, that 'elegant deity' in whose role Felix is cast with the same sustained allusiveness as the Egyptian Joseph.   And there are, above all, the remarkable, and remarkably similar, performances of passionate dexterity given by two French ladies who attach themselves with astounding speed and literalness to the respective and responsive heroes; or more strikingly still, the initiation of both Simplex and Felix into cosmic mysteries, their journeys to the centre of the earth or the beginning of all things —the popular sixteenth- and seventeenth-century device, in fact, of quasi-scientific phantasmagoria, of 'science fiction', which Thomas Mann had used before with Father Leverkühn's 'speculating the elements' or (in direct imitation of the ancient manner) with Adrian's imaginary explorations of the deep sea and cosmic space.[34]   Yet all this is not a matter of 'influence'. *Felix Krull* simply quotes *Simplizissimus*, either with conscious parodistic intent or unconsciously prompted by the spirit of the genre.   And after the great *Bildungsromane* with the roguish heroes, *The Magic Mountain* and *Joseph*, it was at no time improbable that through Thomas Mann this favourite German type of novel, which after Grimmelshausen had emancipated itself from the picaresque, would one day be re-united with it in a parody embracing both species.

Joseph in Aegypten, in Herzog von Braunschweig's *Syrerin Aramena*, and in Philipp Zesen's *Assenat*.   There is work here for the literary detective, whose future entertainments we do not wish to anticipate, but he may be pleased to learn that, to pick two examples, Zesen's Assenat appears in the same baroque setting of ponds and flowers as Thomas Mann's Asnath, and that the motif of her abduction is also used by both authors.

6

Thomas Mann's works have at least this much in common
with Goethe's that they form 'a great confession'. They are
autobiographical, although it would be wrong to think that
all the characters and incidents in them can be traced back
to persons and events in his life. The 'autobiography' is of
a subtler kind: his literary imagination is inextricably bound
up with self-critique, indeed *is* self-critique exercised with
creative freedom. His diary, for instance, contains a brief
discourse on a question asked by the first readers of the manuscript of *Doctor Faustus*; it is one of the many passages in
both the book and the diary which are the frustration of the
critic: why would he not 'show' more of Adrian's personality
(of whom he says in the same place that he never loved a
creature of his imagination as much as him, with the exception,
perhaps, of Hanno Buddenbrook), why would he not make
him more 'alive' after the convention of fiction? If Zeitblom
had to remain almost entirely a 'kindly heart and tremblingly
writing hand', why should Adrian not become more 'recognizable'? Thomas Mann's answer is: 'How easy that would
have been, and yet how impermissible—in a sense never experienced before!' It was a taboo, the taboo of the symbol,
and any transgression of it would have exposed him to
the danger of banality. Nothing could be done about it:
'the peripheral figures of the novel, all these Schildknapps,
Schwerdtfergers, Roddes, Schlaginhaufens, etc. etc., might be
given the usual life of fiction, but *not* the two protagonists.
These had too much to hide, namely the secret of their identity.' [35] The cryptic remark does not, of course, mean that
Leverkühn and Zeitblom are the same, except in the sense
that they represent the 'two identities' of their author.

To write Thomas Mann's 'Life' will probably always mean
to write about his writing. For with him, living and writing
were all but identical activities. This gives to his work its
more than common unity, that unity which he thought *Felix
Krull* would 'round off'. There is not only the unmistakable

idiom, the manner of speech, tone and gesture, identifiable in every line, but also the dominant position of identical themes in volume after volume. Yet there is no monotony (the risk of monotony lies not in the reading but in its discussion—and in the case of *Felix Krull* we shall for once not take it). For Thomas Mann's identical themes were not simply ideas he once had and to which thereafter he clung. They were, in fact, the articulate form of a mind which grew with and within their ever subtler and more complex variations. This is why almost every successive work not only adds to the illumination of his previous writings, but reveals them as actually bigger than they seemed when they first appeared; and for the inevitability of those themes there can hardly be surer evidence than their career, which began in the shadow of pessimism, culminated in myth and tragedy, and ended with the blessings of the comic muse. A great religious thinker once said: 'To shorten the sleep of the night, and jealously to watch over every hour of the day, and not to spare oneself, and then to comprehend that everything was in jest—this indeed is seriousness.' Kierkegaard's words are not altogether inappropriate to Thomas Mann's life.

The most serious concern of Thomas Mann had undoubtedly been the problem of art, and in *Doctor Faustus* we saw how it was raised to a level where it became identified with the problem of civilization. And this is what intrinsically it has always been. All the questions which Thomas Mann has asked about art are questions about civilized existence itself. Of *Felix Krull* he said, at a time when only a fragment existed, that it was 'in essence the story of an artist',[36] and so this novel was bound to become, after *Doctor Faustus*, the comedy of genius, the farce of unauthentic living—the great parody of civilization itself. This story of a charming charlatan who, like the poet of whom Keats speaks, has no 'identical nature', and to whom 'poetry comes easily' by virtue of his 'delicately balanced existence', is made of the stuff of which most great comic creations are made: a grave affliction of the soul resolved in laughter, a laughter which reverberates with many echoes of the writer's anxious passage through a melancholy age. No interpretation can do justice to the comic profundity of the book. It encompasses in its vast parodistic scope every theme we have discussed. To point them out would not only be repetitive: it would be false. For it is one definition of the comic that it puts an end to the debate. If it does not, then it fails in being what it is meant to be: the human spirit's one and only self-inflicted defeat that is almost indistinguishable from victory. Or in other words: the relief from tragedy. Thomas Mann found it with *Felix Krull*, the laughing farewell of a great artist, one of the few writers who, by giving valid form to the chaotic mind of this century, will have helped it to be remembered with at least a measure of friendliness and respect.

Bibliography

THE following list gives Thomas Mann's principal works as they were originally published, except where otherwise stated, by S. Fischer Verlag (for some time Bermann-Fischer Verlag), whose varying domiciles—Berlin, Vienna, Stockholm, Frankfurt-am-Main—reflect, like the works themselves, the recent upheavals in the history of Europe. This is followed by the titles of works and collections as they are most easily available now in German: the individual volumes of the 'Stockholmer Gesamtausgabe der Werke von Thomas Mann', again published by S. Fischer Verlag, begun in Stockholm, and continued in Frankfurt-am-Main. In the third section the reader will find the available English translations. Their publishers are Messrs. Martin Secker and Warburg Ltd., London, and Alfred Knopf Inc., New York.

The editions which are quoted in my text are marked by asterisks.

The list does not claim to be complete. The occasional contributions to journals which have not yet been included in any of the collected volumes are omitted. For bibliographical completeness, and above all for the enormous mass of literature about Thomas Mann, the student of his works is referred to the most recent bibliography, *Fifty Years of Thomas Mann Studies*, by Klaus W. Jonas, University of Minnesota Press, Minneapolis, 1955.

FIRST EDITIONS IN GERMAN:

Der kleine Herr Friedemann, tales, 1898; *Buddenbrooks*, novel, 1901; *Tristan* (contains *Tonio Kröger*), 1903; *Fiorenza*, drama, 1905; *Königliche Hoheit*, novel, 1909; *Der Tod in Venedig*, short novel, 1913; *Das Wunderkind*, tales, 1914; *Friedrich und die Grosse Koalition*, essay, 1915; *Betrachtungen eines Unpolitischen*, autobiographical reflections, 1918; *Herr und Hund*, idyll, 1919; *Wälsungenblut*, tale, Munich, Phanatasus Verlag, 1921; *Bekenntnisse des Hochstaplers Felix Krull*, fragment of a novel, Vienna, Rikola Verlag, 1922, and Amsterdam, Querido Verlag, 1948; *Bemühungen,** essays, 1922; *Rede und Antwort,** essays, 1922; *Der Zauberberg*, novel, 1924; *Unordnung und frühes Leid*, short novel, 1926; *Kino*, fragment of a novel, Gera, Friedrich Blau & Co., 1926; *Pariser Rechenschaft*, travelogue, 1926; *Deutsche Ansprache*, address, 1930; *Die Forderung des Tages*, essays, 1930; *Mario und der Zauberer*, short novel, 1930; *Goethe als Repräsentant des bürgerlichen Zeitalters*, lecture, 1932; *Joseph und seine Brüder*, novel in four volumes: *Die Geschichten Jaakobs*, 1933, *Der junge Joseph*, 1934, *Joseph in Aegypten*, 1936, *Joseph der Ernährer*, 1943; *Leiden und Grösse der Meister*, essays, 1935; *Freud und die Zukunft*, lecture, 1936; *Ein Briefwechsel*, exchange of letters, Zürich, Dr. Oprecht & Helbling A.G., 1937; *Schopenhauer*, essay, 1938; *Achtung, Europa!* manifesto, 1938; *Das Problem der Freiheit*, essay, 1939; *Lotte in Weimar*, novel, 1939; *Die vertauschten Köpfe*, short novel, 1940; *Deutsche Hörer*, broadcasts, 1942; *Das Gesetz*, short novel, 1944; *Doktor Faustus: Das Leben des deutschen Tonsetzers Adrian Leverkühn, erzählt von einem Freunde*, novel, 1947; *Neue Studien*, essays, 1948; *Die Entstehung des 'Doktor Faustus': Roman eines Romans*,* reflections and diary notes on the writing of *Doctor Faustus*, 1949; *Meine Zeit*,* address, 1950; *Der Erwählte*, novel, 1951; *Die Betrogene*, short novel, 1953; *Altes und Neues*,* essays, 1953; *Bekenntnisse des Hochstaplers Felix Krull: Der Memoiren erster Teil*, novel, 1954; *Versuch über Schiller*, essay, 1955; *Nachlese: Prosa 1951–1955*,* essays, 1956.

Available in the 'Stockholmer Gesamtausgabe':

Buddenbrooks, Königliche Hoheit, Der Zauberberg, Joseph und seine Brüder (the four novels in two volumes), *Lotte in Weimar, Doktor Faustus, Die Entstehung des 'Doktor Faustus', Der Erwählte, Bekenntnisse des Hochstaplers Felix Krull, Ausgewählte Erzählungen, Betrachtungen eines Unpolitischen*,* *Adel des Geistes*, essays, *Altes und Neues*,* *Nachlese: Prosa 1951–1955.**

English Translations:

(unless otherwise stated, the translator is Mrs. H. T. Lowe-Porter)

Novels and separately published Stories

Royal Highness,* trans. by A. Cecil Curtis, 1916; *Buddenbrooks*,* 1924; *Death in Venice*, trans. by Kenneth Burke, 1925; *The Magic Mountain*,* 1927; *Early Sorrow* and *Mario and the Magician*, 1934; *The Tales of Jacob*, 1934; *Young Joseph*, 1935; *Joseph in Egypt*, 1938; *Joseph the Provider*, 1944; *Lotte in Weimar*—*The Beloved Returns*,*

1940; *The Transposed Heads*, 1941; *The Tables of the Law*, 1945; *Doctor Faustus*,* 1948; *The Holy Sinner*, 1951; *The Black Swan*, trans. by Willard R. Trask, 1954; *Confessions of Felix Krull*,* trans. by Denver Lindley, 1955; *Joseph and his Brothers** (the four novels in one volume), 1956.

Collections of Stories

Children and Fools, trans. by H. G. Scheffauer, 1928; *Stories of Three Decades*,* 1936 (contains *Little Herr Friedemann*, 1897—*Disillusionment*, 1896—*The Dilettante*, 1897—*Tobias Mindernickel*, 1897—*Little Lizzy*, 1897—*The Wardrobe*, 1899—*The Way to the Churchyard*, 1901—*Tonio Kröger*, 1903—*Tristan*, 1902—*The Hungry*, 1902—*The Infant Prodigy*, 1903—*Gladius Dei*, 1902—*Fiorenza*, 1904—*A Gleam*, 1904—*At the Prophet's*, 1904—*A Weary Hour*, 1905—*The Blood of the Walsungs*, 1905—*Railway Accident*, 1907—*The Fight between Jappe and Do Escobar*, 1911—*Felix Krull*, Fragment, 1911—*Death in Venice*, 1911—*A Man and his Dog*, 1918—*Disorder and Early Sorrow*, 1925—*Mario and the Magician*, 1929).

Collections of Essays

Three Essays, 1932 (contains 'Goethe and Tolstoy', 1923—'Frederick the Great', 1915—'An Experience in the Occult', 1924); *Past Masters and Other Papers*, 1933; *Order of the Day*, trans. by H. T. Lowe-Porter, Eric Sutton, and Agnes E. Meyer, 1943; *Essays of Three Decades*,* 1947 (contains 'Goethe's *Faust*', 1938—'Goethe's Career as a Man of Letters', 1932—'Goethe as Representative of the Bourgeois Age', 1932—'*Anna Karenina*', 1939—'Lessing', 1929—'Kleist's *Amphitryon*', 1926—'Chamisso', 1911—'Platen', 1930—'Theodor Storm', 1930—'The Old Fontane', 1910—'Sufferings and Greatness of Richard Wagner', 1933—'Richard Wagner and the *Ring*', 1937—'Schopenhauer', 1938—'Freud and the Future', 1936—'Voyage with Don Quixote', 1934); *Last Essays*, in preparation, trans. by Richard Winston and James Stern—critical appreciations of Schiller, Goethe, Nietzsche, and Chekhov.

References

EXCEPT for quotations from Thomas Mann, the editions of works to which my text refers are specified. Translations are my own.

Thomas Mann I have quoted either from the original German in my own translation or, whenever possible, from published English translations, which frequently I have adjusted to suit my own taste or the nuance of meaning required by my context. Only the titles of the quoted works are given below; the particular editions are marked by asterisks in the Bibliography.

I. INTRODUCTION: A TRIBUTE

1. *Joseph and his Brothers*, p. 30.
2. *Stories of Three Decades*, pp. 106–7.
3. *Joseph and his Brothers*, p. 937.
4. Hugo von Hofmannsthal, *Gesammelte Werke, Prosa II*, Frankfurt-am-Main, 1951, pp. 12 ff.
5. Franz Kafka, *Beschreibung eines Kampfes*, New York, 1936, p. 44.
6. *Die Entstehung des 'Doktor Faustus'*, p. 83.
7. *Altes und Neues*, p. 297.
8. *Doktor Faustus*, pp. 55–6.
9. *Betrachtungen eines Unpolitischen*, p. 529.
10. *Stories of Three Decades*, p. 132.

II. PESSIMISM AND SENSIBILITY

1. Schopenhauer's *Sämmtliche Werke* in 5 Bänden, Grossherzog Wilhelm Ernst Ausgabe, Leipzig, I, pp. 537–8.
2. *Dichtung und Wahrheit*, Part I, Book IV (Goethe's *Sämmtliche Werke*, Jubiläums-Ausgabe, Stuttgart, XXII, p. 165), slightly misquoted by Thomas Mann in *Neue Studien*, p. 164.
3. *Doctor Faustus*, p. 478.
4. 'Lebensabriss', in *Die Neue Rundschau*, 1930, pp. 472–3.
5. *Betrachtungen eines Unpolitischen*, p. 81.
6. *Oeuvres complètes de Gustave Flaubert, Correspondance*, Paris, 1926, 54, V, p. 260.
7. *Buddenbrooks*, p. 250.
8. Ibid., p. 425.
9. Ibid., p. 598.
10. Ibid., p. 551.
11. Ibid., p. 139.
12. Ibid., p. 120.

13. *Betrachtungen eines Unpolitischen*, p. 130.
14. Georg Lukacs, *Thomas Mann*, Berlin, 1949, p. 18.
15. Schopenhauer, op. cit., II, p. 877.
16. *Buddenbrooks*, pp. 389 ff.
17. Schopenhauer, op. cit., I, p. 259.
18. *Buddenbrooks*, p. 6.
19. Ibid., p. 15.
20. Ibid., p. 22.
21. Schopenhauer, op. cit., II, p. 1373.
22. *Buddenbrooks*, pp. 37–8.
23. Ibid., pp. 177–81.
24. Schopenhauer, op. cit., II, p. 798.
25. *Buddenbrooks*, p. 303.
26. Ibid., p. 307.
27. Schopenhauer, op. cit., II, p. 1261.
28. Ibid., p. 1266.
29. *Buddenbrooks*, p. 9.
30. Cf. Schopenhauer, op. cit., II, pp. 1118–19, and Nietzsche, *Gesammelte Werke*, Musarionausgabe, Munich, 1926, XVIII, pp. 32 ff.
31. *Buddenbrooks*, p. 264.
32. *Stories of Three Decades*, p. 107.
33. Cf. Schopenhauer, op. cit., I, pp. 237 ff. (the chapter entitled: 'The Platonic Idea: the Object of Art').
34. Nietzsche, op. cit., III, p. 46.
35. Ibid, XIX, p. 229.
36. *Buddenbrooks*, p. 468.
37. Ibid., p. 227.
38. Ibid., pp. 524–7. Cf. also Schopenhauer, op. cit., II, pp. 1258 ff.
39. *Stories of Three Decades*, p. 132.
40. *Betrachtungen eines Unpolitischen*, p. 83.
41. *Buddenbrooks*, pp. 535–6.
42. Ibid., p. 597.
43. Ibid., p. 593.
44. Ibid., p. 408.
45. Ibid., p. 334.
46. *Betrachtungen eines Unpolitischen*, p. 82.

III. THE EMBARRASSED MUSE

1. Letters published for the first time in Alfred Kantorowicz, *Heinrich und Thomas Mann*, Berlin, 1956, pp. 64, 66, 70, 71, 72.
2. *Die Neue Rundschau*, 1930, p. 739.
3. *Stories of Three Decades*, p. 130.
4. Ibid., p. 86.
5. Ibid., p. 100.
6. Ibid., p. 110.
7. Ibid., p. 118.

8. Ibid., p. 131.
9. Ibid., p. 132.
10. Ibid., pp. 92 and 132.
11. *Betrachtungen eines Unpolitischen*, p. 61.
12. *Stories of Three Decades*, p. 98.
13. Ibid., pp. 110–11.
14. Ibid., p. 104.
15. Ibid., p. 103.
16. Ibid., pp. 106–7.
17. Ibid., p. 109.
18. Nietzsche, op. cit., XV, p. 90.
19. Schopenhauer, op. cit., I, pp. 256–7.
20. Goethe, op. cit., XXXVII, pp. 102–5.
21. Hegel, *Werke*, Berlin, 1835, X_3, p. 243, and X_2, p. 16.
22. Ibid., II, p. 529.
23. Schopenhauer, op. cit., I, p. 359.
24. Nietzsche, op. cit., III, 45.
25. Ibid., XV, 375–6.
26. *Stories of Three Decades*, p. 104.
27. Nietzsche, op. cit., XV, p. 376.
28. *Stories of Three Decades*, p. 107.
29. T. S. Eliot, *Selected Essays*, London, 1948, pp. 17–20.
30. Martin Heidegger, *Holzwege*, Frankfurt-am-Main, 1950, p. 29.
31. Quoted by Alfred Kantorowicz, op. cit., p. 81. Cf. *Betrachtungen eines Unpolitischen*, pp. 62–3.
32. *Stories of Three Decades*, p. 212.
33. Kantorowicz, op. cit., p. 61.
34. Ibid., p. 81.
35. *Rede und Antwort*, p. 348.
36. *Betrachtungen eines Unpolitischen*, p. 65.
37. *Stories of Three Decades*, p. 268.
38. Ibid., p. 269.
39. Ibid., pp. 238–40.
40. Ibid., p. 255.
41. Nietzsche, op. cit., XV, p. 371.
42. Ibid., p. 404.
43. *Stories of Three Decades*, p. 266.
44. Nietzsche, op. cit., XV, pp. 243–4.
45. Ibid., p. 246.
46. Ibid., p. 248.
47. *Stories of Three Decades*, p. 270.
48. Ibid., p. 266.
49. *Altes und Neues*, pp. 627–8.
50. *Stories of Three Decades*, pp. 270–1.
51. Nietzsche, op. cit., XV, p. 371.
52. *Stories of Three Decades*, p. 272.

53. *Essays of Three Decades,* p. 413.
54. *Betrachtungen eines Unpolitischen,* pp. 191–2.
55. Ibid., pp. 104 and 105.
56. *Royal Highness,* pp. 197–8.
57. Ibid., pp. 158–9.
58. *Betrachtungen eines Unpolitischen,* p. 69.
59. *Stories of Three Decades,* pp. 384–5. Cf. *Die Entstehung des 'Doktor Faustus',* p. 21, and *Altes und Neues,* pp. 38 ff.
60. Ibid., p. 386.
61. Ibid., pp. 378–9.
62. Ibid., p. 379.
63. Ibid., p. 380.
64. Ibid., p. 389.
65. Ibid., p. 389–90.
66. Nietzsche, op. cit., XXV, p. 205.
67. *Stories of Three Decades,* pp. 393–5.
68. Ibid., pp. 396–403.
69. Ibid., p. 434.
70. Ibid., pp. 405–9.
71. Ibid., p. 413.
72. Ibid., pp. 417–18.
73. Ibid., p. 412.
74. Ibid., pp. 424–5.
75. Ibid., p. 427.
76. Ibid., pp. 429–35, and p. 386.
77. *Kritik der Urteilskraft,* I, §§ 5 and 6. (Immanuel Kant, *Sämmtliche Werke* in 6 Bänden, Leipzig, 1921, VI, pp. 60–3.)
78. Nietzsche, op. cit., XV, p. 379.

IV. THE CONSERVATIVE IMAGINATION

1. *Stories of Three Decades,* p. 382; cf. also letter to Heinrich Mann, 26 January 1910, published in Kantorowicz, op. cit., p. 87.
2. Heinrich Mann, *Macht und Mensch,* Munich, 1919.
3. *Betrachtungen eines Unpolitischen,* p. 4.
4. Ibid., p. 10.
5. *Stories of Three Decades,* pp. 384–5.
6. *Altes und Neues,* pp. 97–101.
7. Ibid., p. 82.
8. Heinrich Mann, *Macht und Mensch,* Munich, 1919, p. 94.
9. *Altes und Neues,* p. 101.
10. *Betrachtungen eines Unpolitischen,* p. 181, and Heinrich Mann, op. cit., p. 94.
11. Lionel Trilling, *The Liberal Imagination,* London, 1951, pp. 98 and 81. Cf. William Hazlitt, *The Complete Works,* ed. P. P. Howe, London, 1930, IV, p. 214 (on *Coriolanus*).

12. *Betrachtungen eines Unpolitischen*, p. 507.
13. Ibid., p. 522.
14. Ibid., pp. 94–7.
15. Letter to Richard Woodhouse, 27 October 1818.
16. *Betrachtungen eines Unpolitischen*, p. 101, cf. *Stories of Three Decades*, p. 154.
17. Ibid., pp. 536–7.
18. Quoted from the German *Gesammelte Werke*, Jena, 1922, XII, p. 93.
19. *Betrachtungen eines Unpolitischen*, pp. 215–22.
20. Kierkegaard, op. cit., VII, p. 3.
21. *Betrachtungen eines Unpolitischen*, p. 505. Cf. Nietzsche, op. cit., XVII, p. 259.
22. Kierkegaard, op. cit., VII, p. 18.
23. Ibid., p. 177.
24. *Betrachtungen eines Unpolitischen*, p. 251.
25. Kierkegaard, op. cit., VII, p. 23.
26. *Betrachtungen eines Unpolitischen*, p. 527.
27. Ibid., p. 7.
28. Ibid., p. 125.
29. Schopenhauer, op. cit., III, pp. 569–70.
30. *Betrachtungen eines Unpolitischen*, p. 436.
31. *The Magic Mountain*, p. 340. Cf. *Stories of Three Decades*, p. 293, and *Betrachtungen eines Unpolitischen*, p. 391.
32. *The Magic Mountain*, p. 382.
33. F. W. H. Myers, *Essays—Modern*, London, 1883, pp. 268–9.
34. *Betrachtungen eines Unpolitischen*, p. 526.
35. Ibid., p. 496.
36. Ibid., p. 526.
37. Ibid., p. 510.
38. Ibid., p. 136.
39. *The Magic Mountain*, p. 32.
40. Letter to his brother August Wilhelm, 1791.
41. Nietzsche, op. cit., III, p. 155.
42. Ibid., XV, p. 194.
43. *Zur Kritik der Hegelschen Rechtsphilosophie* (1844), Marx-Engels Gesamtausgabe, First Section, I (First Half-Volume), Frankfurt-am-Main, 1927, p. 612.
44. Nietzsche, op. cit., XII, p. 287.
45. Ibid., XV, pp. 199–200.
46. Schopenhauer, op. cit., I, p. 40, and Nietzsche, op. cit., IV, p. 175.
47. Nietzsche, op. cit., VIII, p. 4.
48. *Betrachtungen eines Unpolitischen*, pp. 106–7.
49. *The Magic Mountain*, pp. 25–6.
50. Ibid., pp. 20–2.
51. *Betrachtungen eines Unpolitischen*, pp. 25–6.
    T*

52. Special Thomas Mann number of *Die Neue Rundschau*, 6 June 1945, pp. 8–10.
53. *Die Neue Rundschau*, October 1945, p. 17.
54. *Essays of Three Decades*, pp. 305–6.
55. *Betrachtungen eines Unpolitischen*, pp. 71–4.
56. *Buddenbrooks*, p. 376.
57. *Betrachtungen eines Unpolitischen*, p. 32.
58. Ibid., p. 93.
59. Ibid., p. 208.
60. Ibid., p. 577.
61. *Joseph and his Brothers*, p. 1155.
62. Klaus Mann, *The Turning Point*, New York, 1942, p. 38.
63. Kantorowicz, op. cit., pp. 32–40 and 110–14.
64. *The Magic Mountain*, p. 373.
65. *Nachlese, Prosa 1951–1955*, p. 31.
66. Ibid., pp. 49–51.
67. Ibid., p. 32.
68. Ibid., pp. 45–6.
69. *Betrachtungen eines Unpolitischen*, pp. 91–2.
70. *The Magic Mountain*, p. 159.
71. Ibid., p. 539.
72. *Nachlese*, pp. 40–1.
73. Ibid., p. 55.

V. Conversation on the Magic Mountain

1. *Neue Studien*, pp. 101–2.
2. *Altes und Neues*, pp. 310–11, 678–9, and *Joseph and his Brothers* (Foreword to the edition in one volume), p. vi.
3. *Altes und Neues*, pp. 567 and 295.
4. *Essays of Three Decades*, p. 173.
5. *Die Entstehung des 'Doktor Faustus'*, p. 83.
6. Weigand, *Thomas Mann's Novel Der Zauberberg*, New York and London, 1933, p. 159.
7. *The Magic Mountain*, pp. 265–7.
8. Friedrich Schlegel, *Kritische Schriften*, ed. Wolfdietrich Rasch, Munich, 1956, p. 274.
9. *The Magic Mountain*, p. 511.
10. Ibid., pp. 251 ff.
11. Ibid., pp. 276 ff.
12. Schlegel, op. cit., p. 12.
13. Ibid., p. 270.
14. *The Magic Mountain*, p. 229.
15. Ibid., p. 183.
16. Ibid., p. 140.
17. Schlegel, op. cit., p. 37.
18. Novalis, *Fragments*, ed. Ernst Kamnitzer, Dresden, 1929, pp. 632–3.

19. Ibid., pp. 652–6.
20. *The Magic Mountain*, p. 192.
21. Schlegel, op. cit., pp. 270–1.
22. Ibid., p. 98.
23. *The Magic Mountain*, p. 478.
24. Ibid., pp. 480–1.
25. Ibid., p. 480.
26. Ibid., p. 154.
27. Ibid., p. 487.
28. Ibid., p. 486.
29. Ibid., p. 496.
30. Ibid., p. 200.
31. Ibid., p. 9.
32. Ibid., pp. 51–2.
33. Ibid., pp. 57–8.
34. Ibid., pp. 229–30.
35. Ibid., p. 32.
36. Ibid.
37. Ibid., p. 231.
38. Ibid., p. 283.
39. Cf. ibid., pp. 219 and 292.
40. Schlegel, op. cit., p. 311.
41. *The Magic Mountain*, p. 342.
42. Ibid., p. 97.
43. Novalis, op. cit., p. 345.
44. Nietzsche, op. cit., XIX, p. 220.
45. *The Magic Mountain*, p. 385.
46. Weigand, op. cit., p. 47.
47. *Betrachtungen eines Unpolitischen*, pp. 367 ff.
48. *The Magic Mountain*, pp. 119 ff.
49. Ibid., p. 489.
50. Ibid., pp. 596 and 511.
51. Ibid., pp. 229–30.
52. *Stories of Three Decades*, pp. 415–16.
53. Goethe, op. cit., XXXV, p. 319.
54. Novalis, op. cit., p. 738.
55. *The Magic Mountain*, p. 468.
56. Ibid., pp. 511–12.
57. Ibid., p. 651.
58. Ibid., pp. 490 ff.
59. Kierkegaard, op. cit., VII, p. 176.

VI. The Theology of Irony

1. Schlegel, op. cit., pp. 306–7.
2. Ibid., p. 310.

3. Schlegel, op. cit., pp. 307–8.
4. Ibid., p. 139.
5. Ibid., p. 141.
6. Pascal, *Pensées*, No. 768 in the numbering of Léon Brunschvieg's edition, Paris, 1904.
7. *Betrachtungen eines Unpolitischen*, pp. 106–7.
8. *Essays of Three Decades*, pp. 361–8.
9. *Joseph and his Brothers*, p. xi.
10. Ibid., p. 948.
11. *The Magic Mountain*, p. 497.
12. *Joseph and his Brothers*, pp. 1099–1100.
13. Ibid., p. 23.
14. Ibid., pp. 23–5.
15. Schopenhauer, op. cit., II, pp. 1451–4.
16. *Joseph and his Brothers*, p. 29, cf. also p. 1155.
17. *Betrachtungen eines Unpolitischen*, p. 32.
18. *Joseph and his Brothers*, pp. 26–7.
19. Ibid., pp. 29–30.
20. Ibid., p. 38.
21. Ibid., p. 843.
22. Ibid., p. 845.
23. Ibid., pp. 284 and 290.
24. Ibid., pp. 850–1.
25. In the German translation by H. H. Schaede: *Ueber den Begriff der Ironie, mit ständiger Rücksicht auf Sokrates*, Munich and Berlin, 1929.
26. Goethe, op. cit., XL, p. 63.
27. *Bemühungen*, p. 56.
28. *Betrachtungen eines Unpolitischen*, p. 560.
29. Ibid., p. 565.
30. *Altes und Neues*, p. 101.
31. *Bemühungen*, pp. 174–80.
32. *Rede und Antwort*, p. 225.
33. *Betrachtungen eines Unpolitischen*, p. 83.
34. Cf. *Lotte in Weimar*, pp. 64–8.
35. *Joseph and his Brothers*, p. 1100.
36. *The Magic Mountain*, p. 344.
37. *Joseph and his Brothers*, p. 266.
38. Ibid., p. 124.
39. Schopenhauer, op. cit., II, pp. 1259–61.
40. Nietzsche, op. cit., XIV, p. 179, XVIII, pp. 45 and 291.
41. *Joseph and his Brothers*, p. 69.
42. Ibid., p. 317.
43. *Die Neue Rundschau*, 1930, p. 765.
44. *Joseph and his Brothers*, pp. 64–7.
45. Ibid., pp. 18–19.
46. *Stories of Three Decades*, pp. 23–6.

47. *Buddenbrooks*, p. 527.
48. *Essays of Three Decades*, p. 421.
49. *Joseph and his Brothers*, p. 81.
50. Ibid., p. 81.
51. Schopenhauer, op. cit., II, p. 1361.
52. Ibid., p. 1266.
53. *Joseph and his Brothers*, p. 281.
54. *Neue Studien*, p. 180.
55. J. G. Frazer, *The Golden Bough*, part V, vol. II, London, 1925, p. 40.
56. *Joseph and his Brothers*, p. 318.
57. Ibid., p. 562.
58. *The Castle*, London, 1953, p. 284.
59. *Joseph and his Brothers*, p. 389.
60. *Essays of Three Decades*, p. 426.
61. *Joseph and his Brothers*, pp. 1052–3.
62. *Neue Studien*, pp. 178–9.
63. *Essays of Three Decades*, p. 221.
64. *Joseph and his Brothers*, p. 1056.
65. Ibid., pp. 863, 904, 1089, 1114.
66. Ibid., p. 1116.
67. Ibid., p. 1041.
68. Ibid., p. 1042.
69. Ibid., p. 1155.

VII. PARODY, TRAGIC AND COMIC

1. *Doctor Faustus*, p. 3.
2. Ibid., p. 497.
3. Ibid., p. 499.
4. J. Scheible, *Das Kloster*, Stuttgart and Leipzig, 1846, II, pp. 943–50.
5. *Doctor Faustus*, p. 372.
6. Cf. Ibid., p. 241.
7. Cf. Ibid., p. 180; cf. also Nietzsche, op. cit., XIX, p. 224.
8. Ibid., pp. 239–40.
9. Lukacs, op. cit., p. 79.
10. *Doctor Faustus*, pp. 499–50.
11. Ibid., p. 238.
12. Ibid., p. 45.
13. Ibid., p. 68.
14. Ibid., pp. 372–3.
15. Ibid., pp. 373–4.
16. *Die Entstehung des 'Doktor Faustus'*, p. 60.
17. *Doctor Faustus*, p. 240.
18. Ibid., p. 239.
19. Ibid., p. 241.
20. Ibid., p. 237.
21. Ibid., p. 271.

22. Dostoevsky, *The Brothers Karamazov*, trans. Edward Garnett, London, 1927, II, p. 298.

23. *Doctor Faustus*, p. 243.

24. Ibid., p. 321.

25. Ibid., pp. 375-8.

26. Ibid., pp. 489-91.

27. Ibid., p. 218.

28. *Die Entstehung des 'Doktor Faustus'*, pp. 77-8.

29. *Doctor Faustus*, p. 209.

30. *Stories of Three Decades*, pp. vii-viii.

31. *Die Entstehung des 'Doktor Faustus'*, p. 24.

32. *Felix Krull*, p. 367.

33. *Joseph and his Brothers*, pp. 943-4.

34. Cf. Grimmelshausen, *Der Abenteuerliche Simplizissimus*, edition in three volumes, Leipzig, 1908: I, p. 248; III, pp. 80 ff.; III, pp. 21 ff.; II, pp. 62 ff.; III, pp. 60 ff.; *Felix Krull*, pp. 226 ff.; pp. 260 ff.; pp. 394 ff.; pp. 287; pp. 185 ff.; pp. 283 ff.; *Doctor Faustus*, pp. 13 ff.; pp. 266 ff.

35. *Die Entstehung des 'Doktor Faustus'*, pp. 81-2.

36. *Stories of Three Decades*, p. vii.